T0295554

Blockchain Technologies, Applications and Cryptocurrencies

Current Practice and Future Trends

Highly Recommended Titles from World Scientific

Inclusive FinTech: Blockchain, Cryptocurrency and ICO
by David Kuo Chuen Lee and Linda Low
ISBN 978-981-3238-63-3 (hardcover)
ISBN 978-981-3272-76-7 (paperback)
ISBN 978-981-3238-64-0 (ebook for institutions)
ISBN 978-981-3238-65-7 (ebook for individuals)

Electronic Trading and Blockchain: Yesterday, Today and Tomorrow
by Richard L Sandor
ISBN 978-981-3233-77-5 (hardcover)
ISBN 978-981-3233-78-2 (ebook for institutions)
ISBN 978-981-3233-79-9 (ebook for individuals)

Blockchain Economics: Implications of Distributed Ledgers: Markets, Communications Networks, and Algorithmic Reality
edited by Melanie Swan, Jason Potts, Soichiro Takagi, Frank Witte and Paolo Tasca
ISBN 978-1-78634-638-4 (hardcover)
ISBN 978-1-78634-639-1 (ebook for institutions)
ISBN 978-1-78634-640-7 (ebook for individuals)

Blockchain Technologies, Applications and Cryptocurrencies

Current Practice and Future Trends

Sam Goundar

Victoria University of Wellington, New Zealand

World Scientific

NEW JERSEY • LONDON • SINGAPORE • BEIJING • SHANGHAI • HONG KONG • TAIPEI • CHENNAI • TOKYO

Published by

World Scientific Publishing Co. Pte. Ltd.

5 Toh Tuck Link, Singapore 596224

USA office: 27 Warren Street, Suite 401-402, Hackensack, NJ 07601

UK office: 57 Shelton Street, Covent Garden, London WC2H 9HE

Library of Congress Cataloging-in-Publication Data
Names: Goundar, Sam, 1967– editor.
Title: Blockchain technologies, applications and cryptocurrencies : current practice and
future trends / Sam Goundar, Victoria University of Wellington, New Zealand.
Description: New Jersey : World Scientific, [2020] | Includes bibliographical references and index.
Identifiers: LCCN 2020004857 | ISBN 9789811205262 (hardcover) |
ISBN 9789811205279 (ebook) | ISBN 9789811205286 (ebook other)
Subjects: LCSH: Blockchains (Databases) | Cryptocurrencies.
Classification: LCC QA76.9.B56 B562 2020 | DDC 005.75/8--dc23
LC record available at https://lccn.loc.gov/2020004857

British Library Cataloguing-in-Publication Data
A catalogue record for this book is available from the British Library.

Copyright © 2021 by World Scientific Publishing Co. Pte. Ltd.

All rights reserved. This book, or parts thereof, may not be reproduced in any form or by any means, electronic or mechanical, including photocopying, recording or any information storage and retrieval system now known or to be invented, without written permission from the publisher.

For photocopying of material in this volume, please pay a copying fee through the Copyright Clearance Center, Inc., 222 Rosewood Drive, Danvers, MA 01923, USA. In this case permission to photocopy is not required from the publisher.

For any available supplementary material, please visit
https://www.worldscientific.com/worldscibooks/10.1142/11410#t=suppl

Desk Editors: Herbert Moses/Jiang Yulin

Typeset by Stallion Press
Email: enquiries@stallionpress.com

Printed in Singapore

About the Editor

Sam Goundar is an international academic and has taught at 11 different universities in nine different countries. He is the Editor-in-Chief of the *International Journal of Blockchains and Cryptocurrencies* (IJBC), Inderscience Publishers; Editor-in-Chief of the *International Journal of Fog Computing* (IJFC), IGI Publishers; Section Editor of the *Journal of Education and Information Technologies* (EAIT), Springer; and Editor-in-Chief (Emeritus) of the *International Journal of Cloud Applications and Computing* (IJCAC), IGI Publishers. He is also on the Editorial Review Board of more than 20 high-impact factor journals.

He is also the author of seven books: three published titles, namely, *Architecture and Security Issues in Fog Computing Applications*, *E-Services (e-Commerce, e-Business, e-Government, and e-Learning)* and *Impact of Digital Transformation on Security Policies and Standards*, and four forthcoming titles, namely, *Innovations in the Industrial Internet of Things (IIoT) and Smart Factory*, *Applications of Big Data in Large- and Small-Scale Systems*, *Enterprise Systems for Management: Applications and Practice* and *Convergence of Blockchain and Artificial Intelligence*. A number of PhD and Master's students have successfully completed their theses under his supervision.

As a researcher, apart from Blockchains, Cryptocurrencies, Fog Computing, Mobile Cloud Computing, Cloud Computing, and Educational Technologies, Dr. Sam Goundar also focuses on Management Information Systems, Technology Acceptance Model (TAM), Massive Open Online Courses (MOOC), Gamification in Learning, Cyber Security, Artificial Intelligence, ICT in Climate Change, ICT Devices in the Classroom, Using Mobile Devices in Education, e-Government, and Disaster Management. He has published on all these topics. He was a Research Fellow with the United Nations University.

Dr. Sam Goundar has been teaching Information Systems (IS), Information Technology (IT), Management Information Systems (MIS) and Computer Science (CS) over the last 35 years at the undergraduate, postgraduate, Master's and PhD levels. Currently, he is a Senior Lecturer in Information Communications Technology at the British University, Vietnam. Prior to this, he was a Senior Lecturer in Information Systems at the University of the South Pacific, Affiliate Professor of Information Technology at Pontificia Universidad Catolica Del Peru (Peru), and Lecturer in Information Systems at the Victoria University of Wellington (Malaysian Partner Campus). He was also a Visiting Professor and Researcher at Hassan 1st University, Morocco (June–July 2019), and Bahir Dar University, Ethiopia (June–July 2018).

Dr. Sam Goundar is a Senior Member of IEEE, a member of ACS, a member of the IITP, New Zealand, Certification Administrator of ETA-I, USA and Former President of the South Pacific Computer Society. He also serves on the IEEE Technical Committee for Internet of Things, Cloud Communication and Networking, Big Data, Green ICT, Cyber Security, Business Informatics and Systems, Learning Technology and Smart Cities. He is a member of the IEEE Technical Society and a panelist with the IEEE Spectrum for Emerging Technologies.

Contents

Introduction to Blockchains and Cryptocurrencies

Sam Goundar

The University of the South Pacific, Suva, Fiji

sam.goundar@gmail.com

Blockchains and cryptocurrencies are now topics of substantial impact that academia, practitioners and the IT industry need to contemplate, study, research, publish, innovate, exploit and adopt. This book titled *Blockchain Technologies, Applications and Cryptocurrencies* intends to provide information on the innovative, scholarly and professional research pertaining to the management, organization and technological use of blockchains and cryptocurrencies. The chapters in this book will be essential for anyone interested in these areas. This book is one of the few dedicated entirely to blockchain technologies, applications and cryptocurrencies.

Blockchain technologies are being claimed to be as disruptive as the Internet. A white paper, written by Satoshi Nakamoto (a pseudonym), "Bitcoin: A Peer-to-Peer Electronic Cash System" appeared in 2008, setting everything into motion. The white paper detailed how an electronic cash transaction can take place between peers without the need for a third party (financial institution). Since then, the paper has been cited 5,687 times at the time of writing this introduction. Digital signatures and cryptography would be used to secure the financial transaction, and peers on the bitcoin network running on the blockchain technology would verify, validate and authorise the transaction to eliminate the "double spend problem".

According to Nakamoto (2008), this would make the system and transaction transparent, immutable and under the control of peers, thus eliminating control of financial institutions and their exorbitant fees. The bitcoin network would timestamp transactions by hashing them into an ongoing chain of hash-based proof-of-work, forming a record that cannot be changed without redoing the proof-of-work. The longest chain will not only serve as proof of the sequence of events witnessed, but proof that it came from the largest pool of CPU power. Messages are broadcast on a best effort basis, and nodes can leave and rejoin the network at will, accepting the longest proof-of-work chain as proof of what happened while they were gone.

The website BlockGeeks.Com (2019) defines "blockchain" as a growing list of records, called *blocks*, which are linked using cryptography. Each block contains a cryptographic hash of the previous block, a timestamp and transaction data (generally represented as a Merkle tree). By design, a blockchain is resistant to modification of the data. It is "an open, distributed ledger that can record transactions between two parties efficiently and in a verifiable and permanent way". Blockchain use with peer-to-peer electronic cash transactions enabled a number of Financial Technology (FinTech) applications, Distributed Ledger Technology (DLT) applications and introduction of more than thousand other Cryptocurrencies. Bitcoin still remains the most popular cryptocurrency.

Blockchains have now moved from electronic cash to other applications in government, supply chain management, healthcare, agriculture, real estate, international development and almost any application that utilize databases that can be replaced with a more secure, immutable, consensus-based, transparent and trust-based database. Apart from FinTech applications, other applications based on blockchains are emerging in every sector and industry as everyone is intent on taking advantage of the special properties of blockchains mentioned in the previous sentence. After bitcoin's success or failure (it depends), people are trying to apply it to procedures and processes beyond financial transactions. In effect, they are asking: What other agreements can a blockchain automate? What other middlemen can blockchain technology retire?

Some examples of real-world blockchain applications in use are as follows:

- **Land Ownership and Management:** Dubai, USA, UK, Sweden, Ukraine, Georgia and Ghana.
- **Development Aid:** Aid Transfer Efficiency, South African Early Childhood Development.
- **Supply Chain Management:** Diamond Tracking (De Beers), Food Safety (Walmart), Oil Supply (ADNOC), Agricultural Products Supply (LDC).
- **Renewable Energy:** WePower (Estonia), Power Ledger (Australia), Acciona Energy (Spain), The Brooklyn Micro Grid (US), The Sun Exchange (South Africa).
- **Remittances:** Blockchain Wallet, TransferWise, Ripple's XRP, BitSpark, MoneyFi, Chynge.
- **Digital Identity:** Civic, ValidatedID, THEKEY, Trusti, PeerMountain, Edge, BlockAuth, BlockVerify, CryptID, ExistenceID.
- **Agriculture:** Food Traceability, Fair Trade Farming, Organic Farming Certifications, Food Safety (Pesticides Use), New Markets, Logistics.
- **Democracy and Governance:** Voting, Decentralisation of Services, GovCoin, Democracy.Earth, FollowMyVote, Smart Participation, Liquid Democracy.
- **Manufacturing and Industrial:** Provenance, JioCoin, Hijro, SKUChain, BlockVerify, STORJ.io, RFID Integration, Anti Counterfeiting, Compliance.
- **Health:** Modum.io, Gem, SimplyVital Health, MedRec, Electronic Health Records (EHR), Ambr0Sys, Hashed Health, Medical Change, Change Health.
- **Financial Inclusion:** MojaLoop, ABRA, Bank Apoalim, Maersk, Augur, Regalii, Ripple, World Remit, Stellar, Oridian, Credits.Vision, OneName, ShoCard.
- **Retail:** OpenBazaar, Loyyal, Blockpoint.io, Customer Data Management, Transparency, Warranty, Goods Tracking, Customer Loyalty.
- **Climate Change:** Power Ledger, ClimateCoin.io, Carbon Emission Trading, Clean Energy, GHG.

- **Environment:** SOLshare, PlasticBank, Agora Tech Lab, EnergiToken, CarbonX, Veridium, IBM, United Nations, Waste Reduction, GiveTrack.
- **Human Rights:** Stop the Traffik, Dash Venezuela, Micro Trade, OpenGarden, RightMesh, Media Freedom, Social Media Awareness.
- **Access to Water:** Clean Water Coin, Decentralized Water Management, Water Quality Assurance Regulations, Water Trading.
- **Cyber-security:** GuardTime, REMME, IoT Security, Decentralized Storage Solutions, Safer DNS, Security in P2P Messaging systems.

Cryptocurrencies are "digital money" that do not physically exist but can be converted to any popular physical currency. Bitcoin, the first digital money, was hatched as an act of defiance. Unleashed in the wake of the Great Recession, the cryptocurrency was touted by its early champions as an antidote to the inequities and corruption of the traditional financial system. Bitcoin sought to replace the services provided by financial institutions with cryptography and code. When you pay your mortgage, a series of agreements occur in the background between your financial institution and others, enabling money to go from your account to someone else's. Bitcoin and other cryptocurrencies replace those background agreements and transactions with software — specifically, a distributed and secure database called a Blockchain.

If you could piece together a running tabulation of who held every dollar, then suddenly the physical representations would become unnecessary. Bitcoin achieved the running tabulation by creating a single, universally accessible digital ledger called a blockchain. Bitcoin's blockchain, unlike the ledgers maintained by traditional financial institutions, is replicated on networked computers around the globe and is accessible to anyone with a computer and an Internet connection. A class of participants on this network, called miners, is responsible for detecting transaction requests from users, aggregating them, validating them and adding them to the blockchain as new blocks. It's called a chain because changes can be made only by adding new information to the end. Each new addition, or block, contains a set of new transactions — a couple of thousand that reference previous transactions in the chain.

"CIO Insights Reflections: Cryptocurrencies and Blockchains — their Importance in the Future" by Notling & Muller (2017) reports the following: "With the help of cryptography and a collective booking system called Blockchain, cryptocurrencies build a distributed, safe and decentralized payment system, which does not need banks, intermediates, an organization or a central technical infrastructure to work. The main difference to the current types of money we know is that an intermediate, which is responsible for production (e.g. central bank) or exchange (banks) is not needed. Exchanges of digital values and goods are made directly between two individuals." Known cryptocurrencies are Bitcoin, Ethereum, Ripple, Litecoin and IOTA. In a sense, they are scarce commodities as the amount of available currency units is in this case limited by mathematical algorithms. After every digital currency unit is issued, there is no way to generate additional currency units from it (e.g. Bitcoin is limited to 21 million units). Furthermore, every cryptocurrency has its own currency generating process. The main factors likely to affect the future development of cryptocurrencies are, in Notling & Muller's (2017) opinions, interventions by the government and central banks and questions on how the sector will be regulated.

The chapters in this book are as follows:

Chapter 1: A Literature Review in Support of Blockchain Technologies

Blockchain technology has to be one of the biggest innovations of the 21st century given the ripple effect it is having on various sectors from financial to manufacturing as well as education. Unknown to many is the fact that Blockchain history dates back to the early 1990s. Since its popularity started growing a few years back, a number of applications have cropped up all but underlining the kind of impact it is destined to have as the race for digital economies heats up. This chapter examines the literature on Blockchain technologies and potential benefits of Blockchain technologies wherever it is used. This research is being carried out because there is no literature review on Blockchain Technology, and so, this chapter will ease the research of the scholars who want to know about Blockchain Technology. This research is important because this chapter will make people aware about Blockchain and all the places it is used and how people can benefit from this technology. Search terms identified more than 30 papers in support of blockchain technologies. The methodology used to carry out the research is also discussed in this chapter, such as various databases that were searched using different search terms. From the papers identified, specific criteria were then applied to identify appropriate articles. Data analysis verified the purpose of blockchain, categories of blockchain and alternatives to blockchain. The findings revealed that blockchain is one of the leading technologies in the world currently that possesses one of the more secure platforms for carrying out any task.

Chapter 2: A Taxonomy of Blockchain Applications

A taxonomy of blockchain application discusses cases — uses and apps. A major obstacle identified in several disciplines is the categorization of objects in a particular area of interest into a specific taxonomy. Blockchain is an innovation of decentralized and value-based information distributed over a vast network that contains untrustworthy users. Developing a taxonomy for blockchain application is a complex process, and thus, the purpose of this chapter is to discuss what internal factors contribute to the success of a blockchain application. This is followed by a discussion of which organizations use blockchain and which applications and apps they use. Finally, the chapter aims to classify blockchains according to what they are used for, e.g. blockchains are used in finance, agriculture, education, and research and development.

Chapter 3: Blockchain Means More Than a Software to Democracy: Access to Fundamental Rights of Sixth Dimension

Throughout history, five dimensions of basic needs have been created to establish the existential minimum. This chapter aims to demonstrate that Human Rights attained the position of the Sixth Dimension in 2009 when the right of access to technology became fundamental to generating peace, dignity and a sustainable world. Establishing technology as a fundamental right is useful to guide the Annual Budget Plan developed by the leaders who use these fundamental rights to establish the margin of investment to be made in each sector proportional to the level of importance it occupies in a citizen's life. For these reasons, research has been done which brought to light the fact that that blockchain and cryptocurrencies are much more than payment systems. The method used was scientific with analysis being done of historical documents as well as social observation and seeking of laws, doctrines and jurisprudence confronted with data taken from socioeconomic statistical reports collected in 2017. This research was enough to show that the Blockchain Technology and Cryptocurrencies combined with AI and IoT is the Smart Economy. Through poverty reduction, physical borders will be protected by virtual borders. The authors conclude that technologies are a powerful accelerator of economic flow and act as a vehicle for the sustainable world requiring investments like Human Rights being the Sixth Dimension, one that cannot be separated from others' rights.

Chapter 4: Autonomous Agriculture Marketing Information System Through Blockchain: A Case Study of e-NAM Adoption in India

The National Agricultural Market, through networking of the APMCs, provides electronic trading for agricultural produce. Under e-NAM, all the trading is to be done through a digital platform as prescribed to ensure transparency in the transactions and provide a fair price to the farmers. The study was conducted in three APMCs of Uttar Pradesh to analyse the ground-level practices taking place in these APMCs and level of adoption of e-NAM. It was found that there is a considerable variation in the arrival and bidding prices obtained from the APMCs when compared with the data available on the agriculture market information system (Agmarknet). The study proposes a blockchain-based infrastructure to facilitate a more transparent, autonomous system to empower the information system and efficient application of government rules and regulations pertaining to agricultural transactions in the APMCs through the utilization of smart contracts.

Chapter 5: Attack Vectors for Blockchain and Mapping OWASP Vulnerabilities to Smart Contracts

Smart contracts powered by Blockchain render transaction processes more effective, secure and efficient when compared with conventional contacts. Smart Contracts facilitate trustless process, time efficiency, cost effectiveness and transparency without any intervention by third-party intermediaries like lawyers. While Blockchains can counter traditional cyber-security attacks on Smart Contract Applications in a significantly good manner, cyber-criminals keep creating new threats and attack vectors that can hack Blockchain technologies. This chapter presents a unique framework to perform Application Security Testing on Blockchain-based

Smart Contracts and compares Manual Penetration Testing with two automated Smart Contract tools to detect critical vulnerabilities on a commercial production Blockchain environment.

Chapter 6: Blockchain Application in Fiji's Aviation Industry
In today's high-technological era, organizations have accelerated the use of blockchain technology to enhance their business processes. Blockchain is somewhat an updated version of database, which is a powerful technology in terms of managing data when compared with normal SQL databases. In Fiji, flight information is a mission critical system as a large number of stakeholders depend on it, such as hotels, airlines, airports, ground handlers and, overall, the general public. Current flight information is meeting the day-to-day organizational needs, but there are information technology problems associated with it, such as inconsistent information, data silos, and availability. With the introduction of blockchain technology, the aviation industry can become more powerful in terms of providing high-quality flight data to all its stakeholders. By the end of the research, we should be able to build a conceptual model that solves the flight data problem in Fiji.

Chapter 7: Blockchain-Based e-Voting Application
Voting has been the fundamental part of a democratic system as it allows individuals to voice out their opinions. For the past few years, voting turnout has diminished as concerns regarding security, privacy, accessibility and integrity escalated. In order to address these issues, e-voting was introduced; however, only few countries managed to use the application due to cost and central authority approvals. Hence, blockchain technology is an emerging platform as it allows decentralization through the use of distributed technology, thereby expanding industries and processes. In this chapter, the researchers discuss the significance of blockchain e-voting application as well as provide details of the issues faced by current blockchain technologies. The chapter will also provide a comparative analysis of existing mechanisms in order to understand and mitigate the gaps before fully adopting blockchain technologies for e-voting applications. Thus, this chapter will be a roadmap for blockchain-based e-voting application to improve the current voting practices and processes.

Chapter 8: Blockchains for Supply Chain Management Networks
Blockchain is a distributed and digital ledger which has transformed supply chain in various ways. In this chapter, we will investigate how blockchain can add value to the supply chain management (SCM) system. This chapter will further investigate the influence of integrating blockchain technology to the current supply chain system and its long-term implications. In essence, the research has been carried out to verify if blockchain technology is capable of providing the transparency and the accountability the current SCM systems lacks. The chapter looks at advantages and disadvantages of such integration and provides feedback and recommendation on the same. The research findings aim to provide a better insight into current practices used by large logistic and supply industries and what the future holds for such companies using supply chain management system.

Chapter 9: Comparison of Three Different Darknet Cryptocurrencies in e-Commerce in Our Digital Era
The emergence of the internet has opened a world of possibilities to connect and interact through web portals to exchange information over the network. In the past decade, buying and selling of goods and services online has become more common through e-commerce. With the advent of Cryptocurrencies, the possibilities of e-commerce have reached new heights for all web users who see potential in this technology. Cryptocurrencies have opened new dimensions based on a Blockchain technology for e-commerce through decentralization — increased privacy and digitalization of coins to allow users to anonymously trade online. This has become more common in the Darknet, which is simply the unindexed side of the Internet. This paper compares the three Cryptocurrencies, namely Bitcoin, Ethereum and Monero, in the Darknet used for e-commerce.

Chapter 10: Cryptocurrencies — An Assessment of Global Adoption Trends
Government and state approaches to any venture first begin with regulation to safeguard its interests as well as those of its citizens. Cryptocurrency adoption globally has been led by major players such as

the U.S and China while some smaller states have achieved comparable success. In this chapter, we analyse and assess a country's level of cryptocurrency adoption via its regulatory framework. We then classify this approach according to the business function that regulates the use of cryptocurrencies. We also derive a gradual approach to cryptocurrency adoption and regulation that can be used by fledgling countries new to the world of cryptocurrency.

Chapter 11: An Overview of Cryptocurrencies for Online Payments of Enterprise Systems

Cryptocurrencies have evolved erratically and at unprecedented speed over the course of their short lifespan. Since the inception of Bitcoin in 2009, more than 1,600 cryptocurrencies have been developed with majority successful in the market. With the advent of cryptocurrencies, the possibility of online trading has reached new heights. Thus, this chapter focuses on enterprise cryptocurrencies and provides a thorough analysis of the various opportunities that lie in the usage of cryptocurrencies for online payments. This chapter was prepared as there is a need to draw a fine line between using fiat currencies and using cryptocurrencies for online transactions, as there is not much research done on using cryptocurrencies in Enterprise systems, and this chapter will give a fair idea to researchers and organizations in making decisions while making corporate payments. We are basing our research using grounded theory, and focus on the certainty of using cryptocurrencies.

As the editor, writer and the co-author of all chapters of this book, I am proud to present this book to the readers. I would like to thank all the reviewers that peer-reviewed all the chapters in this book. I also would like to thank the administration and editorial support staff of World Scientific Publishing who have ably supported me in getting this book to press and publication. And finally, I would like to humbly thank all the authors and co-authors who submitted their research articles as chapters to this book. Without your submission, your tireless efforts and contribution, we would not have this book.

Publication of any book is not easy. Publication of a new book on a relatively new technology with a reputable publisher is even harder. The first step is to find a publisher that is willing to publish such a book. Given the dynamics of academic publishing today, disruptive transformation of academic publishing by the Internet, delivery and access of published research papers by PDF downloads, and Open Access academic journal models, many established publishers are now reluctant to publish a new book. This book on *Blockchain Technologies, Applications and Cryptocurrencies* is indeed privileged to be published by World Scientific Publishing — a publisher that is second to none. Disruptive technologies like blockchains and cryptocurrencies have been seen by many as a passing fad. The publication of this book is proof that they are not a fad but a mainstream disruptive technology.

I hope everyone will appreciate reading the chapters in this book. Additionally, I feel that it will inspire and encourage readers to start their own research on blockchains and cryptocurrencies and submit their articles and chapters to journals and books.

Once again, I take this opportunity to congratulate everyone involved in the writing, review, editing and publication of this book.

Any comments or questions can be emailed to *sam.goundar@gmail.com*.

Happy Reading.

References

Blockgeeks (2019). What is Blockchain Technology? A Step-by-Step Guide for Beginners. Retrieved from: https://blockgeeks.com/guides/what-is-blockchain-technology/. Accessed on May 19, 2019.

Nakamoto, S. (2008). Bitcoin: A Peer-to-Peer Electronic Cash System.

Notling, C., Muller, M. (2017). CIO Insights Reflections: Cryptocurrencies and Blockchains — Their Importance in the Future. Deutsche Bank Wealth Management. Retrieved from: https://www.db.com/newsroom_news/cio_insights_reflections_-_cryptocurrencies_and_blockchains_-_EMEA_-_client_ready.pdf. Accessed February 29, 2020.

Chapter 1

A Literature Review in Support of Blockchain Technologies

Sam Goundar*,‡, Zaahid Shah*,§, Neha Singh*,¶, Goel Lal*,‖ and Anil Singh†,**

*The University of the South Pacific, Suva, Fiji

†Fulton Adventist University College, Nadi, Fiji

‡sam.goundar@gmail.com

§zads.shah@gmail.com

¶tashasingh33@gmail.com

‖amangoellal@gmail.com

**asingh@fulton.ac.fj

Abstract

Blockchain technology has to be one of the biggest innovations of the 21st century given the ripple effect it is having on various sectors, from financial to manufacturing as well as education. Unknown to many is that Blockchain history dates back to the early 1990s. Since its popularity started growing a few years back, a number of applications have cropped up all but underlining the kind of impact it is destined to have as the race for digital economies heats up. This chapter examines the literature on Blockchain technologies and potential benefits of Blockchain technologies wherever they are used. This research is being carried out because there is no literature review on Blockchain Technology and this chapter will ease the research of the scholars who want to know about Blockchain

Technology. This research is important because it will make people aware about Blockchain and where all it is used and how people can benefit from this technology. Search terms identified more than 30 papers in support of blockchain technologies. The methodology used to carry out the research is also discussed in this report such as various databases searched using various search terms. From the papers identified, criteria were determined to identify further appropriate articles. Data analysis verified the purpose of blockchain, categories of blockchain and alternatives of blockchain. The findings revealed that blockchain is one of the leading technologies in the world currently with a more secure platform for carrying any task

Introduction

Blockchain is defined as a "distributed, decentralized, public ledger". Block, which is referred to as digital information, is stored in a chain known as a public database. Each block on the Blockchain is made up of digital pieces of information. It is made up of the following three specific parts:

1. Information about a transaction, which is stored on a block; this may include information such as date, time and dollar amount.
2. Information about the participant of the transaction, which is stored on a block; this may include the participants' username, which is unique for each user.
3. Information about each block, which is stored on the block that will distinguish one from the others. This will be useful when a particular participant makes two different transactions one after the other, in which case the information on each transaction will be stored on two different blocks. These blocks will have similar information but will still be distinguished from each other because of their unique codes.

Moving on, new data are added to the chain as they are stored in a block. There are four requirements that need to be fulfilled that would allow these blocks to be added to the chain.

1. There must be occurrence of a transaction.
2. There must be verification of a transaction.
3. Transaction has to be stored in a block form.
4. Transaction has to be unique.

Furthermore, new block of information is added in a chronological order onto the chain. Once the block has been added to the chain, it becomes difficult to modify the contents of the block. The reason for this is that each block is made up of its own hash, together with the hash of the block before it. Mathematical functions are used to create the hash, which turns digital data into a set of letters and numbers. If any of the data are tampered with in any way, the hash code varies as well (Fortney, 2019).

There are three categories of Blockchain: Public Blockchain, Private Blockchain and Federated Blockchain. Public Blockchain is created on Proof or work (PoW), and the consensus algorithms are open source and are not permissioned. Using public Blockchain anybody can join without authorization, download the code, run a public node on local device, validate the transaction and then create a block, which is added to the chain. People can carry out transactions through the network, but it should be contained within the Blockchain after validation. They can also read transactions on the public block. Some examples of public Blockchain are Ethereum, Bitcoin, Moero, Dash and Litecoin. The advantage of public Blockchain technology is that it is useful to current business models mainly because of the property of disintermediation. Public Blockchain has no infrastructure costs or server maintenance, it also decreases the costs of developing and running decentralised applications (Buterin *et al.*, 2016).

Federated Blockchain, on the other hand, functions under the guidance of a team. It is different from public Blockchain in that the federated Blockchain does not give any individual with access to the internet to take part in verifying the transactions. Federated Blockchain is less slow and can provide extra transaction privacy. This Blockchain is usually used by the banking sector. The harmonization procedure is controlled by a preselected set of nodes. Some instances of federated Blockchain are R3 (Bank), EWF (Energy) and B3i (Insurance). Federated Blockchain reduces transaction cost, clears data redundancy and replaces legacy systems. This could simplify document handling, thereby reducing costs (Buterin *et al.*, 2016).

Lastly, for private Blockchain, read approvals may be public or limited to an arbitrary extent. An example of this is auditing which is internal to a company, so public readability may not be necessary at all. Blockchain can validate transactions internally and contains security risks just like centralized systems. Private Blockchain has its use case, such as scalability, but it is also subject to data privacy rules and other regulatory issues. Some examples of private Blockchain are MONAX and Multichain (Buterin *et al.*, 2016).

All the users can share public Blockchain, and it does not require any special tool to join in. No one owns public Blockchain, so anyone can see the data transmitted. In a public Blockchain, the network is already created, and so one integration could work for all business parties involved; hence, there is no need to create separate networks for each industry to manage privacy. For security and fraud purposes, private Blockchain would be very helpful because it ensures the network security that is given to the other parties. On the other hand, federated Blockchains are chained together on the distributed ledger. By integrating federated Blockchain technology, the solution supports the auditing models without the necessity to centralize the training data.

In the article titled "Blockchain Beyond the Hype — A Practical Framework for Business Leaders," Mulligan *et al.* (2018a) talk about the hype around Blockchain in 2018, as it was being suggested as a solution to a range of issues that organizations are facing.

"One of the biggest reasons for Blockchain's sudden popularity is its number of believers, people who truly believe that Blockchain Technology can resolve any given problem from Global Financial Inequality to helping people sell their properties without even needing an estate agent" (Mulligan *et al.*, 2018b).

Further, in another article titled "Blockchain Beyond the Hype — What is Strategic Business Value", by Carson *et al.* (2018), the authors try to answer the question of how companies can determine if there is enough planned value in Blockchain to justify key investments.

"Blockchain Technology is making headlines for its increasing prices and unpredictability, especially after the launch of its first successful and slowly becoming famous application — Bitcoins" (Carson *et al.*, 2018).

The paper by Carson *et al.* (2018) focuses on the strategic importance of Blockchain in major organizations. Further analysis revealed three important factors of strategic value of Blockchain, and these are as follows: it encourages commercial applications, the short-term value greatly reduces cost before transformative business models, and due to difficulty of resolving the coopetitions, it makes it hard to establish common standards, which means that Blockchain is still a couple of years from feasibility in terms of scale.

There are some structured approaches in a Blockchain strategy that every organization should follow, first by identifying values practically and assessing the impact and feasibility at a high level which than can be addressed to find the main points with specific use cases within selected organizations.

It can then capture the values by tailoring strategic approaches of Blockchain, keeping in mind the measures that can be taken such as the opportunity to shape the ecosystem, establish standards and address regulatory obstacles (Carson *et al.*, 2018).

Moreover, the importance of this project is to show the originality of effective literature review in support of Blockchain technology by justifying the proposed methodology. The method that was used to compile the information was determining search terms, database search and selection of papers. Furthermore, by doing the literature review on Blockchain technology we discovered the importance of Blockchain, such as the places where Blockchains are used (bitcoin, solar energy, government sector, taxation, digital identity, agriculture, food, fishing industry, supply chain, business, smart contract, robotics, smart cities, oil industry, railway, gaming, car leasing, insurance, endangers species protection, advertising, journalism, tourism, shipping, mobile payment, cat bonds, healthcare, waste management, border control, music, carbon offsets, diamonds, real estate, fine art, LGBT) as well as further information regarding such characteristics as costs, advantages and disadvantages and risks.

The main aim of the research in this chapter is to systematically evaluate the benefits and challenges of Blockchain technology and determine how it is better than any third-party institute keeping track of or having control over your transaction.

The objective of this research is to demonstrate where, when and how the Blockchain technology is best applicable considering that it is considered to be disruptive in some respects since there is an absence of understanding in regard to Blockchain technologies. It is disruptive in the sense that there are already working systems in the society that are slowly being replaced by Blockchain Technology. This research will also highlight alternatives to Blockchain.

Method

Data collection

Databases search

The databases searched during this project included those that are of importance in regard to computing education and Blockchain technology and information systems, such as Google Scholar and the USP Library ProQuest database; other relevant electronic databases were also searched to find articles that were related to our research topic.

Search terms

The search terms that we used included terms for blockchain in combination with terms for likely results, effects or impacts of blockchain. These search terms helped us determine our definition of blockchain. The following search terms were used to successfully answer our research question:

("Blockchain benefits" OR "Blockchain challenges" OR "Blockchain transactions" OR "Effective Blockchain" OR "Blockchain performance and Security" OR "Types of Blockchain" OR "Blockchain alternatives")

Selection of papers

Various criteria were identified in order to select all the articles that were appropriate to be included in the review. These criteria were: papers had to (a) include empirical evidence relating to the outcomes of blockchain applications and (b) articles were chosen from the year 2009 to 2018. These two criteria were used to analyze 40 papers that had met the above criteria.

Data analysis

Purpose of blockchain technology

We found out the purpose of blockchain and what benefits we get from blockchain and what can be replaced by blockchain.

Categories of blockchain

Blockchain is of three types: Public Blockchain, Private Blockchain and Federated Blockchain. Our research is based on private and public blockchain, but we will also include papers on federated blockchain.

Alternatives to blockchain

We were able to find two alternatives to blockchain. These alternatives are Tangle and Hashgraph.

Platforms: Various platforms were identified that use blockchain technology. For instance, Bitcoin, Litecoin and Ethereum.

Quality of the studies

The following are the four criteria that were used to evaluate the quality of the papers:

1. How applicable is the research structure in order to address the question or sub-question of the review?
   - High = 3
   - Medium = 2
   - Low = 1
2. How applicable are the methods and analysis?
3. How appropriate is the particular purpose of the study for addressing the question or the sub-question of this review?
4. To what extent can the study findings be trusted in answering the study question?

Result

Bitcoin

The article "What is Bitcoin?" explains that Bitcoin uses blockchain technology when there is a transaction made using bitcoins that is verified by the network of computers. Bitcoin has two traits: it is in a digital form and it can be considered as an alternative currency (Palumbo & Macadam, 2017). Bitcoins are not like normal currency, i.e. coins and notes, but exist online only. In some countries, bitcoins are issued via ATMs as virtual tokens. Bitcoin is not government printed, which means it is not legal to pay taxes or debit with bitcoins. Bitcoins are created by a "mining" process (see Figure 1) which is very complex and get monitored via a network of computers around the world (Palumbo & Macadam, 2017). Bitcoin miners use special software to solve math problems.

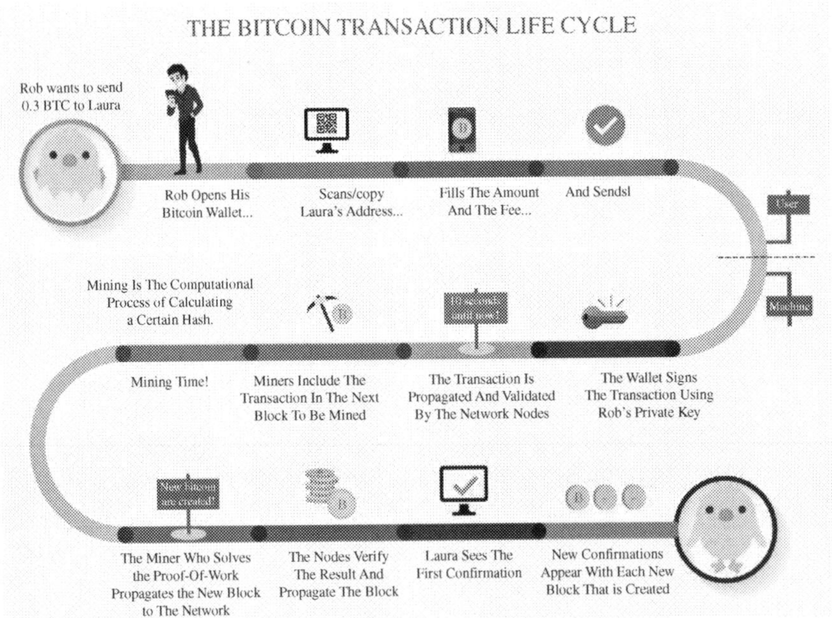

Figure 1: The Transaction and Mining Process of Bitcoin

Source: https://twitter.com/bigchonis/status/1009139509936652290.

Bitcoin miners also help in keeping the network secure by approving the transactions (Bitcoin Mining, 2018).

Moreover, in another article titled "Bitcoin — risky bubble or the future", Rory Cellan-Jones says with his experience that he bought 0.17 Bitcoins for $87 in April 2016 and after 18 months he opened his Bitcoin wallet on his smartphone with increasing frequency where he found the worth of his bitcoin was US$1,713, equal to £1,300. People who own bitcoins do not want to spend them because they are going to have more worth tomorrow. Bitcoin is said to be wasteful in energy because the mining process consumes more electricity each year than is used by Ireland (Cellan-Jones, 2017).

Figure 2 shows the price fluctuation in yearly basis in USD, Horizontal Axis shows the Date range and Vertical Axis shows the price range in US Dollars.

Furthermore, in another article titled "Bitcoin Mining on Track to Consume All of the World's Energy by 2020" (Cuthbertson, 2017), the author Anthony Cuthbertson says that it is estimated that the network that supports Bitcoin will require all the current energy in the world to support itself within the next 3 years. The power required to support bitcoin has improved significantly in recent months. The Bitcoin mining process generates a new unit of cryptocurrency that uses blockchain technology, which needs computing power, which solves the difficult mathematical puzzles used in the mining process.

Furthermore, the problems are becoming more complex when additional computers join the cryptocurrency's network system. A study on the amount of energy Bitcoin mining process revealed that what it consumes is more than the existing energy consumption of 159 individual countries including Ireland, Nigeria and Uruguay (Cuthbertson, 2017). Bitcoin Energy Consumption Index assessed by the cryptocurrency platform Digiconomist puts the usage on par with Denmark, consuming 33 terawatts of electricity per annum. Mining provides a solid stream of revenue, and people are eager to use power-hungry machines to get a piece of it. Digiconomist confirms that Bitcoin network's energy consumption has increased by 25% in the last month, and it is believed that if this continues the energy consumption of Bitcoin mining will consume as much power and energy as the US by 2019. Computer server farms in warehouses are

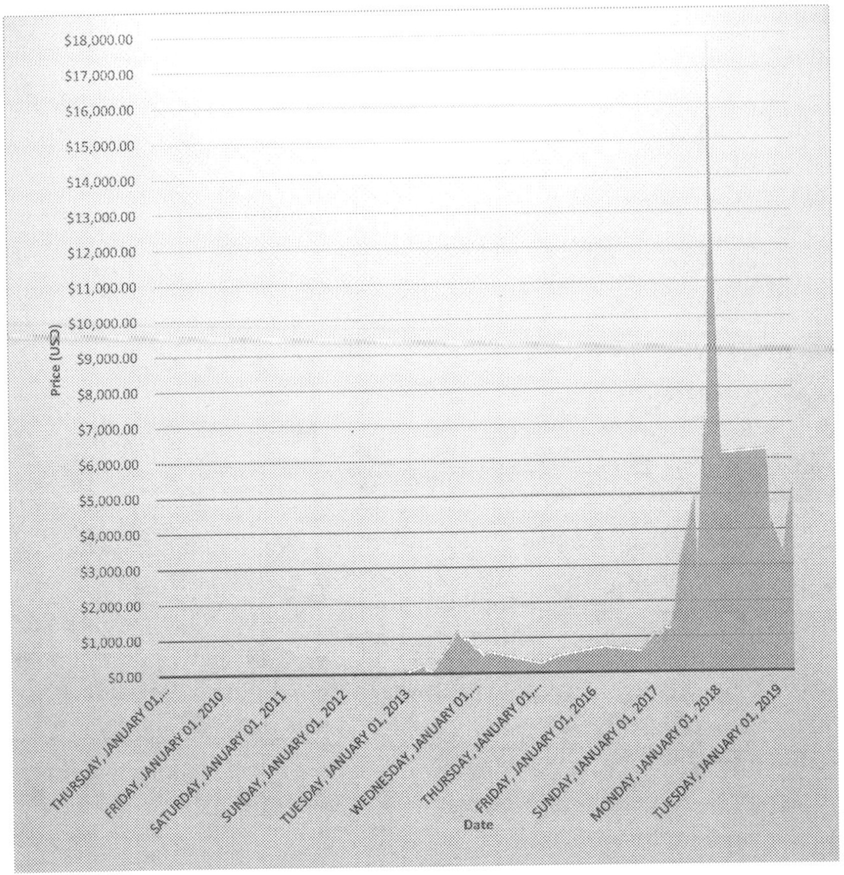

Figure 2: The Price History of Bitcoin Over the Years

used to mine the bitcoin, and cyber-criminals have turned to botnets to exploit the processing power of prey computers (Cuthbertson, 2017).

According to the ad blocking firm AdGuard, approximately half a billion people or more are involved in mining bitcoins from their computers, smartphones and other devices as unknown software were found embedded within 220 popular websites. The mining tool hijacks the CPU of the devices that runs the mining software in the background process of a computer or any other device. Some websites which have been embedded with the mining software are Showtime and torrent websites. PirateBay is one of the torrenting sites that is known to be using such mining software. The joint profit for these sites is estimated to be over $43,000, according to data from AdGuard researchers who also said that at the time during which the incident occurred, Bitcoin was worth $5,000 (Cuthbertson, 2017).

Moving on, despite all the benefits of Bitcoins, limitations are discussed in the article "Where Is Current Research on Blockchain Technology? — A Systematic Review" (Yli-Huumo *et al.*, 2016), where it was highlighted that Blockchain was initially developed for bitcoin cryptocurrencies. The authors stated the reasons of security, anonymity and data integrity for the interest in blockchain in terms of technical challenges and limitations. While doing the research, the authors stated a benefit that blockchain is a public ledger that cannot be altered or erased once the data has been accepted by all nodes. Some of the challenges and limitations that they highlighted were as follows:

- **Throughput:** The possible throughput of challenges in the Bitcoin network is presently significantly reduced to 7 transactions per second. VISA (2,000 tps) and Twitter (5,000 tps) are other forms of transaction processing networks. When the transaction frequency in Blockchain grows to comparable levels, the Blockchain networks' throughput needs to be improved.
- **Latency:** Currently, it takes around 10 minutes for Bitcoin to complete one transaction and create sufficient security. More time must be spent on a block to achieve security efficiency, because it must be greater than the cost of double spending attacks. Double spending is more than just the outcome of successful money spending. Bitcoin defends in contradiction of double expenditure by checking each transaction added to the blockchain to ensure that the transaction inputs were not previously spent. The transaction of the block should be created and confirmed in seconds while maintaining security.
- **Size and bandwidth:** The size of the blockchain in a bitcoin network is presently around 15 GB. When the throughput rises to VISA levels, Blockchain could expand to 214 PB annually. The Bitcoin community

has assumed that the size of one block is 1 MB and that every 10 minutes a block is created. Thus, the number of transactions that can be handled (on average, 500 transactions in one block) is therefore limited. If more transactions need to be controlled by the blockchain, the size and bandwidth problems must be resolved.

- **Security:** The existing Blockchain has a 51% attack likelihood. A single entity would have complete control over the majority of the mining hash rate of the network in a 51% attack and would be able to manipulate the Blockchain. In order to overcome the security issue, more security research is needed.
- **Wasted resources:** Bitcoin mining leads to wastage of enormous amounts of energy ($15 million/day). This waste is produced due to the effort of proof-of-work. In industry fields, there are some substitutes for this such as proof-of-stake. With Proof-of-Work, the likelihood of mining a block is determined based on the miner's work. However, the resource compared in Proof-of-Stake is the amount of Bitcoin a miner holds. For instance, someone holding 1% of the Bitcoin may undermine 1% of the "proof-of-stake blocks". The problem of waste resources in Blockchain needs to be resolved in order to have more effective mining.
- **Usability:** It is difficult to use the Bitcoin API to develop services. A more developer-friendly API for Blockchain is needed. This might look like REST APIs.
- **Versioning, hard forks, multiple chains:** A small chain consisting of a small number of nodes has a greater chance of an attack of 51%. When chains are divided for managerial or versioning purposes, another issue emerges.

The authors also added that blockchain could be applied to various other environments as long as there are some transactions to be done. They conducted the research by approaching "a systematic mapping study with the goal of collecting all relevant research on blockchain technology". They started by searching the databases for relevant papers, followed by screening those papers based on the title. Those papers that crossed the first and second phase were selected to read the abstracts based on which papers that focusing on blockchain were selected. After this, the papers were read and categorized according to clusters. Scientific databases were used to extract 41 primary papers. After the research had been done, the authors demonstrated that results of over 80% of the papers focused on Bitcoin system and that less than 20% dealt with other Blockchain applications. A greater part of the research was concentrated on enlightening and improving the drawbacks of Blockchain in terms of privacy and security viewpoints, but many of the proposed resolutions lacked concrete evaluation on their effectiveness. Many other Blockchain scalability associated challenges including throughput and latency have been left unstudied. On the basis of this study, recommendation on future research guidelines are provided for researchers (Yli-Huumo *et al.*, 2016).

The next article titled "Bitcoin exchange Youbit shuts after second hack attack" (BBC, 2017) explains how due to being hacked twice in less than eight months, a cryptocurrency exchange in South Korea is shutting down. Youbit, which allows people to buy and sell bitcoins and other virtual currencies, filed for bankruptcy in the cyber-attack after losing 17% of its assets. It did not reveal the value of the assets at the time of the attack. Youbit, previously known as Yapizon, lost 4,000 bitcoins worth $73 million (£55 million) to cyber-thieves in April 2017 (BBC, 2017). Upon further investigation conducted by South Korea's Internet and Security Agency (KISA), it was found that the first attack on Youbit was done by cyber-spies working for North Korea, but the origin of the second attack is not clear (BBC, 2017).

Furthermore, Youbit promised their customers that they would receive 75% of the value of the cryptocurrency they had lodged with the exchange and they also said that "they are very sorry that they were forced to shut down" (BBC, 2017). The hackers were not able to steal all the bitcoins since a lot were lodged in a "cold wallet," which is a safe store used to hold non-traded assets. Youbit was South Korea's smallest exchange that was active. Many cyber-criminals have tried to cash in on the boom in virtual currencies like Bitcoin. Many have developed malware to use victim's computers to create or "mine" valuable currencies, while the rest have attacked exchanges and other cryptocash service firms (BBC, 2017).

Solar energy

A new project focusing on distributed energy and water systems is using blockchain technology in the Australian City of Fremantle. Solar panels are used to capture electricity in the sunny region, and this energy is then used to heat water and supply power as well as keep track of data in the blockchain. The National Energy Commission of Chile has started to use blockchain technology to verify data related to the energy use in the country. To secure and modernize the electrical infrastructure of this South American nation, blockchain will be used to store sensitive data (Zago, 2018).

In yet another article in a similar vein titled "Blockchains Will Allow Rooftop Solar Energy Trading for Fun and Profit" (Peck & Wagman, 2017), the authors Peck and Wagman highlighted that blockchain can be used with electronic currency to record electricity production and can also be used for selling it. A study that was conducted by Research and Markets stated that the international market for rooftop photovoltaic panels amounted to nearly US$30 billion and was likely to increase over the next years. The article also stated that if the technology is used efficiently, "additional energy sources at the edge of the grid could help manage demand more efficiently" (Peck & Wagman, 2017). In addition, some specialists argued that this would take place only if the individuals who owned these assets were completely united into an energy market where prices are set in real time. This enables energy manufacturers to realize at which point in time their product is most desirable; thus, they will be able to gain maximum profit (Peck & Wagman, 2017).

Furthermore, Orsini's company used the blockchain technology to send economic signals. LO3 Energy, in a project named "TransActive Grid", has connected 200 smart meters in few neighborhoods in the region of Brooklyn, New York City (Peck & Wagman, 2017). Also, LO3 Energy developed blockchain-based innovations to reform how energy can be generated, stored, bought, sold and used, all at the local level (LO3 Energy, 2018). The smart meters measure the energy production and communicate with the network to collectively manage energy that has been installed in the houses that produce renewable energy. These records for TransActive Grid will assist by being a substitute accounting system to Consolidated Edision Co. (Peck & Wagman, 2017).

There is yet another similar project from Germany, in which, Sonnen (battery supplier) partnered with TenneT Holding (grid operator) to coordinate and record the operation of a thousand odd residential energy storage systems. A product of Hyperledger, known as Fabric — a variant of blockchain — is yet another joint blockchain project which is executed in Linux Foundation. The records will be built on Fabric (Peck & Wagman, 2017).

Government sector

Numerous governments expressed their interest in Blockchain technology to keep public records on a decentralized framework for data management. Essentia is evolving into an e-government pilot with the Agricultural Producers and Forest Owners' Central Union of Finland. Blockchain will allow access to records for urban and rural people across Finland. Other uses include applications from the government such as education, public records and voting (Zago, 2018).

Furthermore, the U.S. Department of Homeland Security (DHS) announced a project in 2016 that would implement Blockchain to securely store and transmit the data it captures. Using the Factom Blockchain, data are encrypted and stored from security cameras and other electronic security devices using Blockchain to mitigate the dangers of data breaches. The project is still underway (Zago, 2018).

Moving on to the article "Blockchain Technology and Decentralized Governance: Is the State Still Necessary" (Atzori, 2015), blockchain is considered as a hyper-political tool capable of achieving social interaction on a large scale and a decentralized platform. In November 2008, Satoshi Nakamoto addressed the first bitcoin electronic payment system (consisting of a digital ledger based on decentralized network). Blockchain-based models of governance are not available at the academic level. The main purposes of blockchain-based governance are as follows:

- Centralized organization and the problem of Scale, State as a Single Point of Failure (SPOF).
- Distributed architecture and trust-by-computation: "Code is Law".
- Power of Individual and politics by instant, atomic interactions.

- "Putting a nation on the blockchain" 16: A Starbucks-style public administration.
- Borderless, globalized government services, Systems of direct democracy.
- Futarchy: "Vote for values, but bet on belief", A decentralized society, still based on the State authority.
- A new social contract, characterized by Decentralized Autonomous Societies and the final demise of the State Franchulates.
- Authority floating freely, cognitive dissonance and societal maturity.

Blockchain-based governance has major technical and managerial benefits for markets and societies. Thus, it plays a major role in economic benefits (Atzori, 2015).

In the same vein, another article titled "The economies of crypto-democracy" discussed how the application of Blockchain technology in government reduces the cost of monitoring information. Blockchain could be useful in the voting system and in the electronic processing of information, leading to a form of crypto-democracy. Democratic technologies include distribution of information and gathering of information about democratic ideas and policies. In 2008, Satoshi Nakamoto introduced Blockchain technologies, and using cryptography enables the coordination of information in a decentralized manner. Blockchain is an effective way to implement the voting system by means of an electronic process. Blockchain technology for voting could decrease various costs associated with voting. To ensure a crypto-democracy for better voting system, Blockchain technology will be the best methodology to follow because of its high level of security. Quadratic voting (QV), which is a new voting system implemented by Lalley and Weyl (2018), works by introducing payment methods into voting systems. QV has implementation challenge, and the cost of transaction is also high. Thus, Blockchain technology is currently the best option to create a decentralized institution (Allen *et al.*, 2017).

The next article titled "Economics of Blockchain", blockchain is creating new types of economies in government. This revolutionary Blockchain technology is a secure distributed ledger. Economies of Blockchain help lighten how this new technology affects the economy.

The study of "Ethereum-based platform" shows a decentralized Blockchain that follows a basis protocol for a cryptography-secured transaction machine called Backfeed. The economic perspective on Blockchain provides technical solutions (cryptographic consensus) for government use. Backfeed is a social protocol on top of Blockchain-based infrastructure to enable the development of individual creation and distribution of economic reputation. "Backfeed" is an engine for decentralized cooperation. It implements a *Social Operating System* for decentralized organizations, enabling massive open source Collaboration without any form of centralized coordination. Thus, backfeed demonstrates one example of how Blockchain can build new type of economies based on crypto-economic institutions (Davidson *et al.*, 2016).

Yet another article on Blockchain technology titled "Block-Chain Based E-Voting for Indonesia" suggests that implementing Blockchain features in each of the key elements of election in Indonesia is the key to its success. "Blockchain Technology is being implemented on an e-voting system in Indonesia based on the basic principles of Voting that was put in place in 2017 by the Indonesian government (Winarno *et al.*, 2018).

Some examples of these principles and their appropriate Blockchain feature are as follows:

- Direct Principle: where the voting must be down directly and not to be embodied by anyone; this principle has an Accuracy feature from Blockchain which indicates that only the owner of the private key can access their voting rights and not everyone.
- Similarly, the other feature is "General", which indicates that elections can be followed by all citizens who have the right to use votes without any exception; this principle uses two features of Blockchain — accuracy and transparency.

These features give voters their right to vote if they follow and fulfill the demographic rules prevalent in Indonesia such as being over seventeen years of age, and it also allows everyone to view in a tabulated form all the details and even provides them the option to audit the system. In order to facilitate a successful election in Indonesia, it is important to implement Blockchain-based features in the e-voting design, which would consist of the issuance of a permanent vote list and the selection and tabulation process.

It would seem as though there are a lot of advantages when it comes to e-voting with Blockchain, some of which are voters having the choice to make a selection anywhere they wish directly, voter's identities being kept confidential and safe, and having the ability to verify that their ballot has been entered. After thorough research, this paper concludes that Blockchain is in fact helping countries like Indonesia in aspects such as e-voting as its principles can be fulfilled by Blockchain systems, thus making it easier to conduct elections based on the internet (Winarno *et al.*, 2018).

Similarly, in the article "NZ companies embrace the revolutionary potential of blockchain", Harris (2017) highlighted that blockchain is a much more secured platform, which means that it is impossible for the hackers to hack, and so government agencies like the Ministry of Health and NZ Qualification Authority are discovering the myriad possibilities of using this technology. As mentioned by Phil Williams, who is an advisor to the Edmund Hillary Foundation, the health ministry is unlikely to put actual health records on "the chain", but it would be an excellent way of linking records scattered in multiple places, with the idea and hope that the blockchain would be adopted by the government. Further, he added that the blockchain technology will provide a gateway for industries and also enable various companies to efficiently make transactions between and among each other (Harris, 2017).

In addition, Mark Pascall, of business consultancy Blockchain Labs NZ, said that before blockchain evolved, the government and other agencies relied upon a centralized database to store information. He also added that "Blockchain has become one of the most potentially world-changing technologies, alongside the Internet, nanotech, genetic engineering and AI" (Harris, 2017).

Furthermore, Air New Zealand thought of adopting blockchain for various uses such as, baggage and cargo tracking, while Webjet thought of using this technology to document hotel bookings. Also, a power company based in Auckland, which has been keeping an eye on blockchain system, thought that this would help keep track of transactions that occur between communities that buy and sell their own power. With this article,

William and the others desire for the government to aid New Zealand grow into a leader rather than a supporter in blockchain. Finally, "Pascall believes that blockchain will ultimately lead to greater globalization" (Harris, 2017).

Conversely, in the article "Illinois vs. Dubai: Two Experiments Bring Blockchains to Government" (Nordrum, 2017), it is mentioned that the government agencies believe that blockchain technology could "regenerate the public sector" (Nordrum, 2017). Those in support of the above statement have argued that employees would be kept accountable due to its transparency, the records will be protected from fraudsters due to immutability and it would make the agencies more efficient because of its capability to process new entries automatically. This allowed the city, state and federal governments to launch the first batch of public-sector blockchain experiments.

The US state of Illinois and the city of Dubai in the United Arab Emirates adopted the unlikely strategy of incorporating blockchain into the government.

First, the city government in Dubai took a "highly centralized approach" where they built a single software stage through which various blockchain projects will be launched by the agencies. On the other hand, the US state of Illinois designed the processes to be more experimental, where individual projects tested various types of blockchain stages and applications to find the best fit for their particular needs. Despite all these activities, it is still not known to anyone whether or not "blockchain can deliver meaningful outcomes for public agencies"; therefore, the government may be hesitant to invest in new technologies. As argued by an expert in IT risk management, Robert Charette, simple cloud database is more effective than a blockchain would prove to be, and he supplemented this fact by stating that it's more of solving an issue that's previously been resolved (Nordrum, 2017).

The platform that the city government had proposed to build, on the other hand, would support both a distributed ledger code base known as Fabric and the public blockchain called Ethereum. Once the platform is launched, it is expected that the city government would go paperless by 2020.

If the blockchain is being implemented in Dubai, the following would be the process. When a property is being purchased, the transaction is recorded by the buyer and the seller on one of the two blockchains that are authorized by Dubai. The buyer and the seller will receive instant approval, as long as the buyer's account has sufficient money that would cover the sale and the deed is filled out properly. After the transaction has come to an end, the blockchain will be considered as the official record, which cannot be altered by anyone, including the government employees. This will result in a blockchain allowing the government transactions to be more secure and streamlined (Nordrum, 2017).

Digital identity

Zug in Switzerland, commonly known as "Crypto Valley," developed a Blockchain project in partnership with Uport to register resident identity cards, giving them the opportunity to take part in online voting and prove their residency status (Zago, 2018).

In the article "Wall Street Firms to Move Trillions to Blockchains in 2018", Nordrum (2017) highlighted that their way of thinking in relation to blockchain was contradictory to the paper that was published by Satoshi Nakamoto in 2008. On the one hand, Nakamoto stated that even if we do not use our real name, we could still own bitcoins and the history of a transaction can be checked by anyone, while the author of the 2017 paper argued that the financial industries' blockchain are closed or, more specifically, require permission for access. That is, identity must be revealed to a system administrator in order to get your entry approved. The author also stated that a permission to enter a network would mean a client's privacy is protected (Nordrum, 2017).

The paper written by Nakamoto also focused on peer-to-peer financial network, which had no collection of fees. A digital key would be assigned to the transactions and recorded in public ledgers so that the previous records of the transaction cannot be tampered with. Thus, only those who have identified themselves through the digital key will have access to the blockchain network. This kind of limited access would allow easy maintenance and also ensure that the ledgers could be customized to meet a company's specific goals (Nakamoto, 2008).

Furthermore, Robert Palatnick, a managing director and chief technology architect of the Depository Trust and Clearing Corporation

(DTCC), a financial utility in New York City, has led various schemes to include Blockchain into the organization's daily operation. The hope is that the permissioned blockchain for their database to be run on will save them money. DTCC's blockchain network would be controlling $11 trillion worth of Credit-Default-Swaps, which is a "type of contract that allows a firm to pass risk to another firm". DTCC has been in partnership with IBM and the blockchain startup Axoni to create a swap network on a unified code base called AxCore (Nordrum, 2017).

Another article on blockchain titled "Forget iris scans, Canadians to use blockchain for digital IDs" (Alexander, 2017) highlighted that just as Estonia used digital identity card and India used iris scans to authenticate money transfers, with the help of the blockchain and mobile phone, Canadians will be able to authenticate their personal information for everything ranging from such simple tasks as obtaining a driver's license, etc. According to Greg Wolfond, chief executive officer of Toronto-based organization SecureKey, this will allow banks, the government and other officials to immediately recognize a consumer using apps on their devices. He also stated that blockchain technology would enable private sharing of these details even without a central system and enable the setting of control over personal information in the hands of the consumer that would avoid the hackers. He further added that due to Canada's concentrated banking system, provincial government and participation from telecommunications, it had a competitive advantage in a commercial roll-out. The article also highlighted that Estonia started to adopt blockchain identity system after a nationwide cyber-attack in 2007, thus making it easier for its population to vote over the internet. Other countries such as Japan, Kazakhstan and India have also incorporated such initiatives (Alexander, 2017).

The article "Do Blockchain Have Anything to Offer Identity" (Olshansky & Wilson, 2018) focuses on IAM as it is slowly becoming central to online interactions. It notes that a number of IAM start-up companies have introduced identity registration solution on the Blockchain. "Blockchain uses a variety of new data security methods which potentially makes it valuable to the Identity and Access Management System (IAM)" (Olshansky & Wilson, 2018).

Some are developing new Blockchain-based structure for distributing attributes, which happens to be a significant element of IAM. This paper gives an impartial view on how Blockchain technology and IAM can come together as one, as the original Blockchains are usually not a good fit for identity management whereas new Blockchain progresses could suit the requirements of IAM.

The goal of cryptocurrency is to give users the ability to trade online currency without the trust issues of involving third-party intermediaries, which is basically different from that of enterprise IAM, as it needs a more rigorous key lifecycle management and access controls than public Blockchain offers. However, there are still some new developments in Blockchain that do show potential for improvements in aspects of IAM, such as the provenance of identity attributes and keys (Olshansky & Wilson, 2018).

Agriculture

In the article "Blockchain Technologies in Agriculture and Food Value Chains in Kerala" (Kerala Development and Innovation Strategic Council (K-DISC), 2018), significant opportunities to improve the agri-food supply chain are provided. Agri-food supply chain is very convenient when planning to focus on the quality and the safety of transactions as it reduces transaction cost. When using Blockchain technology, the process is trusted and database supports financing process. Cold chain is useful for the supply chain management aspect, and when used high accuracy was observed. The Blockchain helps to store and share data, checking and triggering smart equipment and storing information. The advantage of this value chain technology is that the user can share information and track items they have purchased. Blockchain technology is still in the stage of development, but the adaptation process of creating a new value chain can help the agriculture sector in development (Vasudevan & Neelakantan, 2018).

The five possible uses of Blockchain in agriculture are in food safety, traceability, transaction costs, opening new markets and logistics. Food safety ensures that the process from farm to market is quick and saves time and money. Traceability ensures that it will be easy to track where the food comes from and what happens to the food at each step, as this prevents food fraud. Using Blockchain technology, transaction costs becomes more transparent and effective. Opening new market uses AgriLedger, which evaluates each person's trust and their ability to operate. Logistics enables smart logistics of the future. Thus, in agriculture these are only five of the major uses of Blockchain (Hammerich, 2018).

Moving on to the article, "Blockchain for Agriculture and food" (Ge *et al.*, 2017), it states that Blockchain technology aims to have database consistency and integrity in relation to a decentralized database. AgriFood has an advantage because of the presence of transaction information management problems. Blockchain technology reduces the risk of fraud or adulteration. As consumers are getting more and more concerned about the safety and sustainability of food and other requirements on Agrifood chains, Blockchain helps maintain a record and ensures the security of data. Adapting new technologies takes time, but it does play an important role as well (Ge *et al.*, 2017).

Food

Supply chain traceability

With the use of technologies, machine-intensive technologies began to operate on a unique scale. Factories support food production, and it becomes faster and cheaper for food producers. However, the supply chain became a very complex chain, as illustrated (Figure 3). The reason the

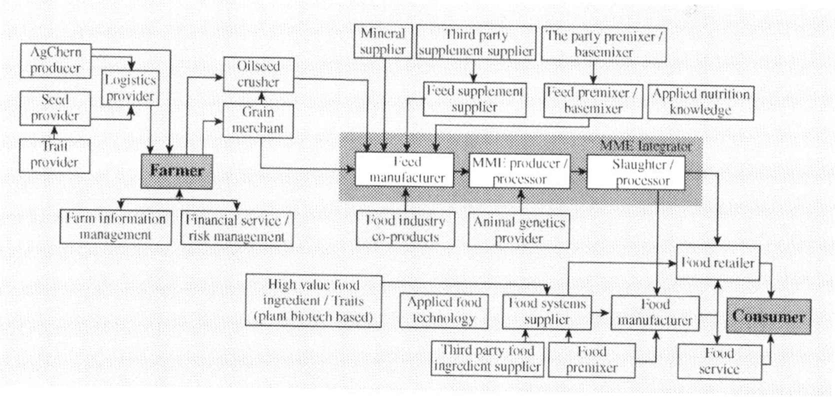

Figure 3: Supply Chain Traceability

Source: https://ec.europa.eu/home-affairs/sites/homeaffairs/files/what-we-do/policies/industry-for-security/docs/dg_home_cou_mapping_en.pdf.

supply chain became more complex is because consumers became disconnected from their food, thus making it difficult for them to track their food and ensure if it is hygienic and sustainable.

In the article "How Blockchain Technology Could Track and Trace Food from Farm to Fork" (Pretz, 2018), the author discusses how several organizations are exploring Blockchain technology as businesses increasingly have their own record-keeping systems. An advantage of Blockchain technology is that it provides proof of ownership because each food product has some kind of code so it is easier for the consumers to identify the product. It is for the farmers to use because according to Palombini, "Farmers now can advertise their produce on Blockchain exchanges monitored by verified wholesalers and distributors". Thus, farmers have digital proof of inventory (Pretz, 2018).

Similarly, in the article "A Framework for Blockchain Technology in Rice Supply Chain Management" (Kumar & Iyengar, 2017), the solution for the problem increasingly arising in rice supply chain in Blockchain technology is provided. Multi-Stage supply chain is used in the rice supply chain management. The production link details are entered into the Blockchain with a digital profile. The information is stored as a digital profile, and this includes every detail with regard to the farming. A new trade was introduced among the farmers and processing companies where the product is traded after signing a Smart contract that is stored on the Blockchain. This thus ensures the integrity of information (Kumar & Iyengar, 2017).

Supply chain management is considered one of the most positive examples of the use of blockchain, as it is ideal for industries in which goods pass through several hands and move through several rounds, from start to finish. Walmart and IBM joined forces to introduce the Food Safety Alliance Blockchain in China. Together with the Fortune 500 Company JD.com, the project is considered to improve tracking food and security, making it easier to authenticate that food is safe for consumption.

China has proven to be a mature test bed for blockchain projects, because it is also home to the world's first commodity agronomic blockchain. Louis Dreyfus Co, a leading food agent, has set up a mission with French and Dutch banks to sell soybeans to China using blockchain technology to settle transactions faster than traditional methods (Zago, 2018).

Fishing industry

Blockchain is being used to promote sustainable fishing. Illegal catching of fish is a common issue seen in the industry, and blockchain technology provides a way to prove where fish have been caught, processed and sold. This net-to-plate chain enables examiners to regulate whether the fish came from a region known for human rights abuses or from countries affected by economic sanctions (Zago, 2018).

An article titled "Startup to Solve Traceability Issues in Seafood Industry Via Blockchain" (Balursky, 2018) focuses on a Blockchain-based startup known as Fishcoin that plans to apply a decentralized ledger technology (DLT) to seafood supply chains, connecting fisherman and fish farmers at the point of harvest to the international seafood supply chain, thus including in the process suppliers, processors, dealers and vendors. In this article, the business aimed to use blockchain technology that would bring traceability to the seafood industry, creating an ecosystem that will permit seafood manufacturers and supply chain intermediaries to get rewards via micro-transactions (Balursky, 2018).

Their startup was mostly known for its parent company, Eachmile Technologies, as the founder developed a mobile application for their fisherman termed as mFish. This application was intended for small-scale fishers; it permitted them to keep track of their catch and get valuable information such as weather and market conditions like prices, all via electronic means. The application has since then been adopted by over 80% of almost 1,800 fishermen, and it has been reimagined to become a means for small-scale fish farmers to share data with the Fishcoin Blockchain Network (Balursky, 2018).

Business

Microsoft Azure Enterprise customers can access as a service the Ethereum Blockchain. In a secure host environment, this offers businesses the right to use smart contracts and blockchain applications.

It is also reported that Google is working on a proprietary blockchain to backup its cloud-based business. The parent company, Alphabet, is developing a distributed ledger that parties can use to store data in connection with Google's cloud services for businesses, with a white-label version for businesses in the works as well (Zago, 2018).

One particular article titled "These 11 Questions Will Help You Decide If Blockchain Is Right for Your Business" (Mulligan *et al.*, 2018) talks about how any innovative development of Blockchain must of necessity have a good fit between particular benefits of Blockchain and uses that enable the realization of such benefits.

"One of the biggest reasons for Blockchain's sudden popularity is its number of believers, people who truly believe that Blockchain Technology can resolve any given problem from Global Financial Inequality to helping people sell their properties without even needing an estate agent" (Mulligan *et al.*, 2018). In some ways, this can be considered as overpromotion of the technology as it is still a growing industry and so could have a negative impact in the possible future.

The research analyzes different aspects of Blockchain and its uses and the authors came up with some questions that a business needs to answer in order to realize if Blockchain can solve any of its problems. For example, the software that a special effects company uses face issues with providing large-scale graphics processing units to work on and deliver customer projects.

A company like this needs access to a large amount of processing power for as little money as possible; this is because the consumer-grade processors may already be installed on the devices, thus allowing anyone that could contribute their processing power to do so at a cost. When one does need the processing power, they could sell the downtime to the special effects company that could use that extra processing power for their new software and receive a token on the Blockchain for it. This paper basically tries to encourage people to practice finding business problems that can be solved by Blockchain technology rather than overhyping the technology (Mulligan *et al.*, 2018).

Smart contracts

In the project "Protecting Farmers in Emerging Markets with Blockchain", the three applications of Blockchain solution were supply

Figure 4: Origin of Smart Contracts

Source: Blockgeeks — Smart Contracts.

chain traceability, smart contract and crop insurance, and micro-financing and bitcoin.

Smart contracts origin

The smart contracts origin that is depicted above (Figure 4) shows automated contracts that have to fulfill certain conditions, such as execution only when a certain clause or requirement has been satisfied. This can be used to track money, property and physical assets without middlemen.

In the article, "A Blockchain Research Framework", blockchain technology has been discussed as receiving a lot of public attention owing to its unique technologies characteristics. Regardless of its popularity, there is currently a serious lack of information concerning where and how blockchain technology is successfully applicable and where it can offer actual societal effects. Blockchain research seems to be limited, disconnected and focused on a limited number of topics; therefore, further study on the Blockchain research framework can help provide meaningful information. Blockchain technology cannot process monetary transactions, but it ensures that the transactions deal with programmable rules, which is "smart contracts". Multidisciplinary research has since been conducted to create more knowledge of blockchain technologies (Risius & Spohrer, 2017).

Robotics

The article by Manuj Aggarwal titled "Blockchain In Robotics — A Sneak Peek Into The Future" states that if blockchain is combined with robotics, it is going to make the robotics operations more secure, flexible, autonomous and profitable. The networks are combined with cryptographic algorithms, and it is possible for the parties concerned to reach an agreement on a particular transaction and even record that agreement without any centralized control authority. Together with robotics, this technology has the potential to completely redesign the digital business (Aggarwal, 2018).

Blockchain would play a vital role in distributing information to enable a group of robots to perform the desired task or effectively solve problems. Swarm Robotics work with robots that function together to perform a certain task. For commercial applications, the main obstacle to deploying these robots on a large scale is that they need to be secured. Swarm robotics security basically encompasses data integrity, data confidentiality, authentication of data origin and authentication of the entity. Blockchain technology can address the security issue in swarm robotics as it not only provides a reliable and private communication network for swarm agents but also provides ways to address vulnerabilities, potential threats and attacks (Aggarwal, 2018).

The use of encrypted techniques such as digital signature cryptography and public key cryptography in blockchain technology is not only the recognized means of proving the identity of a specific agent in a network but also of making transactions that are using unsafe and shared channels. In order to enable such transactions, a pair of private, public and a corresponding key are made for each agent (Aggarwal, 2018).

Under swarm robotics, the public keys can be shared between robots that want to communicate using public key cryptography. Any robot can therefore send information to a specific robot in the network, and only a robot with a matching private key can read the message. Therefore, there is no risk involved even if it falls into the wrong hands because a public key cannot be used to decrypt the message (Aggarwal, 2018).

Thus, implementing blockchain technology will allow the robots to operate in various and changing environments. This will be possible if different blockchain ledgers using different parameters are in sync with their operation and without modifying their basic control algorithms (Aggarwal, 2018).

Smart cities

Smart cities are no longer considered the realm of science fiction. With the help of Blockchain Technology, Taipei seeks to place itself as a future city. A partnership has been announced with IOTA, and they have already employed temperature, light, humidity and pollution detection cards (Zago, 2018).

Oil industry

S&P Global Platts, one of the prominent players on the commodity market, trialed a blockchain solution utilized to keep track of data from oil storage. Weekly inventories on the blockchain will be stored to diminish the need for physical data management and reduce the likelihood of humanoid errors (Zago, 2018).

Railways

Blockchain technology has been used by rail operators to advance the speed of their operations in Russia, i.e. Novotrans. The company, one of the country's major rolling stock operators, will use blockchain to keep track of requests for repair, inventory and other operational issues. The main reason for using blockchain records is that it becomes tougher to manipulate and corrupt the data (Zago, 2018).

Gaming

One of the gaming industry's most dominant companies, Ubisoft, is researching how blockchain can be implemented in their video games.

In particular, it focuses on owning and transferring in-game items such as digital collectibles and rewards. Successful demonstration has been recorded with the use of Ethereum blockchain (Zago, 2018).

Car leasing

The distributed ledger technology of Blockchain is ideal for safely and unalterably registering records of any kind. One such use case that Essentia is developing is in the renting of vehicles. Many large leasing businesses will be able to use Essentia's blockchain protocol to store fully encrypted customer data and share the same with relevant parties on an authorized basis (Zago, 2018).

Insurance

There is often talk of blockchain use in the insurance industry, but the fact that many are not aware of is that this technology has already been executed, for example, Insurer American International Group Inc. has accomplished a so-called pilot "smart contract" multinational policy intended for Standard Chartered Bank PLC in partnership with International Business Machines Corp. and aims to accomplish complex international coverage by blockchain (Zago, 2018).

Endangered species protection

A man is another man's wolf, and to animals an even bigger wolf. "Care for the Uncared" is a non-profit organization working with the brightest developers to find a way of preserving and protecting endangered species using Blockchain technologies (Zago, 2018).

Advertising

In partnership with Nasdaq, the New York Interactive Advertising Exchange uses blockchain to generate a marketplace where ads can be purchased by brands, publishers and agencies. The procedure is simple and as safe as can be using the Ethereum blockchain's open protocol (Zago, 2018).

Journalism

One of the hottest topics in the journalism industry is permanence. One mistake, and all the hard work and research would be wasted. Blockchain is one intelligent solution to this problem. Apart from the obvious benefits of blockchain, Civil, a decentralized journalism marketplace, offers an economic incentive model for quality news content, coupled with the capability to permanently archive content that can be accessed at any time (Zago, 2018).

Shipping

The suitability of Blockchain to record shipment data is self-evident. Several projects have used distributed ledger technology to work in this field, using it to bring transparency to the inevitable bureaucracy in international trade within the maritime logistics industry. Maersk, one of the world's biggest shippers, was one of the first to use Blockchain, and ZIM has now picked up the torch (Zago, 2018).

Tourism

Blockchain is under research in order to improve the economy of Hawaii by providing tourists with the opportunity to pay with bitcoin and other currencies for local goods and services. The government of the state thus hopes to attract tourists, particularly from Asia, to spend more money and ultimately aid Hawaii develop economically (Zago, 2018).

Land registry

Blockchain proves again that it cannot only be used in the crypto space but also by small businesses in this aspect. Georgia's government is using it to list land titles. They designed a custom Blockchain system and integrated it into the National Public Registry Agency's (NAPR) digital records system. Georgia is now taking advantage of the benefit of Blockchain technology to improve transparency and reduce fraud (Zago, 2018).

Mobile payments

Cryptocurrencies are used in a wide range of projects along with the fundamental Blockchain technology to enable mobile payments. A consortium of Japanese banks have been involved in one of the recently announced initiatives launched in the fall of 2018. They will use the technology of Ripple to allow instant mobile payments (Zago, 2018).

Cat bonds

Cat bonds will be the only hope for those who are a victim of tsunami, earthquakes and other forms of natural disasters. Blockchain permits fast and transparent settlements among parties and generates certainty that even without human operation, the system will remain operational. Blockchain has now been used successfully as a settlement mechanism for cat bonds (Zago, 2018).

Healthcare

Medical records are disreputably discrete and flawed, with unpredictable processing of data. This means that the hospital and clinic will be forced to work with incorrect or partial records of patients. Healthcare projects such as MedRec use blockchain to facilitate the sharing of data while ensuring confidentiality and providing authentication (Zago, 2018).

Waste management

A Smart Waste Management System in China is using RFID technology from Waltonchain. This project will allow the monitoring of waste levels by using Walton's blockchain to increase operational efficiencies and enhance resources (Zago, 2018).

Border control

Essentia met with the Netherlands government to create a new system to check passengers traveling between Amsterdam and London. Currently, at multiple points, passengers on Eurostar trains between the two countries are subject to border checks. Essentia is studying a blockchain-based solution that would store passenger data securely, allowing UK agencies to audit the metrics recorded in the Netherlands. Blockchain would ensure that the data were not altered and verifiably accurate (Zago, 2018).

Music

One of blockchain technology's main advantages is the way intermediaries are removed. The music business is a major illustration of an industry that has seen artists poorly paid for their efforts. A number of blockchain-based projects have sprung up, seeking a fairer deal for music creators, including Artbit, overseen by former Guns N Roses drummer Matt Sorum (Zago, 2018).

Carbon offsets

China's environmental footprint is substantial owing to its status as a heavily industrialized nation. In March 2017, together with Energy-Blockchain Labs, IBM launched the Hyperledger Fabric blockchain as a way to track carbon assets in China. This creates an assessable and auditable emissions tracking system and facilitates a tradable market for businesses seeking to offset their energy consumption while encouraging greener industrial practices (Zago, 2018).

Diamonds

One of the most famous diamond companies in the world, The De Beers Group, uses its own blockchain to create a "digital record for every diamond registered on the platform". Because of concerns about the source of diamonds and their country of origin ethics, coupled with the risk of stones being swapped along the line for less valuable ones, blockchain is a natural fit. Because each record is indelible, the data for each stone will last as long as the diamonds themselves (Zago, 2018).

Real estate

Ukraine is one of the first countries to use blockchain to make property deals easier. A property in Kiev was sold by TechCrunch's founder Micheal Arrington, a prominent cryptocurrency advocate. The deal was made possible with the help of smart contracts of the Ethereum blockchain and is meant to be the first of many to be completed by Propy, a start-up specializing in blockchain-based real estate transactions (Zago, 2018).

Fine art

Similar to the trade in diamonds, the art industry depends on the origin and validity of the arts. Although blockchain cannot verify a painting to determine if it is real or a fake, it can be used to identify the former owners of the item. Furthermore, blockchain is now used as a means of acquiring art. Blockchain technology can be used to make touchable objects transferrable from anyplace in the world without transferring them from secure storage physically (Zago, 2018).

LGBT

Blockchain can help build the "pink economy" and help the LGBT community fight for their rights without revealing the identities of individuals. The latter is a tremendously important problem because hate crimes are a frequent problem amongst the gay community, particularly in nations known for abuse of human rights and where homosexuality is illegal or at least frowned upon (Zago, 2018).

Blockchain alternatives

Two alternatives to blockchain that have been identified are Tangle and Hashgraph. Both the technologies promised to yield remedies for blockchain's performance bottleneck. Blockchain is sequential in nature, which means once the first block is approved, the next block will be placed above the previous block, and this cannot be changed. Because of the sequential nature of blockchain, the process of adding the blocks to the chain is greatly affected in terms of speed. Furthermore, Tangle and Hashgraph can also be considered to be distributed technologies even though they are fundamentally different to the blockchain. The basic difference is that they are "blockchains without blocks and chains".

Furthermore, Tangle and Hashgraph are "Directed Acyclic Graphs". First of all, tangle does not utilize "blocks" in the conventional sense. Instead, Tangle will require a user to approve two previous transactions before carrying out a new transaction. Thus, it can be said that when a new transaction is added to the Tangle, the user will be assigned two preceding transactions that he or she will be required to authorize.

It is essential to note that by authorizing a preceding transaction, Tangle combines the transaction making process with the consensus reaching process. A user will not be required to wait for approvals from the community once he or she has initiated a transaction. Also, Tangle applications can attain harmonization without the contribution of any miners, as this technology does not require a fee. A user may assume that the work that they approve will serve as a payment for their transaction. Additionally, as more participants join the Tangle network, it speeds up.

Second, Hashgraph uses a completely different technique of "sharing information and establishing consensus: gossip". This means that one network participant is required to share all the data on transactions with various other network nodes that are selected randomly. The next node will then collaborate the information with the information that is received from other nodes and include any information about recent transactions. This set of combined information will then be handed on to the next randomly chosen nodes until all nodes are aware of the information created at the start. The sharing of information includes a timestamp as well as the information about the preceding receivers of the information. All in all, rather than Hashgraph making use of the gossip, it also uses gossip of gossip.

To add on, Hashgraph is extremely fast, as it can handle more than 250,000 transactions per second. Even though Hashgraph's transaction per second is fast, it has only been implemented in private distributed ledger. Thus, Hashgraph may face similar challenges as other public distributed ledger technologies in terms of security and performance.

Risks of blockchain

In the article "10 Blockchain Implementation Risks in International Development", the focus is on the risks of implementation due to people not completely understanding Blockchain technology and trying to implement them anyway. "Distributed Ledger Technology (DLT) uses a decentralized system to store transactions which can later be processed, verified and stored on a permanent ledger" (Vota, 2019).

Even though Distributed Ledger Technology (DLT) is on the rise and becoming more popular in the current era, it still is not mature enough, which opens it up to risks especially during implementation phase. Understanding of such risks is key when it comes to deciding which DLT is more appropriate for any particular scenario. One of the major risks being faced by DLT is not having any set standards at such a rapid development stage. The lack of these international standards puts customer privacy and security, among other factors, at risk. Considering that Blockchain uses public and private keys of an individual to perform transactions without actually keeping track of each key, in case of any issues with law enforcers this will become a problem since it will be difficult to identify individuals with their keys.

Considering the number of successful attacks on DLTs and the privacy and security risks involved with DLTs along with other numerous vulnerabilities such as malware, phishing, etc., it can be concluded that at this stage of the development of Distributed Ledger Technologies Blockchain is not the safest mode to use to exchange transaction, but with further development in terms of safeguarding the customer's personal information, security and privacy, it could be one day (Vota, 2019).

Moving on to the article "Blockchain — A Survey on Functions, Applications, and Open Issues", the focus is on why society deems

Blockchain technology disruptive and also on Blockchain features and its practical applications. "Blockchain technology is slowly making headlines especially after its successful development of Cryptocurrency, as this technology is gradually replacing already in place systems, it is being considered as a disruptive technology to the society" (Lu, 2018).

There have been many developments in cryptocurrencies, and the significance of Blockchain is starting to gain recognition and is mostly being considered as disruptive. The paper discusses how Blockchain uses data structures to authenticate and store data and uses distributed algorithms to create and update data. It also uses encryption to ensure secure data transfer and access and uses an automated scripting code to form a new distributed infrastructure. Blockchain technology does not need any third party support or hardware intervention or even central supervision.

This gives Blockchain a decentralized network feature through P2P protocol in which all nodes have the same encryption rights and obligations and must follow the same encryption rules to equally maintain data records throughout the network system. Another feature of Blockchain is its openness and transparency as it is built on open source software and freely available to everyone. Being a Distributed General Ledger Technology, all nodes of the network system can view all data records and operations of the system. These are just some of the features of Blockchain technology; there are many more characteristics such as Independence, Unforgeability and Anonymity. These features prove that Blockchain technology has a lot to offer when it comes to practical application and that it is not as disruptive as society makes it seem like (Lu, 2018).

Advantages of blockchain

In a similar article titled "In Blockchain We Trust", the focus was on why Blockchain is so significant in the current technological era and how wild speculations in regard to Blockchain could slow down its rise. "There have been a lot of speculations regarding the importance of Blockchain Technology, but in order to truly comprehend it we must look past these speculations to what is actually being built underneath the technology (Casey & Paul, 2018).

This paper suggests that Blockchain is not about making millions overnight or about hiding your financial activities from nosy governments but rather a way to drastically decrease the cost of trust by means of a thorough, decentralized approach to accounting and, by extension, making innovative ways to structure economic organization.

Blockchain is considered a special kin of ledger because rather than using a centralized institute for management such as banks and government agencies do, it uses a decentralized network to store data in independent computers using multiple copies which means no single entity will be in control of the ledger.

Any of these computers on the network can make changes to the ledger as long as they follow instructions uttered by a consent protocol; once you follow proper consensus protocol measures, all the computers on the network would update their copies of the ledger simultaneously. Although if any computer tries to add a new entry on the ledger without this consensus, the rest of the network will automatically reject the entry as invalid. With all this information, the paper concludes that Blockchain technology can provide an entirely new paradigm for innovators ready to deploy world-changing applications (Casey & Paul, 2018).

Moving on to another paper on Blockchain technology titled "Is Blockchain Hype, Revolutionary, or Both? What We Need to Know", the authors are trying to answer if Blockchain technology is going to transform the economy or whether it is just publicity. "Some are considering Blockchain Technology to be a revolutionary technology as it gives users the ability to engage in day to day trusted transactions without the need for a third-party intermediary" (Oh & Wallsten, 2018).

Economies need their transactions to be trusted, that is, a buyer needs to know for sure that the supplier truly owns the assets he/she claims to be marketing and, on the other hand, the seller should be able to validate that he/she will receive the agreed payment for transferring ownership of the asset. The lesser the cost of such trusted transactions, the more types of transactions can be conducted, which will thus help the economy to function more efficiently.

This brings us to Cryptocurrency. Cryptocurrency such as bitcoins have incorporated features of money into private digital currencies like Facebook Credits, Microsoft Points and Litecoins, and entrepreneurs have made a new ecosystem of electronic transactions, settlement and reconciliation of non-money digital tokens.

Its social value is still unclear, however, since cryptocurrency does not yet appear to offer much improvements over the already existing trusted electronic currencies such as Visa or MasterCard (Oh & Wallsten, 2018).

Discussion

Figure 2 shows the price fluctuation of bitcoins. When Bitcoin first started, it did not have any value, but as the years progressed Bitcoin started gaining popularity as it was the most secure platform for any transactions. The value of Bitcoins increased by day, until Bitcoin exchanges got hacked in some countries and since then Bitcoin users started losing trust in Bitcoin, and that is the reason Bitcoin went down.

Criteria used to rank the articles used in this study were the number of citations: high-ranked articles have 50+ citations, medium-ranked articles have between 15 and 25 citations and low-ranked articles have less than 10 citations (Figure 5). Journals indexed on various publication websites such as Springer, Amoral, Sub Journals, Taylor and Francis, and Science Direct were also used to rank the articles.

Figure 6 shows that the majority usage of blockchain is in Bitcoin technology as there are numerous banks around the world using bitcoin

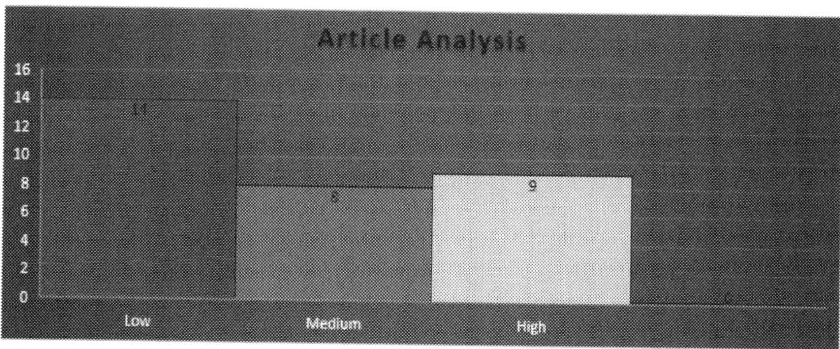

Figure 5: The Ranking of Articles Used in Compiling the Report (High, Medium and Low)

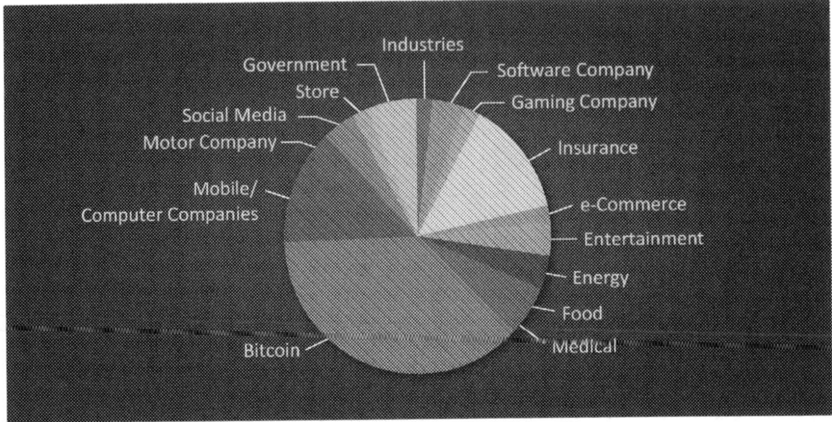

Figure 6: The Usage of Blockchain in Various Fields

for the transactions. Banks also use blockchain to protect the identity of their customers. The second major use of blockchain is in insurance companies, where it is used for balancing their exposure risk. Food industries use blockchain for traceability. Food is tracked from harvest/manufacture till it reaches the customers for consumption. Moving on to mobile and computer companies, the two major companies that use blockchain are Apple and Samsung, and they use it for timestamping and traceability of their products. Finally moving to the government, blockchain is used to store public records on a decentralized framework.

With regard to the advantages and disadvantages of blockchain technology, in the articles on Blockchain Technology that were analyzed, we came across certain points pertaining to this. Figures 7 and 8 show the analysis of the Advantages and Disadvantages with regard to different aspects of Blockchain Technology.

The pie charts show the major advantages and disadvantages we were able to identify when analyzing the papers that formed part of our overrall literature review. The percentage value indicates the proportion of papers or articles that had that particular advantage or disadvantage. For example, out of all the articles we selected and read, most of them identified disintermediation as their prime advantage; hence, it has the highest percentage. The same was observed for disadvantage, i.e. performance was the most common disadvantage of Blockchain technology.

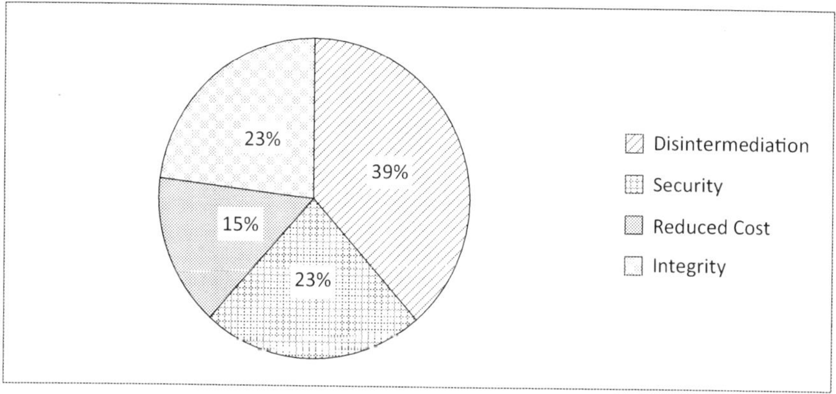

Figure 7: Pie Chart Showing Major Advantages of Blockchain Technology

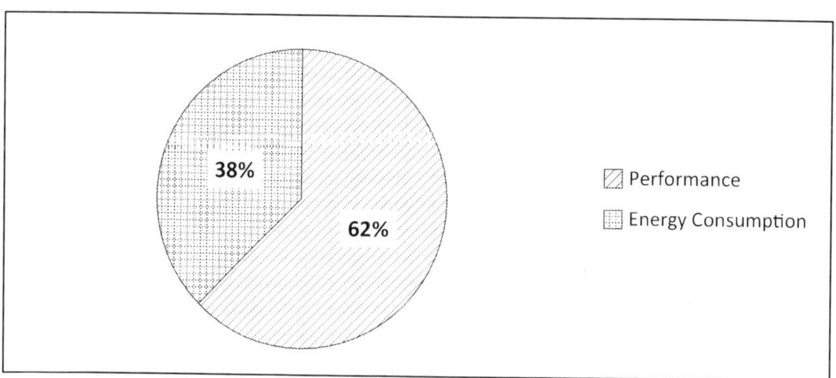

Figure 8: Pie Chart Showing Major Disadvantages of Blockchain Technology

One of the most major advantages we came across during the analysis of these articles and papers was disintermediation. The reason for this is because it gives you the ability to independently verify and process the transactions. This is better than relying on a computer system that is being run by a third party, even if it is a trusted organization such as banks, because the contents that are saved in the database of this computer system can be easily corrupted if someone gets access to the system. Thus, by implementing Blockchain you could save the time and money of hiring people and designing processes in order to secure that database. It is

Blockchain's use of distributed database and cryptography that helps keep the database more secure.

There are other aspects of Blockchain that can also be beneficial. In many of the articles we analyzed, reliability and security were the two main benefits, as Blockchain does not have a central point of failure, thus making it more immune to malicious attacks.

As transactions are usually added to a single public ledger, ledgers are more manageable and efficient in terms of access. Considering the business aspects of Blockchain, it provides reduced transaction time as it is processed 24/7. Also, by eliminating third-party intermediaries and overhead costs for exchanging assets, Blockchain can potentially reduce transaction costs.

Moving on to the disadvantages, from the articles that we analyzed we determined that the 2 major drawbacks of Blockchain technology were Performance and Energy Consumption. Even though having a distributed database works as an advantage, a centralized database is faster due to the fact that Blockchain does all the same things as a regular database but has additional factors that need to be taken into consideration. One such factor is Signature Verification, which requires the Blockchain transaction to be digitally signed using a public and private cryptography scheme, as without this the source cannot be proven since transactions need to propagate in a peer-to-peer fashion. In a central database, however, once a connection is established, there is no need to verify each request individually.

The second factor is known as Consensus Mechanisms, i.e. in order for the nodes in a Blockchain network to reach consensus, effort must be expended. Depending on this consensus mechanism, there could be a lot of back-and-forth communication, and their associated rollbacks. A centralized database would also deal with conflicting and rejected transactions, but it is less likely to end up being queued and processed in a single location.

The third and last factor to take into consideration is Redundancy: a centralized database would process transactions once or twice, whereas in Blockchain it needs to be processed individually by each node in the network, which means more work is being done for the same result.

The other major disadvantage of Blockchain is the amount of energy it consumes. In our analysis, we came across a couple of articles suggesting that Blockchain technology, specifically Bitcoin, consumes a lot of energy. The Bitcoin network requires a lot of energy and processing power to support itself, and the level of energy it needs has only been increasing over the years.

There are also some other minor disadvantages of Blockchain such as the amount of throughput and latency it requires while processing.

Conclusion

To conclude, we could state that Blockchain definitely has its issues, but considering the benefits of it in different aspects in terms of the current trend and technology field, i.e. how it is helpful not only in the IT field but other fields as well, it can be said that Blockchain Technology has a promising future. On this note, we proved that Blockchain is a disruptive technology. Thus, we can say that blockchain is going to replace the currently existing technologies. Moreover, we were able to achieve the aim and objectives of our research.

Acknowledgements

In order to complete this research project successfully, several people were involved who need to be thanked. We would specifically like to thank Dr. Sam Goundar for providing us with the resources to carry out the research in blockchain technology and also his guidance in compiling the systematic literature review.

References

Aggarwal, M. (2018). Blockchain in Robotics — A Sneak Peek Into The Future. Retrieved from A Medium Corporation: https://medium.com/@manuj.aggarwal/blockchain-in-robotics-a-sneak-peek-into-the-future-4e115ccf4931. Accessed on April 30, 2019.

Alexander, D. (2017). Forget Iris Scans, Canadians to Use Blockchain for Digital IDs. Retrieved from STUFF: https://www.stuff.co.nz/technology/digital-living/98893860/forget-iris-scans-canadians-to-use-blockchain-for-digital-ids. Accessed on April 29, 2019.

Allen, D. W., Berg, C., Lane, A., Potts, J. (2017). SSRN. The Economics of Crypto-Democracy, p. 11. Retrieved from: https://papers.ssrn.com/sol3/papers.cfm?abstract_id=2973050.

Atzori, M. (2015). Blockchain Technology and Decentralized Governance: Is the State Still Necessary?, p. 37. Retrieved from: https://papers.ssrn.com/sol3/papers.cfm?abstract_id=2709713.

Balursky, N. (2018). Startup to Solve Traceability Issues in Seafood Industry via Blockchain. Retrieved from Cointelegraph: https://cointelegraph.com/news/startup-to-solve-traceability-issues-in-seafood-industry-via-blockchain. Accessed on May 12, 2019.

BBC (2017). Youbit Shuts after Second Hack Attack. Retrieved from BBC News Websites: https://www.bbc.com/news/technology-42409815. Accessed on April 15, 2019.

Bitcoin Mining (2018). Retrieved from Bitcoin Mining Website: https://www.bitcoinmining.com/. Accessed on April 2, 2019.

Blockchain Technologies in Agriculture and Food Value Chains in Kerala (2018). Retrieved from: https://mafiadoc.com/blockchain-technologies-in-agriculture-and-food-_5b797efc097c47892f8b45fc.html. Accessed on April 30, 2019.

Buterin, V., Coindesk, Kravchenko, P., Tamayo, D. A., Wood, G. (2016). Blockchains & Distributed Ledger Technologies. Retrieved from Blockchain Hub: https://blockchainhub.net/blockchains-and-distributed-ledger-technologies-in-general/. Accessed on May 9, 2019.

Carson, B., Romanelli, G., Walsh, P., Zhumaev, A. (2018). Blockchain beyond the Hype: What is the Strategic Business Value. Retrieved from Mckinsey Digital: https://www.mckinsey.com/business-functions/digital-mckinsey/our-insights/blockchain-beyond-the-hype-what-is-the-strategic-business-value. Accessed on May 9, 2019.

Casey, M. J., Paul V. (2018). In Blockchain We Trust. Retrieved from MIT TechnologyReview:https://www.technologyreview.com/s/610781/in-blockchain-we-trust/. Accessed on April 9, 2018.

Cellan-Jones, R. (2017). BBC. Retrieved from BBC News: https://www.bbc.com/news/technology-42138370. Accessed on November 27, 2017.

Cuthbertson, A. (2017). Bitcoin Mining on Track to Consume All of the World's Energy by 2020. Retrieved from Newsweek Website: https://www.newsweek.com/bitcoin-mining-track-consume-worlds-energy-2020-744036. Accessed on April 2, 2019.

Davidson, S., Filippi, P. D., Potts, J. (2016). SSRN. Economics of Blockchain, p. 23. Retrieved from Economics of Blockchain: https://papers.ssrn.com/sol3/ papers.cfm?abstract_id=2744751. Accessed on April 30, 2019.

Fortney, L. (2019). Blockchain, Explained. Retrieved from Investopedia: https://www.investopedia.com/terms/b/blockchain.asp. Accessed on May 9, 2019.

Ge, L., Brewster, C., Spek, J., Smeenk, A., Top, J. (2017). Blockchain for Agriculture and Food. Dutch Ministry of Agriculture, Netherlands: Wageningen Economic Research. Retrieved from https://www.wur.nl/upload_mm/d/c/0/b429c891-ab94-49c8-a309-beb9b6bba4df_2017-112%20Ge_def.pdf.

Hammerich, T. (2018). 5 Potential Use Cases for Blockchain in Agriculture. (I. Admin, Producer) Retrieved from Ingeni: https://futureofag.com/5-potential-use-cases-for-blockchain-in-agriculture-c88d4d2207e8. Accessed on April 30, 2019.

Harris, C. (2017). NZ Companies Embrace the Revolutionary Potential of Blockchain. Retrieved from Stuff: https://www.stuff.co.nz/business/innovation/99606942/nz-companies-embrace-the-revolutionary-potential-of-blockchain. Accessed on April 25, 2019.

Kumar, M. V., Iyengar, D. N. (2017). A Framework for Blockchain Technology in Rice Supply Chain Management. *Advanced Science and Technology Letters*, 146 (FGCN 2017), 125–130. Retrieved from: https://www.researchgate.net/publication/323259797_A_Framework_for_Blockchain_Technology_in_Rice_Supply_Chain_Management_Plantation. Accessed on May 1, 2019.

Lalley, S. P., Weyl, E. G. (2018). Quadratic Voting: How Mechanism Design can Radicalize Democracy. In *AEA Papers and Proceedings*, Vol. 108, pp. 33–37.

LO3 Energy. (2018). Reshaping The Energy Future. Retrieved from The Future of Energy: https://lo3energy.com. Accessed on April 14, 2019.

Lu, Y. (2018). Blockchain: A Survey on Functions. *Journal of Industrial Integration and Management*, 3(4): 1850015. Retrieved from: https://www.worldscientific.com/doi/abs/10.1142/S242486221850015X?journalCode=jiim&utm_source=TrendMD&utm_medium=cpc&utm_campaign=Journal_of_Industrial_Integration_and_Management_TrendMD_0&. Accessed on May 5, 2019.

Mulligan, C., Rangaswami, J., Warren, S., Scott, J. Z. (2018a). These 11 Questions will Help you Decide if Blockchain is Right for your Business. *World Economic Forum*, p. 8. Retrieved from: https://www.weforum.org/agenda/2018/04/questions-blockchain-toolkit-right-for-business/. Accessed on May 4, 2019.

Mulligan, C., Scott, J. Z., Warren, S., Rangaswami, J. (2018b). Blockchain Beyond the Hype — A Practical for Business Leaders. *World Economic Forum*, p. 10. Retrieved from: http://www3.weforum.org/docs/48423_Whether_Blockchain_WP.pdf. Accessed on May 9, 2019.

Nakamoto, S. (2008). Bitcoin: A Peer-to-Peer Electronic Cash System. Retrieved from Bitcoin Organisation: https://bitcoin.org/bitcoin.pdf? Accessed on April 20, 2019.

Nordrum (2017). Wall Street Firms to Move Trillions. Retrieved from IEEE Spectrum: https://spectrum.ieee.org/telecom/internet/wall-street-firms-to-move-trillions-to-blockchains-in-2018. Accessed on April 17, 2019.

Nordrum, A. (2017). Illinois vs. Dubai: Two Experiments Bring Blockchains to Government. Retrieved from IEEE Spectrum: https://spectrum.ieee.org/computing/networks/illinois-vs-dubai-two-experiments-bring-blockchains-to government. Accessed on April 11, 2019.

Oh, S., Wallsten, S. (2018). Is Blockchain Hype, Revolutionary, or Both — What We Need to Know. *Technology Policy Institute*, p. 14. Retrieved from: https://techpolicyinstitute.org/wp-content/uploads/2018/04/Is-Blockchain-Hype-Revolutionary-or-Both_What-We-Need-to-Know.pdf. Accessed on May 7, 2019.

Olshansky, S., Wilson, S. (2018). Do Blockchains Have Anything to Offer Identity. *Internet Society*, p. 13. Retrieved from: https://www.internetsociety.org/resources/doc/2018/blockchain-identity/. Accessed on May 3, 2019.

Palumbo, D., Macadam, D. (2017). BBC. Retrieved from BBC News: https://www.bbc.com/news/business-42150512. Accessed on April 2, 2019.

Peck, M., Wagman, D. (2017). Blockchains Will Allow Rooftop Solar Energy Trading for Fun and Profit. Retrieved from IEEE SPECTRUM: https://spectrum.ieee.org/computing/networks/blockchains-will-allow-rooftop-solar-energy-trading-for-fun-and-profit. Accessed on April 10, 2019.

Pretz, K. P. (2018). How Blockchain Technology Could Track and Trace Food From Farm to Fork. Retrieved from IEEE Spectrum: https://spectrum.ieee.org/searchContent?q=How+Blockchain+Technology+Could+Track+and+Trace+Food+From+Farm+to+Fork. Accessed on April 30, 2019.

Risius, M., Spohrer, K. (2017). A Blockchain Research Framework — What We (don't) Know, Where We Go from Here, and How We Will Get There. *Business & Information Systems Engineering*, 59(6), 385–409. Retrieved from Association for Information Systems: https://aisel.aisnet.org/bise/vol59/iss6/2/. Accessed on April 30, 2019.

Vasudevan, U. P., Neelakantan, K. (2018). Blockchain Technologies in Agriculture and Food Value Chains in Kerala. Retrieved from Research Gate: https://mafiadoc.com/blockchain-technologies-in-agriculture-and-food-_5b797efc097c47892f8b45fc.html. Accessed on April 30, 2019.

Vota, W. (2019). 10 Blockchain Implementation Risks in International Development. Retrieved from ICTworks: https://www.ictworks.org/blockchain-implementation-risks/#.XMzf4ugzbIU. Accessed on April 30, 2019.

Winarno, A., Harsari, J., Ardianto, B. (2018). Block-Chain Based E-Voting For Indonesia. *Journal of Engineering and Science Research*, 2(5), 13–17. Retrieved from: https://www.jesrjournal.com/uploads/2/6/8/1/26810285/50032018-jesr-13-17.pdf. Accessed on April 28, 2019.

Yli-Huumo, J., Ko, D., Choi, S., Park, S., Smolander, K. (2016). Where is Current Research on Blockchain Technology? — A Systematic Review. *PLOS One*, 11(10), e0163477.

Zago, M. G. (2018). 50 Plus Examples of How Blockchains are Changing the World. Retrieved from A Medium Corporation: https://medium.com/@matteozago/50-examples-of-how-blockchains-are-taking-over-the-world-4276bf488a4b. Accessed on April 20, 2019.

Chapter 2

A Taxonomy of Blockchain Applications

Sam Goundar[*,§], Shalvin Chand[*,¶], Jalpa Chandra[*,||], Akash Bhardwaj[†,**] and Fatemeh Saber[‡,††]

[*]*The University of the South Pacific, Suva, Fiji*

[†]*University of Petroleum and Energy Studies, Dehradun, India*

[‡]*University of Malaya, Kuala Lumpur, Malaysia*

[§]*sam.goundar@gmail.com*

[¶]*s11120206@student.usp.ac.fj*

[||]*jalpachandra96@gmail.com*

[**]*abhardwaj@ddn.upes.ac.in*

[††]*emeh.saber@gmail.com*

Abstract

A taxonomy of blockchain application uses cases that include application and apps. A major obstacle identified in several disciplines is the categorization of objects in a particular area of interest into a taxonomy. Blockchain is an innovation that is decentralized and characterized by value-based information that is distributed over a vast network with many untrusted users. Developing a taxonomy for blockchain applications is a complex process. This chapter thus attempts to discuss what internal factors contribute to the success of a blockchain application. This is followed by an analysis of which organizations use blockchain and which applications and apps they use. Finally, we classify blockchains according to what they are used for. For example, Blockchains are used in such fields as finance, agriculture, education, development, etc.

Introduction

The 21st century is about innovation. With the expanding requirement for modernization in our everyday lives, individuals need to adapt to new technologies. From utilizing a remote for controlling gadgets to utilizing voice notes for giving directions, today's innovation has made space in our ordinary lives. Technologies like augmented reality have picked up pace in the previous decade, and now there is another addition to the pack, for example Blockchain Technology.

Blockchain — The progressive innovation affecting distinctive businesses miraculously was presented in the business sectors with its absolute first modern application Bitcoin. Bitcoin is only a type of digital currency (cryptocurrency) that can be utilized in the place of fiat cash for exchanging. Furthermore, the underlying innovation behind the accomplishment of cryptocurrencies is named as Blockchain. There is a typical confusion among individuals that Bitcoin and Blockchain are one; however, that is not the situation. Making cryptographic forms of money is one of the applications of Blockchain innovation and, other than Bitcoin, there are various applications that are created based on the Blockchain technology. In simple terms, Blockchain can be depicted as an information structure that holds transactional records, while simultaneously ensuring security, transparency and decentralization. A Blockchain is a disseminated record that is very open to everybody on the system. When a data is entered on a Blockchain, it is incredibly hard to change or modify it. Every transaction on a Blockchain is verified with a computerized signature that demonstrates its credibility. Because of the utilization of encryption and digital signatures, the information stored on the Blockchain is carefully designed and cannot be changed. Blockchain is similar to an engineering organization, which endorses the exchange for claiming advanced information with complex publicizing coding (Figure 1).

Blockchain itself brings the concept of privacy. It is known for providing privacy for its users effectively because of the highly encrypted networks. If someone tries to steal, the cyber-police will be helpless because of the huge amount of encryption. Therefore, using Blockchain

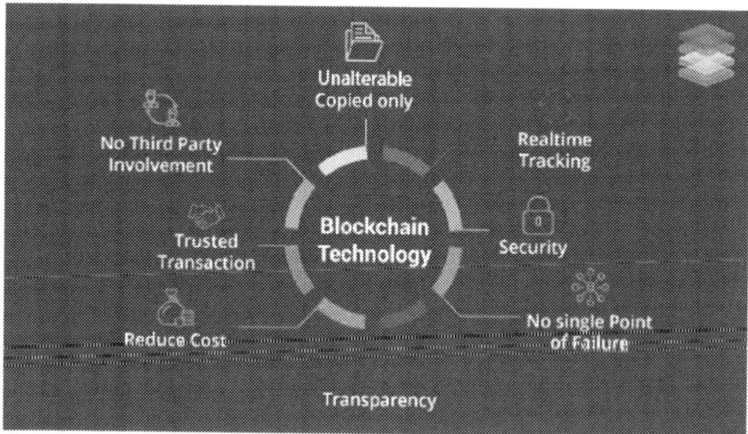

Figure 1: Why is Blockchain Technology Important

Source: Tasca & Tessone (2019).

technology can reduce the cost of getting a third party to work for you. For instance, when we have to send money to people staying in foreign countries, we can send money using Western Union or direct banking. However, in both cases we are involving a third person who is acting as an agent for us. It can be risky as hackers might steal the information or might provide misleading data. Hence, we use Blockchain technology, i.e. using a mobile app to send money, which is free, safe and convenient.

Furthermore, a taxonomy tree is used to summarize the study and provide a navigation tool across different Blockchain architectural configurations (Tasca & Tessone, 2019). For the purpose of this research, we will be opting to use inductive, deductive and intuitive reasoning and methodology. Inductive methodology includes watching observational cases, which are then investigated to decide measurements and qualities in the taxonomy. The deductive approach derives a taxonomy not from empirical cases but instead from theory or conceptualization. It identifies dimensions and characteristics in the taxonomy by a logical process derived from a sound conceptual or theoretical foundation (Nickerson *et al.*, 2013). The intuitive approach is essentially *ad hoc*. The researcher uses his or her understanding of the objects to be classified to propose a taxonomy based on the researcher's perceptions of what makes sense (Nickerson *et al.*, 2013).

This chapter is organized as follows: Literature review, followed by our research question, methodology, results, discussion and, lastly, conclusion.

Literature Review

Blockchain, Chainblock or Block Chain, no matter which way we put it, remains the same, as this technological topic is new in itself. Blockchain is a new technology with strong implications for the current and for the future of exchange of information and currency in globally interconnected societies. Wikipedia defines this as "continuously growing list of records called blocks which are linked and secured using Cryptography" (Wikipedia, 2020). It is so new that there is not much academic work done on the topic, but this trend is gradually changing quickly.

A fundamental problem in many disciplines is the classification of objects of interest into taxonomies. Biology has studied this problem extensively and developed a number of classification schemes that order the complexity of the living world and provide a foundation for biological research. Similar schemes are also found in many social science fields. Taxonomies play an important role in research and management because the classification of objects helps researchers and practitioners understand and analyze complex domains (Miller & Roth, 1994).

The variety, albeit not major, of blockchain innovative work looks at the cross-treatment of thoughts and inventiveness, yet it can likewise result in discontinuity of the field and duplication of efforts. One arrangement is to set up institutionalized structures to outline the field and advance innovative work activities in a regulated manner. Thus, the problem of consistently engineering large, complex blockchain systems remains largely unsolved. We approach this problem by proposing a component-based blockchain taxonomy starting from a base level to a connecting analysis. This taxonomy compartmentalizes the blockchain connectors/components and establishes the relationships between them in a hierarchical manner. The problem, as in many disciplines, is the classification of objects in a domain of interest into a Taxonomy, since basically classifying large information found in one whole complex process is then adequately addressed. Working on that thought and in that context,

Taxonomies play an important role in research and management because the classification of objects helps researchers and practitioners understand and analyze complex domains. Miller & Roth (1994, p. 286) note that "taxonomies are useful in discussion, research and pedagogy".

Thus, this literature review on Blockchain would identify and provide an overview of the current themes in the Taxonomy of blockchain, the implications and the applications of it and our recommendations. At first, we began by collecting sample papers reflecting the different topics and also all relevant topics related to blockchain, thus creating different channels and differing opinions and information. Second, we jotted down prime objectives of this research, i.e. what factors contribute to this blockchain application being successful, the need for blockchain, the ways in which organizations make use of blockchain technology and what are the impacts created by these applications.

A simple way of understanding block chain is this: you are walking in USP, and you see a flying Monkey twice as big as normal land and in the presence of about a 1,000 people dance for around 5 minutes and run away; at the same time a lie detector is placed into the hands of people who have just watched that humorous act, and it records exactly what they have seen. Everyone tells the same story, with identical details.

The first question is "will there be any doubt about the landing and dancing of a flying monkey?"

This is similar to the Taxonomy Blockchain, a data structure in which the information is grouped in sets (blocks) to which meta-information is added to another block of the previous chain in a time line. So that owing to cryptographic techniques, the information contained in the block can only be disowned or edited by modifying all subsequent blocks. This property allows its application in a distributed environment, so that the data structure "Blockchain" can act as a non-relational public database which contains irrefutable historical information. In part it has allowed, with consideration of concepts of asymmetric functions, the implementation of a distributed ledger that allows the support of and guarantees the security of digital money.

Following the appropriate protocols for all the operations carried out on the blockchain, it is possible to reach a consensus on the integrity of your data by all the network participants without having to resort to a technology in which the "truth" (reliable state systems) is built and reached. For these reasons, blockchain technology is especially suitable for scenarios in which it is required to store increasingly ordered data over time, without the possibility of modification or revision and in cases where trust is intended to be distributed instead of residing in a certifying entity (Casavant, 1988). The concepts of blockchain approaches have different aspects:

- **Data storage:** Achieved by replicating the information on the blockchain.
- **Data transmission:** Achieved through peer networks.
- **Data confirmation:** Achieved through a consensus process between the participating nodes.

The whole concept of blockchain was applied for the first time in 2009 as part of Bitcoin. As the data stored in the chain of blocks is usually transactions (for example, Financial), it is commonly called transactions data. Another example could be a chain of blocks that can be used to stamp documents and secure them against alterations (Lee, 2016).

With regard to Bitcoin, Pierro describes each Bitcoin as a number and considers that these numbers are the solution to an equation. Each new solution to the equation generates a new bitcoin, and the act of generating a solution is called "mining". Once mined, a bitcoin can be transferred or exchanged, and every transaction generates an entry into the blockchain's activity log.

This is often referred to as a "ledger". What makes the blockchain stand out is that the ledger is not owned or stored by one agency, but instead every transaction conducted has a copy of the details of that transaction stored on every computer that was a part of the transaction. Di Pierro (2017) goes on to describe the blockchain as "a table with three columns, where each row represents a distinct transaction, the first column stores the transaction's timestamp, the second column stores the transaction's details, and the third column stores a hash of the current transaction plus its details plus the hash of the previous transaction". By providing a time stamp and the previous transaction, parties wishing to verify this data are able to look it up at any point, and since it mentions the previous transaction, it becomes possible to track the history with relative ease. There is some security in place to prevent those who were not a part of the transaction from viewing details about it. The hash mentioned earlier as column three that is populated during the transaction is an encrypted string of letters and numbers that is generated to hide data about the transaction.

Blockchain technology is not limited to currency though; since each transaction in the ledger is just a string value, transactions can always be traced. Cook County in Chicago has been using blockchain technology to track real estate titles as they change ownership. Basically speaking, the blockchain is a linked chain of blocks of data (Pierro, 2017).

We began our Search with the USP library online sever, and searched for the key word "Blockchain", which yielded a solid mix of media sources. Not surprisingly, newspaper articles were the highest proportion of sources, with over 23,000 entries, and the total number of journal articles was about one-tenth the number of newspaper entries. Blockchain has many papers written about it, and since it is an ongoing concept many findings are added to it as time progresses. Looking into the details available, we selected topics on which our research could be based on mainly focusing on journal entries. We selected the articles, using any that were related to the themes on which many of the articles were based, such as finance, government activities, business, land management, education, etc.

Overall, the concept of blockchain technology is seen to possess such a huge appeal, as we have already seen a wide spread of adoption of this in various fields. As nearly every industry aims bigger but wishes to utilize some sort of versatile record-keeping practice, it is not unreasonable to expect to see this blockchain technology in a wide range of applications, some of which have been hinted at in our previous sections, such as the potential for a smarter city and developments. Thus, many more discoveries and new findings are yet to be evolved, bringing more changes to a new technological era, thus enabling a smarter and more highly developed area of study (Pilkington, 2015). Furthermore, due to the peer-to-peer nature of the technology, since every stakeholder has access to their block of the ledger, cooking the books or falsifying data has never been harder.

In conclusion, blockchain technology appears to not only improve tasks in current industries but also holds the potential to revolutionize systems that keep track of the history of artifacts through a vastly improved, transparent ledger system.

Methodology

According to the definition given by March & Smith (1995, p. 257), a method is a "set of steps used to perform a task". For the purpose of our research project, we will be accessing Google scholar and ProQuest to get more information on Blockchain technology through the previous research works that are available. In addition, two approaches are followed: deductive approach and intuitive approach.

First, deductive approach derives taxonomy not from empirical cases but instead from theory or by conceptualization. It identifies dimensions and characteristics in the taxonomy by a logical process derived from a sound conceptual or theoretical foundation. A deductive methodology is about "building up a speculation (or theories) in light of existing hypothesis, and afterward planning an exploration procedure to test the theory". It has been expressed that "deductive method is thinking from the specific to the general. In the event that a specific hypothesis or case precedent by all accounts infers a causal relationship or connection, it may be valid much of the time. A deductive plan may test to check whether this relationship or connection is obtained on increasingly broad conditions". Deductive methodology can be clarified by the methods for theories, which can be obtained from the recommendations of the hypothesis. As it were, deductive methodology is about deducting ends from premises or recommendations.

Intuitive approach is one whereby the researcher uses his or her understanding of the objects to be classified to propose a taxonomy based on the researcher's perceptions of what makes sense. There is no explicit method in this approach. It is an approach that has the ability to make quick decisions when time is short as it is based on previous experience. It is also based on those decisions which are irrational. Intuitive approach is describing something that is known, perceived, understood or believed by instinct, feelings or nature without actual evidence, rather than by use of conscious thought, reason or rational processes.

Table 1: Platform Support Rate for Using Blockchain

Platforms	Percentage
Webpage	25.81
Mac	29.03
Linux	32.26
Windows	32.26
iOS	70.97
android	74.19

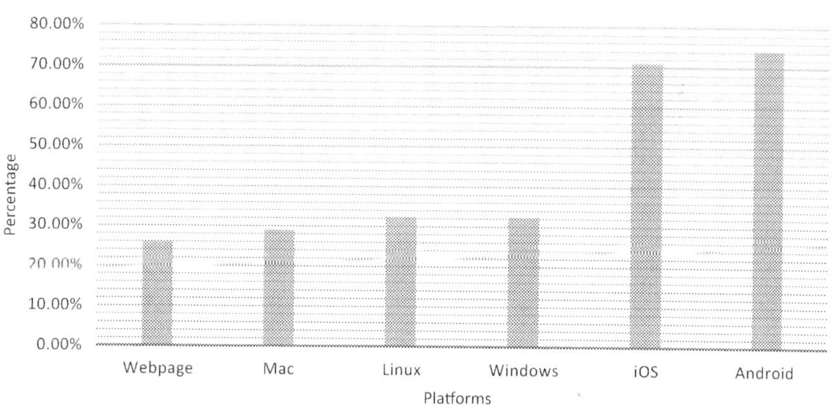

Figure 2: Platforms Using Various Blockchain Applications and Apps

Results

As can be seen from Table 1 and Figure 2, android platform is the most used for blockchain apps. In addition, webpages account for only 25.81%, Mac for only 29.03% and Linux and Windows support 32.26%, but iOS is the second largest platform used for blockchain with a rate of 70.97%.

Discussion

Method of operation — blockchain

Figure 3 shows the process/method of operation using blockchain for a financial transaction. A similar process could be used to trace other types

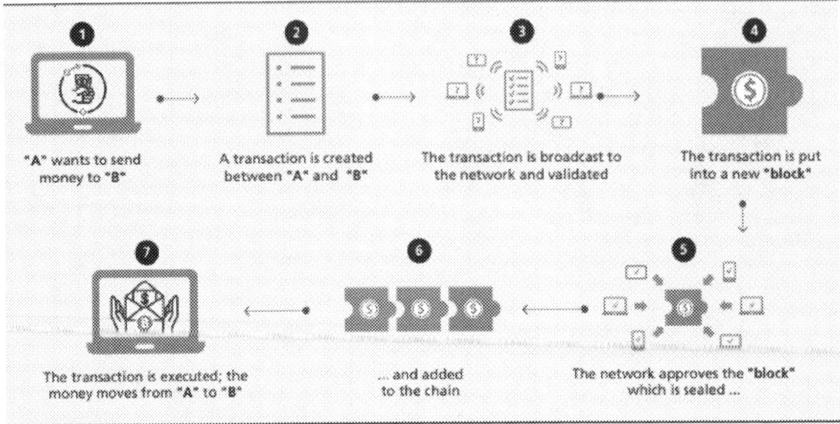

Figure 3: Method of Operation

Source: Sharma (2018).

of asset transfer, to commit new data to a blockchain, and to update data in a blockchain in other services, too. Where Company A wants to send money to Company B, in the second process a transaction is created between the two companies. In the third process, the transaction is broadcast to the network and is put into a new block of information, which then becomes the fourth step. Furthermore, the network approves the block and adds it to the chain. Therefore, the transaction is executed, and finally the money is moved from A to B. Here, public key (publicly known by the sender) and private keys (where a password is required to unlock and which must not be shared to anyone) are used to ensure confidentiality and privacy.

Top businesses that have incorporated blockchain in their operations

Recent years have seen much publicity in regard to cryptographic forms of money from the media and financial specialists. However, at this point, the hype is fading away and is offering a path for the progressively natural and normal development of Blockchain Technology. Furthermore, the clients of Blockchain are not just restricted to financial areas. From coordination to land and computerized ID management, organizations around the globe are making huge steps in the adoption of Blockchain Technology. The following are some examples.

1. Burger King

Burger King is using Blockchain technology for its reward power. What is interesting about this methodology is that unlike traditional reward programs, whopper coin tokens can be put away on the web, exchanged or even transferred to other individuals utilizing the Waves stage. Clients would get a Whopper Coin for each Rouble they spend at Burger King, and correspondingly a Whopper could be purchased for 1,700 Whopper Coins. This is a huge move that can have expansive consequences for a wide range of remuneration programs — from cinemas to frequent flier miles.

2. KIK

KIK is one of the greatest online chat platforms with more than 300 million dynamic clients. "KIK had recently integrated the Kin cryptocurrency in their platform which can be used to make payments to other users of the platform ... KIK's goal is to integrate blockchain-based payments into services that people already use creating an entire economy around their cryptocurrency" (Sharma, 2018).

3. IBM

IBM is turning out to be one of the giants in the cryptographic money space by providing the foundations of Blockchain-related administrations to organizations. Utilizing the Hyperledger Blockchain creator device, they can assist the associations with creating their own disseminated record and smart contract frameworks. "They have already partnered with some businesses that deal with logistics to increase efficiency and lower costs for them ... the partners include logistics giants like Walmart and banks like the Bank of Montreal (BMO), CaixaBank, Commerzbank, Erste Group, and the United Bank of Switzerland (UBS)" (Sharma, 2018). As regards their partnership with Walmart, the objective is to make the production network progressively more secure so that contamination can be reduced.

4. Walmart

"Walmart and nine other food companies have partnered with IBM to create a Blockchain for tracking food globally through its supply chain. Real-time data will be captured at every point, on every single food product on the Food Trust Blockchain, which includes Nestlé SA, Dole Food Co., Unilever, and several others" (Sharma, 2018). This will probably improve the organizations' capacity to recognize issues related to nourishment reviews, for example, tracing outbreaks more quickly to limit customer risk. Walmart seems to have joined the activity after the outbreak of *Salmonella* in its supply chain a year ago.

5. Microsoft

Microsoft is another tech giant that has grasped Blockchain Technology since its initiation. Microsoft had begun allowing Bitcoin installments on its site in 2014 when nobody knew about cryptographic forms of money. Microsoft has likewise verified somewhere in the range of 40 licenses identified with the utilization of Blockchains as installment entryways and for secure storage. Microsoft is additionally giving organizations and designers a chance to send their very own Blockchain utilizing Stratis in Microsoft Azure.

6. Huawei Technologies

Huawei needs to utilize Blockchains to arrange the portable business further to decrease fraud and trickery. Huawei asserted in a recent public statement that "Blockchain Technology offers mobile carriers superb opportunities to support the transformation of business models through new network layers, which can revolutionize how data integrity is verified and values and rights are transmitted and tracked over the infrastructure to subscribers" (Sharma, 2018).

Blockchain access vs. scope matrix

Based on our groups' research and discussions of what and how the businesses use potential blockchain application, we decided to use a 2 × 2 matrix (Figure 4). The 2 × 2 matrix will be displaying the blockchain

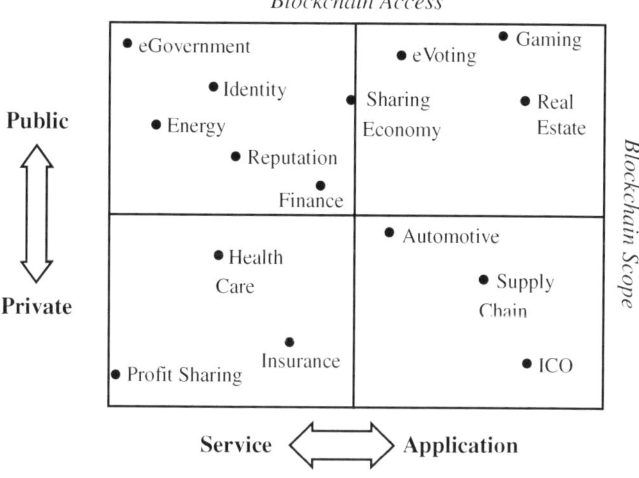

Figure 4: Blockchain Access vs. Blockchain Scope.
Source: Sharma (2018).

access (as a service or as application), and the industry sectors contrary to blockchain scope, that is public versus private.

Figure 4 displays the two criteria that are used to map the horizontal markets against the criteria listed below:

- **Scope** — Is blockchain usage globally unrestricted (public) or enterprise permissioned (private)?
- **Access** — Are blockchain technologies and access to these in the form of services or as applications?

To further elaborate about the above matrix diagram consider the example of real estate and a healthcare (chosen from the above matrix). Via the blockchain, the healthcare industry is trying to make easy and safe transfer of patient records. Therefore, the Access (criteria) is considered a service-oriented business, whereas to the healthcare partners the Scope (criteria) remains private. In contrast, the real estate industry uses blockchain for land records (mainly registration records). The application will be open and easily understood by the public. Overall, these current and envisioned use-cases for blockchain technology can be a trusted value ecosystem that can lead to exciting new economic opportunities in both the public and private sectors.

Taxonomy of Blockchain Application

Table 2 shows the taxonomy of blockchain applications used in financial transactions. Table 3 demonstrates the taxonomy of blockchain applications used in smart contracts. Table 4 lists the taxonomy of blockchain applications used in Data management. Table 5 shows the taxonomy of blockchain applications used in Storage and Communication.

The emergence of the blockchain as the foundation of the first ever decentralized cryptocurrency not only revolutionized the financial industry but also proved to be a boon for peer-to-peer information exchange in the most secure, efficient and transparent manner. The blockchain is a public ledger which works like a log by keeping a record of all transactions in a chronological order, secured by an appropriate consensus mechanism and providing an immutable record.

The blockchain has the capacity to revolutionize the security, stability and transparency of networks in need, provided it is applied appropriately and only if needed, because it is not a panacea for all security applications. Over time, the information and communication technology field has undergone numerous transformations for facilitating easier, quicker, efficient and secure sharing and exchange of data, information and funds in a myriad ways. With the emergence of the Internet, digital communications emerged, empowering all forms of data and information interchange through online transactions, such as financial transactions for making payments and receiving funds. The entire transactional and communication system goes through a trusted intermediary, which not only guarantees safe and secure delivery but also, in case of financial transactions, ensures accurate changes being reflected in multiple accounts.

Based upon several criteria, the blockchain systems are classified as public, private and consortium. A public blockchain provides an open platform for people from various organizations and backgrounds to join, transact and mine. There are no restrictions on any of these factors. Therefore, these are also called "permission-less" Blockchains. Every

Table 2: Taxonomy of Blockchain Applications Used in Financial Transactions

	Reading Access		Writing Access		Event Handling			Data Exchange Type		Encryption		
Taxonomy of Blockchain Applications	**Pr**	**Pu**	**P**	**U**	**N**	**F**	**C**	**T**	**C**	**U**	**P**	**T**
Financial transactions												
Anonymous cryptocurrencies		✦		✦	✦			✦				✦
Cryptocurrencies		✦		✦	✦			✦		✦		
Wealth storage & micro-payments		✦		✦	✦			✦		✦		
Financial services		✦	✦		✦			✦		✦		
Energy-efficient financial services		✦	✦		✦			✦		✦		
Enterprise global and micro-financial transactions	✦			✦	✦			✦			✦	
Global centrally issued financial instruments	✦		✦		✦			✦			✦	

Notes:
✦ — Characteristics that belong to an application case.
Reading Access Pr — Private (only authorized members of a limited community can read blockchain).
Pu — Public (everybody can read a blockchain).
Writing Access P — Permissioned (a user should be authorized to validate transactions).
U — UnPermissioned (a user can validate transactions without authorization).
Event handling N — No (blockchain does not support any events).
F — Fixed (blockchain supports built-in event).
C — Custom (blockchain supports processing of event created by user).
Data exchange Type T — Transaction (logs of actions executed are exchanged among users and recorded on a blockchain).
C — Content (digital assets are exchanged among users and recorded on a blockchain).

Table 3: Taxonomy of Blockchain Applications Used in Smart Contracts

	Reading Access		Writing Access		Event Handling			Data Exchange Type		Encryption		
Taxonomy of Blockchain Applications	**Pr**	**Pu**	**P**	**U**	**N**	**F**	**C**	**T**	**C**	**U**	**P**	**T**
Smart contracts												
Smart contracts		✦		✦			✦	✦		✦		
Testing of smart contracts	✦			✦			✦	✦		✦		
Energy-efficient smart contracts		✦		✦			✦	✦		✦		
Testing of energy-efficient smart contracts	✦			✦			✦	✦		✦		
Community smart contracts		✦	✦				✦	✦		✦		
Enterprise smart contracts	✦			✦			✦	✦			✦	
Global agreements between institutions	✦		✦				✦	✦			✦	

Notes:
✦ — Characteristics that belong to an application case.
Reading Access Pr — Private (only authorized members of a limited community can read blockchain).
Pu — Public (everybody can read a blockchain).
Writing Access P — Permissioned (a user should be authorized to validate transactions).
U — UnPermissioned (a user can validate transactions without authorization).
Event handling N — No (blockchain does not support any events).
F — Fixed (blockchain supports built-in event).
C — Custom (blockchain supports processing of event created by user).
Data exchange Type T — Transaction (logs of actions executed are exchanged among users and recorded on a blockchain).
C — Content (digital assets are exchanged among users and recorded on a blockchain).

Table 4: Taxonomy of Blockchain Applications Used in Data Management

Taxonomy of Blockchain	Reading Access		Writing Access		Event Handling			Data Exchange Type		Encryption		
Applications	**Pr**	**Pu**	**P**	**U**	**N**	**F**	**C**	**T**	**C**	**U**	**P**	**T**
Data management												
Global authentication ownership		✦		✦		✦		✦		✦		
Sharing economies		✦	✦			✦		✦		✦		
Enterprise asset management	✦			✦		✦		✦			✦	

Notes:
✦ — Characteristics that belong to an application case.
Reading Access Pr — Private (only authorized members of a limited community can read blockchain).
Pu — Public (everybody can read a blockchain).
Writing Access P — Permissioned (a user should be authorized to validate transactions).
U — UnPermissioned (a user can validate transactions without authorization).
Event handling N — No (blockchain does not support any events).
F — Fixed (blockchain supports built-in event).
C — Custom (blockchain supports processing of event created by user).
Data exchange Type T — Transaction (logs of actions executed are exchanged among users and recorded on a blockchain).
C — Content (digital assets are exchanged among users and recorded on a blockchain).

Table 5: Taxonomy of Blockchain Applications Used in Storage and Communication

Taxonomy of Blockchain Applications	**Reading Access**		**Writing Access**		**Event Handling**			**Data Exchange Type**		**Encryption**		
	Pr	**Pu**	**P**	**U**	**N**	**F**	**C**	**T**	**C**	**U**	**P**	**T**
Storage												
Open access publishing		✦	✦			✦			✦	✦		
Content preview		✦	✦			✦			✦		✦	
Decentralized storage		✦	✦			✦			✦			✦
Communication												
Broadcasting		✦		✦		✦			✦	✦		
Discussion forum		✦	✦			✦			✦	✦		
IoT communication	✦			✦		✦			✦	✦		

Notes:
✦ — Characteristics that belong to an application case.
Reading Access Pr — Private (only authorized members of a limited community can read blockchain).
Pu — Public (everybody can read a blockchain).
Writing Access P — Permissioned (a user should be authorized to validate transactions).
U — UnPermissioned (a user can validate transactions without authorization).
Event handling N — No (blockchain does not support any events).
F — Fixed (blockchain supports built-in event).
C — Custom (blockchain supports processing of event created by user).
Data exchange Type T — Transaction (logs of actions executed are exchanged among users and recorded or a blockchain).
C — Content (digital assets are exchanged among users and recorded on a blockchain).

participant is given full authority to read/write transactions, perform auditing in the blockchain or review any part of the blockchain, anytime. A Private blockchain system is a set-up to facilitate private sharing and exchange of data among a group of individuals (in a single organization) or among multiple organizations with mining controlled by one organization or selective individuals. It is also called a permissioned blockchain since unknown users cannot access it, unless they receive a special invitation. A consortium blockchain can be considered as a partially private and permissioned blockchain, where not a single organization but a set of predetermined nodes is responsible for consensus and block validation. These nodes decide who can be part of the network and who can mine. For block validation, a multi-signature scheme is used, where a block is considered valid only if it signed by these nodes.

Some of the areas where blockchain finds application and is currently being used owing to its advantages are listed as follows:

Blockchain in Asset Management — It is all about securely transferring assets within a business network. An asset could be a physical one like a server, computer or a laptop or an intangible one like software and services. The blockchain offers shared ledger capability, which means full visibility from end to end into a business network. The blockchain is employed right from serialization to being deployed on the floor and focuses only on five key events, i.e. manufacturing serialization of assets to initiate the blockchain, receiving and validation of assets, asset capitalization, warranty activation and installation of the asset.

Blockchain in Real Estate — Transactions in real estate are cumbersome, not transparent and expensive mainly because of the involvement of the various middlemen like brokers, government property databases, title companies, escrow companies, inspectors and appraisers, notary publics, etc. The blockchain will enable every property, everywhere, to have a corresponding digital address that contains details on occupancy, finance, legal, building performance and physical attributes, that conveys this information as necessary and maintains all historical transactions.

Blockchain in Finance — A very important process, which becomes quite expensive and sluggish, due to the presence of unnecessary middlemen is cross-border payments. It takes several banks (and currencies) before the money can be collected. Services like Western Union can be used which are faster but also expensive. The blockchain can speed up and simplify this process, cutting out the unnecessary middlemen. At the same time, it makes money remittance more affordable.

Blockchain in the IoT — IoT solutions using blockchain can be built to maintain a continuously growing list of cryptographically secured data records protected against alteration and modification. For example, consider an IoT connected object with an RFID tag with sensitive location and temperature information moving along various points in a warehouse or in a smart home, (Dorri, 2017) this information could be updated on a blockchain. This permits all involved parties to share data and the status of the package as it moves among different gatherings to guarantee that the terms of an agreement are met.

Blockchain in Healthcare — A blockchain-based management of patient's health records is proposed. The patient's medical history is stored on a decentralized system, accessible to the treating doctors and medical insurance providers (Ekblaw, 2016).

Some non-financial sectors also use the blockchains, such as the following:

- Ascribe allows artists to claim ownership and issue numbered, limited-edition prints of all kinds of artwork in their digital form using the blockchain technology. It even includes a marketplace and assists in buying and selling art through its website, removing the need for escrow.
- Bit Proof is the most advanced of the many document timestamping apps that have popped up in recent years, making notaries obsolete. Although free versions like Block sign and Origin Stamp exist, Bit Proof offers more services, including one that targets intellectual property protection. Interestingly, Bit Proof has recently partnered with San Francisco's Humberto School to put their student academic certificates on the blockchain, totally reengineering how diplomas and student certificates are handled and used.

- Colu is the first business allowing other businesses to issue digital assets, and the variety of these assets they can "tokenize" is pretty impressive. Although the free Bitcoin wallet Counterparty already allowed simple tokens to be issued and traded between other holders of that wallet, Colu's tokens can come in all shapes and sizes, leave and reenter their system, and even store data on the Bit Torrent network when it's too large to be put on the block chain.
- Filament is perhaps the most ambitious entry on our list. Filament uses small, advanced hardware devices to put all kinds of electronics, especially appliances, on the block chain, creating an Internet of Things for your local area
- Genecoin is not a cryptocurrency but a novel service that "backs up your DNA" by placing a copy of your genome on the block chain. Besides the Sci-fi connotations of making a copy of yourself, there are medical uses for keeping your DNA profile handy and accessible too.
- Provenance seeks to record every last thing that happens in the global retail supply chain on the block chain, and make all of that data searchable in real time for consumers. Imagine scanning a QR code on a can of tuna in the supermarket and knowing exactly where the fish inside it was caught, who certified it, where it was canned, etc., all timestamped at each step.
- Wave has targeted the global supply chain and specifically the incredibly wasteful problem with import documents known as Bills of Lading to be modernized with the block chain. They connect all members of a supply chain to the decentralized block chain, which allows for a direct exchange of documents between them, solving the shipping industry's largest problem. WAVES application manages ownership of documents on the block chain eliminating disputes, forgeries and unnecessary risks.
- The International Bitcoin Real Estate Association (IBREA) is not a company, but more of an advocacy group. We felt they needed a mention because they are a large group of real estate professionals looking to educate and promote the uses of the block chain and bitcoin in real estate. Eventually, it is their plan to help modernize the entire process,

solving problems everyone has with real estate globally including the title process, land registries and even escrow.

Conclusion

This chapter has inspected the topic of scientific taxonomy advancement from a few angles. Apart from these examples, the progressive innovation of Blockchain holds a high potential for application in many industries. While a few industries have already started adopting Blockchain in their organizations, many are still investigating the ideal approaches to start the process. Blockchain is just another name in the world of technology, yet it is certainly the one to last. Indeed, even in the beginning phase, the technology has increased in popularity, beginning with the absolute first use of digital forms of money. Through this research, we have successfully met our aims and objectives. Moving on, more areas of uses are being found and tried as time passes. When the technology is accepted and acknowledged on a worldwide scale, it will change the manner in which we live today.

References

Casavant, T. L. (1988). A Taxonomy of Scheduling in General-Purpose Distributed Computing Systems. *IEEE Transactions on Software Engineering*, 14(2), 141–154.

Di Pierro, M. (2017). What is the Blockchain?. *Computing in Science & Engineering*, 19(5), 92–95.

Dorri, A. (2017). Blockchain for IoT Security and Privacy: The Case Study of a Smart Home. In *Proceedings of the IEEE International Conference on Pervasive Computing and Communications Workshop*, pp. 618–623, Hawaii, USA.

Ekblaw. (2016). *A Case Study for Blockchain in Healthcare: "MedRec" Prototype for Electronic Health Records and Medical Research Data.* Whitepaper.

Lee, L. (2016). New Kids on the Blockchain: How Bitcoin's Technology Could Reinvent the Stock Market. *SSRN Electronic Journal*, 13, 5.

March, S. T., Smith, G. F. (1995). Design and Natural Science Research on Information Technology. *Decision Support Systems*, 15(4), 251–266.

Miller, J. G., Roth, A. V. (1994). A Taxonomy of Manufacturing Strategies. *Management Science*, 40(3), 285–304.

Nickerson, R., Varshney, U., Muntermann, J. (2013). A Method for Taxonomy Development and its Application in Information Systems. *European Journal of Information Systems*, 340(22).

Pilkington, M. (2016). Blockchain Technology: Principles and Applications. In *Research Handbook on Digital Transformations*. Edward Elgar Publishing.

Sharma, T. K. (2018). Top 10 Companies that have Already Adopted Blockchain. Retrieved from Blockchain Council: https://www.blockchain-council.org/blockchain/top-10-companies-that-have-already-adopted-blockchain.

Tasca P. (2016). The Dual Nature of Bitcoin as Payment Network and Money. In SUERF Conference Proceedings, 2016, Chapter VI, Paris, France. https://bravenewcoin.com/insights/ten-companies-using-the-blockchain-for-non-financial-innovation.

Tasca, P., Tessone, C. J. (2019). Taxonomy of Blockchain Technologies. *Principles of Identification and Classification*. ArXiv preprint. arXiv:1708.04872.

Wikipedia. (2020). Blockchain. Retrieved from: https://en.wikipedia.org/wiki/Blockchain. Accessed February 29, 2020.

Chapter 3

Blockchain Means More Than a Software to Democracy: Access to Fundamental Rights of Sixth Dimension

Andrea Garcia*,‡ and Sam Goundar†,§

*Internet Society Chapter, New York, USA

†The University of the South Pacific, Suva, Fiji

‡andgarciar@gmail.com

§sam.goundar@gmail.com

Abstract

Throughout history, five dimensions of basic needs have been created to establish the existential minimum. This research aims to demonstrate that Human Rights has since become the Sixth Dimension (in 2009), and it is one where the right of access to technology is fundamental to generating peace, dignity and a sustainable world. Establishing technology as a fundamental right is useful to guide the creation of an Annual Budget Plan by the leaders who use the fundamental rights to establish the margin of investment to be made in each sector proportionaly to the level of importance it would occupy in a citizen's life. For these reasons, the research demonstrated evidence that Blockchain and Cryptocurrencies are much more than a payment system. The method used was scientific, with analysis of historical documents and social observation as well as observation into laws, doctrine and jurisprudence alongside data taken from socioeconomic statistical reports collected in 2017. This research was enough to show that Blockchain technology and Cryptocurrencies, when combined with AI and IoT, create the Smart Economy. Through poverty reduction, physical borders will be protected by virtual borders. Finally, the authors conclude that technology is a powerful accelerator of economic flow and can be a vehicle for the sustainable world, and this requires investments in such things as a Sixth Dimension of Human Rights that cannot be separated from others rights.

Introduction

Until the year 1800, the world was almost homogeneous: most people were poor and the range of professions was restricted.

Thus, the French Revolution (1789–1799) becomes a milestone for our analysis about the Human Rights evolution embodying the importance of technology to humanity since it was a disruptive period socially, economically and politically.

Civil society was divided between the clergy, the nobility and the bourgeoisie. The bourgeoisie was the part of society that paid taxes that were used to pay for the good life of the court, clergy and nobility.

One special fact must be added, the country went bankrupt and the blame attributed to the poor economic administration of the king who also controlled the courts and passed sentences with the content almost always unjust and impartial.

The bourgeoisie joined the poor classes because the poor economic management of the king did not provide the growth of capitalism. Thus, the greater freedom for trade and the end of high taxes were, among others, the most important causes of the French Revolution.

Thus, *Liberté, Egalité, Fraternité* (Rousseau, 2008) was the slogan for the French Revolution and marked the end of feudal privileges, equality of all before the law and guarantee of property. "The Declaration of the Rights of Man" was approved by the French National Assembly on August 26, 1789, which decided that a declaration of rights should precede the Constitution.

The French Revolution meant the end of the absolutist system and the privileges of the nobility. The people gained more autonomy and social rights came to be respected. In the meantime, the bourgeoisie conducted the process to ensure its social dominance.

We can see that autonomy and social rights were always moving alongside of human evolution. The more the evolution, the more the autonomy to society and the less the interference from State in an individual's life.

Since the "Declaration of the Rights of Man", many constitutions have been created around the world that have democracy as a model of government. This was the first bill of rights and the source of inspiration for the United Nations' universal "Declaration of Human Rights" charter in 1948.

However, as the authors analyze, since the end of World War II the States have developed mechanisms to regain privileges, control the flow of economic growth and interfere with property rights in confiscatory acts that, although legal, are immoral and unconstitutional.

Throughout the text, the authors develop the theme to conclude that human rights are currently the sixth layer of protection for the rights claimed since the French Revolution: the right to technology as a form of financial independence to provide the minimum existential life worthy of form to ensure the survival and development of future generations in all respects in a healthy environment that is available to all.

This is easy to verify. Broadband access is an aspect of technology that causes positive changes in the life of the individual that when accessing the Internet some things happen. First, people are much more satisfied with their lives when they have access to the Internet. When they have access to the Internet, they can see how the world works. They can watch movies or television shows. Satisfaction with life thus increases.

The World Bank Group (WBG) in April 2018, after many studies, said that technology and economics go hand in hand to allow for decent living as reference income increases and individual income, proportionately, also increases.

Alongside these authors, other scientists like Sarma (2018) have been arguing that partnerships among civil society, private companies, governments and non-governmental organizations can improve the economy and facilitate the technological education in developing countries in a focal manner and much faster than governmental actions alone.

Technology will do us a great service by connecting everyone, but the other thing that technology is doing at the same time is modifying the way jobs claim larger investments than those made in the framework of laws to increase the power of state administration through increase of taxes. Raising taxes as a way of generating wealth and reducing poverty is an outdated and insufficient mechanism that does not guarantee sustainability.

About the Goals of the Research to Establish a Legal Doctrine Under a Protective Cover of the Charter of Fundamental Rights

Have no doubts that Interactions between Humans and Machines means the Future of Work. Advances in artificial intelligence (AI), robotics and deep learning change how we work, and jobs that were once widely viewed as safe are increasingly being automated, increasing migration and forced displacement.

The double taxation, high taxes, and the state's seeking for profit from taxes prevent the positive advance of the global economic flow and the technological innovation.

Simultaneously, digital economy is one of the goals in the 2030 Agenda for Sustainable Development created by the Department of Economic and Social Affairs in the United Nations because there is no doubt that it has the potential to accelerate economic and educational development as well as provide a protected environment for future generations. Kofi (2015) pointed to AI and Big Data combined with Blockchain as a useful tool to turn Africa into a barn to feed the world. All these combined measures could reduce by drastic levels the hunger and poverty situation that is now prevalent in just 15 years.

However, to date, we do not have an inclusive standard for regulating the digital economy with Blockchain and Cryptocurrency, and establishing high taxes will create risks to technological innovation.

Watching the landscape, the following three potential problems to humanity's survival arise:

1. Increasing the economy and creating jobs is an urgent necessity, and it must be done now and done fast.

2. High taxes are jeopardizing human survival, and the system of double taxation cannot be allowed to continue because this represents illegal confiscation on the tax base.
3. Governments must manage the State activities at the same time that they assume responsibility for human security on the global field.

This research aims to provide a legal doctrine that will guide the regulatory framework as an inclusive global standard that will also drive the governments to maximize the application of taxes. And finally, it establishes a proposal of application in laboratory tests with AI to simulate the economic behavior, in this way, making it possible to know the effectiveness of the doctrine without the need to wait for the results for 15–20 years, which is the average time required to demonstrate the effectiveness of social and economic policies.

Methodology Adopted for Research

The research method used was the Scientific Method (Knight and Chynoweth, 2008), i.e. analysis of historical documents and social observation as well as looking into laws, doctrine and jurisprudence confronted with data taken from socioeconomic statistical reports collected between 2014 and 2017 from newspaper articles and reports from the United Nations and other agencies.

The Scientific Method is the logical expression of the reasoning associated with the formulation of convincing arguments. These arguments, once placed, are intended to inform, describe or persuade regarding a fact. For this, the authors used the following:

(a) **Terms** — Words, declarations, conventional meanings that refer to an object.
(b) **Concept** — The representation, expression and interiorization about what the thing is. It is the idealization of the object. The concept is a mental activity that drives knowledge, making not only that person or thing become understandable, but all people and things of the same form.

(c) **Definition** — The manifestation and apprehension of the elements contained in the concept, trying to decide about what is doubtful or what is ambivalent.

Knowing how to properly use terms, concepts and definitions means methodologically expressing in science what the individual knows and wants to convey through his/her scientific observation. The object studied was technological innovation.

An Innovative Humanitarian Contribution to Solving the Tax Complexity for Smart Economy with Blockchain and Cryptocurrency

This research is innovative because it involves and credits the Sixth Dimension of Human Rights as a scientific discovery. This means one more layer of fundamental rights for the survival of the human being is added to the set of rights protected in the Universal Declaration of Human Rights (1948), (United Nations, 1948) which provides the common norm to be achieved by all peoples and nations.

Human rights are also guidelines that impact how the law will be treated by the Organization for Economic Co-operation and Development (OECD, 1948), and for these reasons the research is useful and innovative to mankind.

The Organisation for Economic Co-operation and Development (OECD) is an intergovernmental economic organization with 36 member countries, founded in 1961 to stimulate economic progress and world trade. It is a forum of countries describing themselves as committed to democracy and the market economy, providing a platform to compare policy experiences, seeking answers to common problems, identifying good practices and coordinating the domestic and international policies of its members.

The scientific discovery adds to knowledge as it establishes a legal and socioeconomic doctrine that guides all practitioners working in the digital economy, be they government, legal or private sector members.

By the way, the authors' discovery about technology, especially with AI, Big Data, IoT and Smart Economy, with Blockchain and Cryptocurrency has already been presented at the IGF Forum 2018 at UNESCO Headquarter, Paris (Garcia, 2018a), for the technical and scientific community. In the same way, it was presented at the Conference for technology WEBbr 2018 in Brazil (Garcia). It represents an important discovery because fundamental rights serve as the guidelines for the drafting of laws. And specifically in regard to the objective proposed in this research, establishing technology as a fundamental right, treated exclusively in the sixth dimension, will serve to elaborate laws that aim to maximize the application of the rates. To the authors, the high taxation, laundering of money and frauds are leading humanity to widespread impoverishment.

Humanity will benefit from the authors' discovery because humankind will pay lower and fairer taxes. For Smart Economy, it will be possible to establish a tax exception.

The publication of this research, the authors hope, will allow discussion in the technical and scientific community and provide an overview of the inclusive standard in the regulatory framework in terms of a humanitarian approach.

As a consistent and viable thought, the authors affirm that peace on physical borders will be a reality if governments assume joint responsibility for human security by making a joint effort to establish taxation in the Smart Economy with a humanitarian focus.

The stability of humanity has layers that overlap: food, health, legal, social, healthy environment, etc. And the economy is the armor that maintains stability because it protects and provides a means of concreteness to hold the layers of stability. Politics matters only insofar as it serves to structure and maintain stability. The authors feel that if the borders are protected and global peace established, then people do not need to pursue survival in other countries.

The solution lies in education and partnerships between developed and developing countries to accelerate the economy through emerging technologies that are bringing more jobs, new ways to develop business and financial life autonomy.

There is a need for countries with established Smart Economy to help others. This will keep the physical borders protected because, since 2008, with the establishment of the Smart Economy borders are not physical, as globalization has established virtual borders.

Countries with a strong economy will not invade others in search of survival. The biggest example of this was in 2019, when 2,000 Mexican children ended up locked in the United States when their parents tried to illegally enter the United States. The sovereignty of the American government had laws that allowed this, but this characterizes crime against humanity (*Source*: Fonte: *Carta Maior newspaper*) (Esquerda Net).

Another equally common situation in Europe is Libyans entering the Mediterranean trying to reach countries like Italy, Portugal, Spain and others. Most of them die during the crossing of hunger and thirst. Others get to the destination and face the life of illegal immigrants. But it is the price of survival (*Época*).

There is no power without money. Even the toughest rulers and dictators have realized this and invest in diplomatic, political, administrative and social infrastructure because war creates a weak economy and power interests only come correlated with economic power.

For these reasons, there is already a joint desire to invest in disruptive technologies to strengthen the economy around the world, and the authors bring an innovative contribution through the doctrine built through the results obtained with this research.

Dimensions of Fundamental Rights: Universal Right to Technology as the 6th Law of Protection

There is a new Social Contract increasing digitization, and new platforms, digital business models, and non-state actors exert considerable pressure on the government and its legitimacy, creating implications for public policy on issues ranging from taxes to basic accountability. Advances in technology and continual retooling create the need not only for new forms of social protection but also create potential for more efficient service delivery. From the point of view of the authors, increasing urbanization will accelerate innovation, but also create economic shocks.

These economic shocks can be solved with investments in the regulatory framework and by establishing broad and universal access to technologies as a Fundamental Right.

The relationship between the State and the individual has long been given definitions and classifications both to explain and to establish limits of the interference of public interest into private interest.

Human Rights are rights inherent to all human beings, regardless of race, gender, nationality, ethnicity, language, religion or any other condition, and it includes the *right to life*, *Liberty*: opinion and expression freedom, the *right to work*, education and many others. All people deserve these rights without discrimination.

International Human Rights establishes the obligation of governments to act in a determined manner or to abstain from predetermined acts in order to promote and protect the Human Rights and freedom given to groups or individuals.

Jellinek's Theory is concerned with classifying the limitations to which the conduct expected by individuals and rulers is subject.

Created at the end of the 19th century by Georg Jellinek, an important jurist and philosopher, Jellinek's Four Status Theory indicates four conducts that an individual could show to the State: passive, active, negative and positive.

- **Passive Status (status subjectionis):** The individual is subordinated to the Public Powers, being the holder of duties in relation to the State that imposes its will through laws that allow or prohibit conduct.
- **Active Status (status activus civitatis):** The citizens exercise their political rights. Thus, there is the possibility of the individual interfering in the will of the State, which among other ways, includes voting.

Bobbio (2005), an Italian political historian, in 1998 already addressed the decentralization of State power over the individual as healthy under the socioeconomic aspect and as a way of making democracy sustainable.

- **Negative Status (status libertatis):** Indicates the freedom of the individual in relation to the State; he will act as he wants, in some situations, released from the performance of the Public Power in an exceptional way. One example of this is freedom of expression.
- **Positive Status (status civitatis):** The possibility of the individual to demand the State about some provision, and the Public Power then acting in a positive way to favor this individual. One example is the possibility of the individual requiring the right to health.

From this explanation, the importance of the methodological cut is explained by the fact that historically human evolution brings new facts for Legal Science to harmonize the legal structure with human needs.

Often, the collision of rights between free initiative and the autonomy of the private will and the dignity of the human being calls for the maximum effectiveness of Fundamental Rights as a sustainable way of guaranteeing future generations. In case there is Fundamental Rights collision, it is recommended to use the judgment about interests in a reasonable and harmonious way within the system of laws of each country, or in an international environment when applicable.

In the study about human evolution, the Fundamental Rights are given layers of protection that interact harmoniously with rights and duties individually as well as collectively.

Legal doctrine usually divides them into generations or dimensions. The authors prefer to adopt the term dimension because it better reflects the legal treatment that overlaps history in the form of layers, whereas the term generation passes the idea of a right that gives way to another in a successive way. Therefore, establishing technology as a fundamental right is important as it ensures constant human evolution in all its aspects through the application of AI, ICTs, IoT and others that can be combined with Blockchain technology for Smart Economy with Cryptocurrencies.

We have five dimensions of rights enshrined in the current legal doctrine (Lenza, 2009).

The *First Dimension* is a landmark shift from the authoritarian State to the rule of law. They are rights related to public liberties and political rights, that is, civil and political rights translating the value of freedom. The historical documents are: (a) *Magna Carta* (1215), signed by the King João Sem Terra; (b) *Peace of Westphalia* (1648); (c) *Habeas Corpus Act* (1679); (d) *Bill of Rights* (1688) and the *Declaration of American Independence* (1776) and *Declaration of French Independence* (1789).

The *Second Dimension* was driven by the European Industrial Revolution of the 19th century where the poor working conditions represented the motivation for civil revolutions. At the beginning of the 20th century, World War I showed the need to establish social rights. The Second Dimension consists of social, cultural and economic rights corresponding to the rights of equality. The historical documents are *Constitution of Weimar* (1919) in Germany and *Treaty of Versailles* (1919) at the OIT.

The *Third Dimension* is transindividual rights that have resulted from the shifts that the international community and the mass society have undergone. It is the phenomenon of Globalization, developing technology and Legal Science that establishes the right of communication and the property right over the common patrimony of humanity. But economic and sustainable development were not the goal. The focus was on the rights of solidarity, that is the right of everyone to live in a healthy environment.

The advancement of the industry is responsible for several companies emerging, and thus the need also arose to ensure consumer protection mechanisms, making the State responsible for the establishment of norms to regulate consumer relations. The State has the duty to guarantee consumer protection through public policies and access to specific bodies that can solve the problems arising from the commercial relationship.

Documents in this regard include the following: (a) *Consumer Bill of Rights* (1962); (b) *Council of Europe* (1973); (c) *Commission on Human Rights* (UN), in session 29 recognized the fundamental and universal rights of the consumer; (d) *Resolution 39/248* (1985), UN.

The *Fourth Dimension* encompasses individual rights introduced by political globalization. Highlights include the right to direct democracy, information and pluralism. Fundamental Rights belong to an autonomous dimension that must be globalized in the institutional field.

The *Fifth Dimension* is about the right to peace: It encompasses the right of collectivity to guarantee the Human Rights, and peace is the axiom of participatory democracy. Right to life, being an indispensable condition for the progress of all nations and in all spheres, the Fifth Dimension guarantees all peoples the right to self-determination. It is the right of a people not to submit to the sovereignty of another people (or governments) against their will. It is the possibility of this people to determine their destiny and their cultural, social and economic development, without the influence of another. However, it finds limitations in that in no one case, a people will be deprived of its own means of subsistence.

The authors point out that currently most countries are committing to human subsistence with taxes of almost *50–80% payable to the State* (Ortiz-Ospina, 2018). It is a confiscatory encroachment when the Governments hold such a large share. This is one of the causes that is raising poverty rates and the number of starving people. At this point, the authors would like to warn the readers that the world will collapse.

Documents in this regard include the following: *Universal Declaration of Human Rights* (1948, UN) and *Declaration on the Right of Peoples to Peace,* contained in UN Resolution 39, (1984).

The Sixth Dimension of Fundamental Rights was created in 2015 and presented for the first time in 2018 at the International Conference on Cognitive Computing WEBbr 2018, held in Brazil, by the lawyer and legal scientist Garcia (2018b):

> The Sixth Dimension arises from the 4th Industrial Revolution and incorporates the right to social and technological development as a fundamental right that allows the individual to self-management, self-development and self-concept. It concerns the historical period started in 2009, when the first virtual currency (Bitcoin) was introduced to the economy. It brought to the citizen greater financial independence joined to the payments system introduced by Blockchain technology in ecosystem without intermediaries such as banks. Sixth Dimension brings to this century a minimal acceptance of the interference from State in the intimate and financial life of the citizen. Social awareness strengthens the bonds of commercial partnership based on the will to share the gains more quickly and justly than the State is doing it. There is a high degree of collective consciousness where the sense about land borders has been

> replaced by boundaries of virtual boundaries. It sounds like a maximized bloc extracted from all dimensions of Human Rights embodying the sixth dimension.

The Fundamental protection is justified on the grounds that the social and economic benefits that technology has provided to all peoples is undeniable because it has the great accelerating power of development in all spheres of society life. Reliable vehicles and communication officers each provide reports and scientific research that restate this claim. It is the Smart Economy scenario that reveals reasons for concerns, but the advantages have overcome the problems.

One of the evidences of technology as a fundamental value comes from Kofi (2015), former Secretary-General of the United Nations, who passed away on 18 August 2018. In the speech he delivered at the Massachusetts Institute of Technology (MIT) in 2015, he shared his views on how technological advancements could improve the state of the world. He said:

> Two crucial ingredients can help solve these crises: Technology and political will. The use of electronic systems for voter registration and identification and the tallying of votes can increase trust and reduce suspicions in countries with records of electoral fraud. [...] In sum: let us invest in and embrace technology; it makes progress possible. But technology does not free us of the need for leadership; it makes leadership all the more important. So let us not forget that technology by itself cannot absolve us of our political responsibility to ensure that we use it wisely and efficiently for the good of society everywhere.

Renowned researchers point out that technology will take many forms and have an influence in many sectors. Education is an important part of the technological challenge. Let's see below how Sam Goundar (2011), a technology scientist, guides us:

> With the number of mobile devices surpassing the number of computers, there is now a real opportunity for innovative teaching and interactive learning with mobile devices. Mobile devices are ICT devices but with greater flexibility and ubiquitous connectivity, combined with the power of desktop computing. The potential impact of using mobile devices in

> education will result in the production of ground-breaking teaching and learning technologies. Teachers can have instructional support at their fingertips in the learning environment. Students can be empowered with access to learning resources with supplementary multimedia for better understanding regardless of time and physical location.

Along the same lines, the World Bank Group report (2017) puts forth the same evidence to elevate technology as the Sixth Dimension of Human Rights to claim universal access to the connection in internet and technologies:

> Technological progress is a driving force behind economic growth, citizen engagement, and job creation. Information and communication technologies (ICTs), in particular, are reshaping many aspects of the world's economies, governments, and societies. In this context, access to the Internet has become a vital development tool. The so-called Fourth Industrial Revolution is a digital revolution that requires universal and reliable Internet access; without it, many developing countries will not be able to fully participate in an increasingly mobile and digital-based economy.

Technology has been recognized by the United Nations as possessing great transformative potential to ensure a dignified life, and this was stated in the 2030 Agenda for Sustainable Development (United Nations, 2015) by the Department of Economic and Social Affairs. This Agenda is a Plan of Action for people, planet and prosperity. It also seeks to strengthen universal peace by greater freedom and recognizes that eradicating poverty in all ways and its dimensions, including extreme poverty, is the greatest global challenge and an indispensable prerequisite for sustainable development.

The Agenda guides all countries and stakeholders to work in a collaborative partnership. They will implement this plan in a joint effort to release the human race from the tyranny of poverty and to heal and protect the planet directed to change the world to move into a more sustainable and resilient path. To achieve this goal, 17 Sustainable Development Objectives were established, demonstrating the scale and ambition of this new Universal Agenda. They seek to realize Human Rights for all and achieve Gender Equality and the Empowerment of all Women and

Girls. The goals are integrated and indivisible and balance the three dimensions of sustainable development, that is economic, social and environmental.

The Goals will stimulate action over the next 15 years in areas of critical importance to humanity and the planet. Objective number 17 is about development of Partnerships because it has the capacity to life up the world and the life of each person to a better level. Developing education is addressed in objective number 4, and it also talks about actions to stimulate and provide for Technological Education (4b). From these objectives, it will be possible to impact the economy and perform objectives 1–5: exterminating hunger and poverty and creating a sustainable environment.

After all the above arguments, which have not been exhausted, the authors are restating that when it was demonstrated that Technology and Smart Economy with Blockchain and Cryptocurrency came up as the Sixth Dimension of Human Rights at the 2018 WEB Conference for Cognitive Computing, the scientific community agreed on the grounds that the landmark would leave an impact on the history of human evolution and also stated that the positive results would increase the flow of economic and social development. Moreover, it promotes a dignified life and creates new professional positions with a high degree of individual autonomy to generate personal satisfaction in the individual, and consequently throughout society.

The utility to raise technology as the Sixth Dimension Human Rights is to solve the problem that could come up if developing countries and poor peoples are placed out of access: the poverty and hunger would keep growing. But like a Fundamental Right, it now gains the same status as universal rights like health, food, education and others. Thus, this way makes it so that it is the responsibility of the Governments to invest in actions to make technology available to all.

Democracy and Icts: AI, IoT, Blockchain in the Smart Economy to a Sustainable World

Nowadays, the democratic debate confronts challenges within the worldwide social and economic scenario, because corruption is just one of the serious problems. Without adequate governmental investment on social work, there will not be worthy distribution of social justice. In all countries, the social work undertaken by the government is insufficient because tax money is being spent to maintain the high lifestyle standard of public administrators or is diverted to keep the corruption system alive. Therefore, there is accentuated regression of fundamental and individual rights, besides the stimulus to the civil society's depoliticization process, especially in developing countries.

This economic vision reached the 2030 Agenda for Sustainable, through which it was believed possible to solve these issues through partnerships between civil society, private companies, associations and foundations. This partnership model is a showcase of the social benefits–sharing with the rest of humanity that occurs when peoples achieve significant financial autonomy. These partnerships are more efficient than governments because they are faster and act in focal situations without intermediates and with less bureaucracy. More autonomy means bigger democratic exercise, and it can improve the education through sharing of experiences between developed and developing countries, beside provision of financial mutual help.

This is the opinion of others political scientists too. Look at below the extract from an article written in 1997 by Mathew (1997):

> Except in China, Japan, the Middle East, and a few other places where culture or authoritarian governments severely limit civil society, NGOS' role and influence have exploded in the last half-decade. Their financial resources and — often more important — their expertise, approximate and sometimes exceed those of smaller governments and of international organizations. "We have less money and fewer resources than Amnesty International, and we are the arm of the U.N. for human rights," noted Ibrahima Fall, head of the U.N. Centre for Human Rights, in 1993. "This is clearly ridiculous". Today NGOS deliver more official development assistance than the entire U.N. system (excluding the World Bank and the International Monetary Fund). In many countries they are delivering the services — in urban and rural community development, education, and health care — that faltering governments can no longer manage.

With accuracy it can be said that democracy is an essential principle. Therefore, Social Work is an important function of social regulation, as it is a trustee of values like dignity of the human being, self-determination and social justice and, by nature, represents the ideals of democracy. *This allows for peace and lessens interest in physical boundary disputes.*

The work developed here focuses on human needs, thus requiring them to be met, not as a matter of option but as an imperative of basic justice. Therefore, Social Work moves toward considering Human Rights as one of the organizational principles of its professional practice and one that must be preserved by any democratic country that has signed an International Treaty aiming at ensuring Human Rights.

In summary, with regard to the guiding principles of democratic States, the *Supremacy of the Popular Will* underscores popular participation in government decisions like a necessity to holding peace and improving the economic flow to make Gross Domestic Product.

Another important guide driving the democracy is the principle about the *Preservation of Freedom*, understood as the power to do everything that is not harmful to another person, and also it means individual freedom to dispose of himself and property without any interference from the State. The *General Data Protection Regulation (GDPR)* is an example that allows people to sell their own personal information.

Both principles are combined with *Equality of rights*, understood as the prohibition of distinctions in the enjoyment of rights, mainly for economic reasons or of discrimination between social classes.

There is also a paradox between laws and the guarantee of a dignified citizenship owing to values about popular needs versus the possibility of the Government providing social programs when *83 million people being added to the world's population every year* (United Nations, 2017).

More popular financial autonomy is not a whim. Indeed, it is a necessity to ensure human survival that will be achieved with investments in technologies for broad access.

It will not be possible if taxes are not re-treated by governments that must make a regulatory framework with taxes that are more progressive and proportionate than we currently have. This is about the partnership between governments and citizens driving the administration of the State as a democratic ideal.

As for the existence of a sustainable planet and leading a dignified life, rulers cannot argue their defense founded on the principle of the "Possible Reserve" that establishes a limit for the realization of social rights when governments provide insufficient financial and structural resources. The principle is opposed to the *Existential Minimum* required by humanity. The Existential Minimum principle includes everything that is necessary for a dignified life: health, housing, education, leisure, etc. This is why the State cannot deny Smart Economy with *Blockchain and Cryptocurrencies* because the financial interest of the government is a secondary interest. If the government is worried about profits, it is not in public interest. Thus, the State cannot ignore the realization of fundamental and social rights that guarantee the existential minimum for all only because they are afraid of sharing power and the public administration.

The truth is this is a complex issue. But the complexity can be mitigated through Information Technology (ICT) and AI because this technology is maximizing how the human being solves difficult issues. Human intelligence is the ability to know and learn about problem solving. Artificial Intelligence is the simulation of human intelligence by machines and includes the ability to solve problems, ability to act as humans and the ability to rationalize behaviors and activities. Put another way, Boden (1998) enlightens us about AI:

> Creativity is a fundamental feature of human intelligence, and an inescapable challenge for AI. Even technologically oriented AI cannot ignore it, for creative programs could be very useful in the laboratory or the market-place. And AI-models intended (or considered) as part of cognitive science can help psychologists to understand how it is possible for human minds to be creative.
>
> Creativity is not a special "faculty", nor a psychological property confined to a tiny elite. Rather, it is a feature of human intelligence in general. It is grounded in everyday capacities such as the association of ideas, reminding, perception, analogical thinking, searching a structured problem-space, and reflective self-criticism. It involves not only a cognitive dimension (the generation of new ideas) but also motivation and emotion, and is closely linked to cultural context and personality factors [3]. Current AI models of creativity focus primarily on the cognitive dimension.

> A creative idea is one which is novel, surprising, and valuable (interesting, useful, beautiful). But "novel" has two importantly different senses here. The idea may be novel with respect only to the mind of the individual (or AI-system) concerned or, so far as we know, to the whole of previous history. The ability to produce novelties of the former kind may be called P-creativity (P for psychological), the latter H-creativity (H for historical). P-creativity is the more fundamental notion, of which H-creativity is a special case.
>
> AI should concentrate primarily on P-creativity. If it manages to model this in a powerful manner, then artificial H-creativity will occur in some cases-indeed, it already has, as we shall see [...]

In today's scenario modern days, robots with machine learning reinforcement are capable of replacing humans at work, assisting in healthcare, and developing business strategies for the financial market but at a higher level than humans and of mass-scale performance. Also, Blockchain technology is showing high performance in maintaining the integrity in electoral procedures by avoiding fake results (Nguyen, 2018).

Besides that, democracy is being threatened by plutocracy groups and autocratic governments that use fraudulent elections to engage in apparent democratic legitimacy and keep the cycle of corruption and laundering money active.

Meanwhile, hunger has affected millions of people around the world. Africa is expected to double its population to 2.4 billion by 2050. On the other hand, Africa has 60% of the world's uncultivated arable land. These are some of the useful information given in the United Nation's report (2017) that demonstrates access to technology as a Sixth Dimensional Human Right where there is a need to think about the economy in a decentralized and intelligent way to include developing countries. For example, Africa has the potential to feed the world and to develop itself through exporting food. It is the warehouse of the world.

Two crucial ingredients can help solve these crises: technology and political will. AI, IoT and Blockchain in a society using Smart Economy will create a sustainable world. But decision-makers must accept the technology, or it is useless.

Intelligent digital development means using information and communication technologies (ICTs) to improve people's lives. And everyone knows that beyond the positives, we have points that present some problems as well. But for the authors, problems should not be seen as obstacles because they can be possibly solved with one-off measures.

Technology is moving at a fast pace, and major technological advances such as IoT, 5G, AI, Blockchain and Cloud Environment can increase and decrease the gap between developed and developing countries. For this reason, the authors are concerned about establishing grounds for appropriate legislative, economic and educational treatment.

ICTs are strategically important to Smart Economy, and we definitely need to use them to accelerate the achievement of the Sustainable Development Goals in agriculture, education, health and also to propitiate more value for societies and communities. Thus, this requires a people-centered approach.

By 2030, we will see an increase in the number of large cities, especially in developing countries, and so governments programs are required to make possible the management of resources to guarantee the minimum existential level to citizens. ICTs can help support transport networks and electrical networks, among other key systems for development. If technology exists, we must use it to facilitate the future of humanity.

Almost half the world's population is still offline, and most of them live in remote and isolated rural communities where connectivity is difficult. Providing connectivity is difficult for geographical reasons but also because the return on investment in these areas is much poorer than urban areas.

In some countries, the high price of connection service and the tax burden on the service also contributes to this factor. And if we want to keep up with and retain technology benefits, connection is key.

The authors brought to the text many reasons demonstrating that Smart Economy with Blockchain technology, AI and the Cryptocurrencies are the future of the economy.

By analyzing the scenario of Tax Law and International Policies in the Smart Economy and also the practical application of technologies such as AI, IoT, IoE and Blockchain working in the Cloud Environment, is possible to say that this will lead to real benefits. Virtual is just the environment in which the decentralized economy takes place. The repercussions and benefits are real.

The nature of the economic transaction at all levels was altered when Blockchain technology and Cryptocurrencies emerged in the world economy. Before that, the financial nature was money for money in unequal and discriminatory businesses, and now there is a social value in economic transactions that can touch all social levels. Smart Economy with Blockchain is completely *non-discriminatory.*

Tax Morality and the Flow of Economic Growth

The following text reports the authors' concern about the future of Smart Economy in case it does not receive investments and one-off measures because the dictatorship of banks and the flow of laundering money threaten the world economy to protect the corruption that fuels terrorism and others crimes. The abuse from banks, laundering money and corruption is feeding growing poverty and hunger in the world.

"Dictatorship" means all power in the hands of a few: a dictator or a group. This system is seen in cycles because the real power does not die out. What can be extinguished is only the power of a dictator or group. Therefore, the Power will continue circulating and is disputed all the time.

The society has neglected world history since World War II, and today we are living a new cycle of dictatorship that affects the whole world: the Dictatorship promoted by the Banks through using abusive measures against humanity. Proof of this was the crisis experienced by Europe in 2010, where governments were bankrupt and lived by the orders of the banks. This fact has been widely explored by newspapers worldwide, such as the *New York Times* (2016).

The ordinary citizens have borne the brunt of the economy in a lonely way. Note that when banks go into crisis, the Rulers give money to keep the activity under the claim of keeping the economy galloping. This is not the real reason because banks do not perform any social function. They do not create jobs. They work for profit by profit. On the other hand, when the citizen loses his job and fails to pay the banks, he will be taken to task and the bank will take his assets, and in some countries like Brazil put his survival at risk. No one is giving money or employment, and so the citizen continues finding ways to earn income and pay the bills. This was an example about the cycle of power moving within the economic system of plutocracy.

This is why it is so natural for some countries to resist the digital economy. They are feeling threatened by the individual freedom that Smart Economy allows by counteracting the tyranny imposed by dictatorship where banks have power and Plutocracy is a New Economic Strategy.

The system of corruption makes public administrators and organizations manipulate the principle of legality to ban most people from all that is good in the world and reserving for plutocrats or some powerful groups money, food, health, housing, education and comfort. The authors point out that laws are not made by minorities or poor people. The laws are made by the powerful and rich people. Anything that threatens the division of power or money will not be accepted by the corrupt people. Smart Economy gives humanity a chance to get out of this cycle quickly without manipulating laws against the interests of bankers from the classical payment system where they are the middlemen. Currently, banks acquire status as holders of power and controllers of laws. In fact, banks are only part of a country's productive and economic chain, and anything beyond this means abuse against the humanity.

In this regard, Smart Economy is important because it frees governments and citizens by placing banks in their rightful place: a participant in the financial services chain into country. And only this.

Making fairer laws that limit the power of banks has been impossible in all countries since they have plenty of money to create laws that favor them. Legality, morality and constitutionality are different concepts. Not everything that is legal will be moral or constitutional.The developing countries are rife with vulnerable compared to others.

The authors justify this statement because this issue is frequent in reliable international newspapers (Prada, 2015). When rulers authorize laws that allow the excessive use of pesticides in the food, it is the people who will die getting cancer, and that will be fine because it does not threaten the power or wealth of rulers or plutocrats. That will only represent fewer people competing for power or money. Therefore, most countries that prohibit (or deny) Smart Economy are the same ones that authorize the use of agrochemicals. Curious, is it not? What about cancer? Why is there no cure?

In general, taxes must be fair to enable the State administration activity in a manner proportional to maintaining economic and educational growth. But taxation is not allowed to be so high as to make human survival unfeasible. And when we have reports indicating that there are 275 million people living in extreme poverty in Central, Southern and West Africa, West Asia, Latin America and the Caribbean, it is possible stating that there is a lack of investments in generating income and education (Source: *United Nation's report: World Economic Situation and Prospects 2018* from Department of Economic and Social Affairs — UN/DESA; the United Nations Conference on Trade and Development — UNCTAD).

But the gap in investments is not due to the low tax collection. In contrast, there are developing countries with profitable economic activity and with coffers fulls of tax money paid by citizens. But corruption and laundering money are responsible for poverty, hunger and lack of professional opportunity. These added factors weaken the democracy and create fertile ground for dictatorship.

For these reasons, the authors argue that the growth of the economic flow is not resolved by obligating citizens to pay more and more taxes. There are already too many taxes in the world. The time now is to maximize these features.

This is the road of capital flows flight that most people do not see. But by far the biggest chunk of outflows has to do with unrecorded — and usually illicit — capital flight. US-based Global Financial Integrity (GFI) (Hickel, 2017) calculates that *developing countries have lost a total of $13.4tn through unrecorded capital flight since 1980*. Most of these unrecorded outflows take place through the international trade system. Basically, corporations — foreign and domestic alike — report false prices on their trade invoices in order to spirit money out of developing countries directly into tax havens and secrecy jurisdictions, a practice known as "trade misinvoicing". Usually the goal is to evade taxes, but sometimes this practice is used to launder money or circumvent capital controls. In 2012, developing countries lost $700bn through trade misinvoicing, which outstripped aid receipts that year by a factor of five.

Simultaneously, taxes are captured from a larger proportion of the poorest people when expected otherwise. Mathematical calculations distort the principles of social equality that establish the obligation of rulers to create fair and progressive taxes. And in this way the rich become super-rich because they pay lower taxes.

In United States, the IRS found that as you go from being merely wealthy (the 1%) to super-duper wealthy (the 0.001%), your average federal income tax rate actually goes down. In other words, the progressivity of the federal income tax starts to fall apart at the upper reaches of the income distribution. Figure 1 shows this fact (Ingraham, 2015).

These issues are not far from the technological field as Smart Economy uses Blockchain technology and Cryptocurrencies to free humanity from this cycle that violates human dignity and threatens human survival.

Paying taxes is necessary to generate benefits that will be shared between States and citizens, and paying Just Taxes is a real action to establish the Principle of Human Dignity (Kaddous, 2015).

The Organization for Economic Co-operation and Development (OECD) is worried about this scenario. Some countries are establishing the excessive taxation, and the Double Taxation Principle is opposed

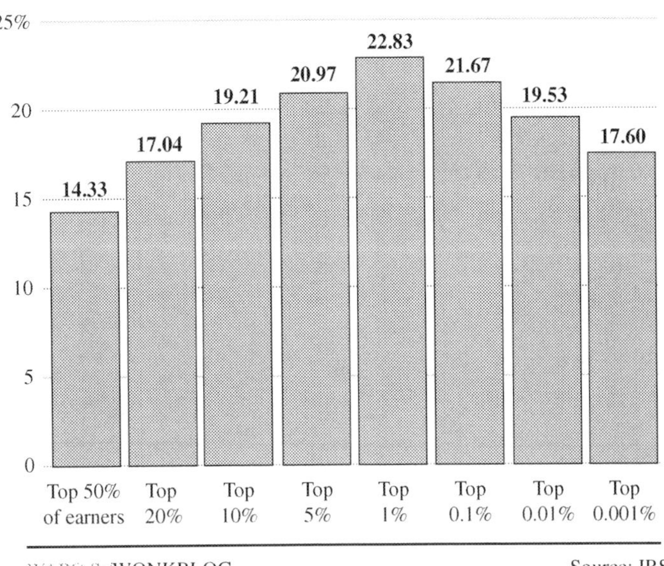

Figure 1: More Money, Less Taxes. Average Income Tax Rates in 2012, by Income Percentile

Source: *The Washington Post* (2015).

by the OECD because it represents a practice that is potentially damaging to the world economy and is unconstitutional. The method for elimination of double taxation is found in article 23A and 23B in OECD Model Tax Convention.

Double Taxation is a principle on Tax Law referring to the Income Tax. It means the tax paid twice On the Same Source of income earned. It occurs when income is taxed at both the corporate and personal levels. Double taxation also occurs in international trade when the same income is taxed in two different countries.

This has been balanced by international agreements such as the Base Erosion and Profit Shifting (BEPS) (OECD, 2018). Convention to Eliminate Double Taxation in Relation to Taxes on Income and Prevent Tax Evasion and Elision.

For the authors, Income Tax is sounds like the tax from the feudal monarchy, and Double Taxation will be set up when governments require tax revenue and, at the same time, are taxing products bought, supplied and transported as well.

In most analyses of income distribution, we are asking for more reasonable sense in establishing tax rates for the rich and poor people. The idea of greater income equality and a more even distribution of wealth reiterates the importance of a progressive income tax structure. It also highlights the economically sensible nature of targeted welfare assistance to those with lower incomes and a tightening of payments away from high-income earners.

This is where the current tax breaks to very wealthy people super annuants and the business sector need to be radically overhauled. Not only will changing policies in these areas enhance economic growth and see a structural lowering in the unemployment rate, they have the other benefit of being fair, decent and compassionate.

The authors are arguing that citizens should pay taxes only on consumer goods and services and not on income from the labor force. This is because it taxes the same source several times. Income from work has a noble social function because it is shared with society through taxes paid when the citizen buys products or uses services. Only income that is spared for short-term financial speculation should be directly taxed on income.

Throughout Smart Economy and the new business opportunities emerging in the Cloud Environment, it is quite possible to be paying for proportional and fair taxes on income because there is no intermediary and it eliminates the legal nexus to set the tax liability directly on the income. Also, the public coffers will become even more full with the investments from stronger consumers through consumption, and investments as a result will become greater.

Smart Economy is imperative for maintaining the growing economic flow.

Sovereignty and Border Protection Requiring Inclusive Standards

From conferences and newspaper articles, some interesting data emerge. In information collected from 2017, "1.6 billion adults have a mobile phone and they can use this technology" (ITU-UN, 2018). According to World Bank, 1.7 billion people are still unbanked (World Bank, 2018) and countries with high mobile money account ownership have less gender inequality. In a world where the statistics is showing us that 1.6 billion adults have a cell phone but do not have access to a checking account, this is able to be used as evidence to prove the statistical relationship that many people are excluded from the banking system because they create rules that exclude portions of the population assuming that these sectors of the population are unprofitable for the banking system. This behavior reflects on the world economy because excluding people from the payment system means restricting access to Free Trade.

The policy established by the banks is far from complying with the corporate principle of the *Company's Social Function* (Galligan, 2012) and the humanitarian principle of the *Social Function of Property* (Coelho, 2007) which requires that every economic activity must generate jobs and also that it must be non-discriminatory. Thus, the classic banks have a great influence and have caused significant damage to the world economy: it increases poverty and causes social inequalities.

The Disruptive Theory refers to the socioeconomic phenomenon we are experiencing in this age. If people find themselves oppressed and unable to escape from hunger, they will manifest this in a revolutionary manner. People will, in a natural and disorganized manner, respond to the aggressive environment they inhabit as a way of survival. Blockchain technology emerged and Smart Economy immediately became the door to survival. This is just and legitimate. This is why the Initial Coin Offering (ICOs) operate and specialize through investments from society, without participation of state investments. Despite this, does not need become a rule?

The authors concludes that Disruptive Theory in a legal concept is:

> "***Disruptive Theory***: It regards to the process of social and business survival while introducing in the same time a foreign element to specific industry modifying the behavior of the whole phases of the sector: production processes, marketing, supply and demand policies, compliance, laws, social and governmental behavior. It isn't a procedure driven only by competitive techniques to free commerce. Indeed, it means a procedure that reverses the order of power in that whole industry through technological practices. There is a balance between supply and demand. In fact it is a "Leverage Process" where was added Social Value".

Democratic Power must recognize the LEGALITY and Social Function necessary for Smart economy and establishing the requisite security to enable survival without changing the legal nature of the virtual economy with Blockchain and Cryptocurrencies.

Capital increases arising from the sale of *stock certificate* (when listed on the responsible bodies) and the capital gains on the disposal of cryptocurrencies acquired as a long-term investment and not intended to trade must be taxed under different rules.

It must be noted that the financial life of the ordinary citizen is a different right from the right that is available to companies when they are acquiring income from a trade or service such as securities or company shares. In this case, it must be reported in the tax return and taxed at the applicable rates because it is impacting all members in the trade society and not just companies in the Cloud Environment or virtual economy.

The ordinary citizen cannot compete in the same level with companies. They do not enjoy legal instruments or tools comparable to those of corporations to enable them to compete. Just as States already guarantee that people are free to seek a cure for their illnesses by acquiring medicines and treatments that may not be available in the country, this is also human dignity. No one can prevent the human being from doing what is necessary for the preservation of life. In the same reasoning and by equality of measure, Money is Equated with the Remedy When in the Proportion of Guaranteeing the Dignified Life.

For this reason, the financial system addressed in Smart Economy enjoys humanitarian protection, has humanitarian value and Social Function and must have different legal and tax treatment. This does not remove the monetary portion of governments to carry out the functions of public administration. Seen the other way, this increases the country's economy by generating more income to the States, which are collected from taxes, because a strong consumer buys more, circulates the currency and heats up the economy.

Soon we will have questions about the *Smart Economy* requisiting resolution in the Courts, and therefore all the professionals that work in this industry need to speak the same legal language. In this way, they will release themselves of crimes such as scams, frauds, laundering money, false currency, tax evasion, civil liabilities for material and moral damages as well as violations of the *Consumer Code.*

This is such a crucial point that Malta, through the Technology Arrangements Service Bill (Tas Bill), has set itself the obligation to draw up a law to establish the concept of Smart Contract before establishing the rules of responsibility.

Szabo (1994) established the *technical concept about Smarts Contracts* in 1994 as a computer protocol designed to facilitate, verify or digitally enforce the negotiation or execution of a contract. Smart contracts enable trusted transactions to occur without third parties.

The authors have developed a broad *Legal Concept* that they consider to be more appropriate to the current Smart Economy:

> "Smart Contract: It means a decentralized management behaving like a mathematical ratio in self-executing contracts after computational codes have been written with predefined business rules. In a broad sense, it is an obligation placed on the machine to deliver rules from a hypothetic fact to a consequential fact under a "Dry Legal Code". In the end, it produces the Individual and Concrete Legal Norm valid between the

> contracting parties (NIC). Legal Nature encompasses technological resources informed by AI and IoT, establishing signs to be interpreted through the learning function of the machine to establish the applicable reality in prescriptive language. The intrinsic relation to the Smart Contract, Blockchain and the AI tools represent the duty to be, that is, establishes the Base Proposition describing a hypothetical business event carrying the Base Proposition of the legal business relational to the consequent effect".

In addition, the legislative body from Malta island was concerned about the validity and was questioning about the use of Smart Contract for the future. The reason for this is because smarts contracts are different from the classic ones in that they are self-executing and work without additional third-party intervention. The system of positive laws was vague about contracts in the intelligent format, and currently we have lead with IoT inserting elements for contract analysis. Therefore, the laws that establish the concept and ways it will be applicable brings a greater degree of legal certainty to the intelligent contracts. Just as an illustration, in Malta Island there was only the Electronic Commerce Act (Chapter 426 of the Laws of Malta) stating that a contract would not be invalid simply because it is in the "electronic" form. It was proposed that a similar provision be introduced to ensure that a contract is not invalidated simply because of its *smart format.*

One of the most unique characteristics of Blockchain is its decentralized quality of performance, which is shared among all parts of the network, thus, eliminating the involvement of third parties or intermediaries. There is a need to shift countries and cities from a government agency-centric model to citizen-centric model. This feature is particularly useful because it avoids the chances of any conflict in the process and saves time as well. While Blockchains have their own set of issues that still need to be resolved, they offer faster, cheaper and more efficient options compared to traditional systems. Because of this, even banks and government organizations are turning to blockchains these days.

Building the regulatory system is much important and should be in line with international law. Taxation has been a worldwide knot and, in that respect, Malta Island has dropped out of the way by building its Regulatory Framework.

Financial transactions and payments with Blockchain are incorruptible and 100% auditable. The entries are intact and immutable, and these keep the laundering of money away from legal businesses and do not feed corruption. Failures of data entry are only capable of being manipulated by humans during first entry. However, the decentralized payment system is auditable, and so this would soon be discovered by the *Consensus*. This feature discourages laundering money.

Smart Contracts do not require an intermediary as an outsourced facilitator. The consequence, essentially, is giving the user user full control of the agreement. Blockchain acts as a mediator by loading the data/signs applicable to trading. It establishes a high trust between the parties and allows reliable exchange of information. No one can steal or lose any of your documents because they are encrypted and stored securely in a shared and secure ledger. Also, you do not have to trust the people you are dealing with or expect them to trust you, because the impartial system of smart contracts replaces trust.

However, establishing inclusive access standards also involves thinking about the legal personality of the Smarts Contracts. Many Smart Contracts will be hosted in the structure of a company that already has consolidated many contracts in a traditional way, and the registration of this contract will follow this pattern. But this is not always the rule. It can happen that there are many Smart Contracts managing businesses on the Cloud Environment, without a physical property or structure. This could result in transactions occurring without an appropriate "legal entity" as the counterparty. Therefore, there is a need for a specific legal structure with requirements different from those in the Classical Register itself given the complexity of the technology involved.

For the authors, the emerging economy calls for a regulatory framework with inclusive standards in order to allow broad access in such a non-discriminatory and egalitarian way that a country cannot outgrow it. Compliance in this case will result in equalizing the individual benefits that are shared and help develop the economic flow in a secure manner.

Tilmes & Kanehira (2018) from The World Bank Group suggests that in order to realize this technological aspiration, we need to engage governments and people, coordinate development partners and mobilize the private sector to:

1. **Build:** Develop the foundational building blocks for sustainable, technology-led economies.
2. **Boost:** Expand the capacity of people and institutions to thrive in a resilient society in the face of disruption.
3. **Broker:** Harness disruptive technology, data and expertise to solve development challenges and manage risks.

Fatca Law and GDPR represent a legal control system for Laundering Money. Of course, it is positive. On the other hand, this has made it difficult for developing countries to access income because they are excluded from the system of bank payments and because financial activities become suspect because there is a lack of registration for the origin of the income. Failure to fully comply with the requirements of these laws is not the same as practicing crimes. These have been trade barriers for some countries.

Going through this scenario, either the Smart Economy or just the financial system that communicates within the Blockchain with the Cryptocurrencies is the way for developing countries or small economies to access income through new professional positions, dignified and humanitarian taxation, and free financial autonomy from suspicious blockages imposed by international banking regulations.

For the authors, the typical man–machine interaction will make man better than he is today. AI will improve the way a man makes decisions in all industries because it will increase access to multiple sources of information in a short time. This will require great educational and technological development of the people.

For example, in medicine, AI will not provide a cure for spinal cord injuries, but it will provide patients with the same healing effect. That means a more dignified life.

Human reality will be interpreted by the machine that has been previously analyzed and fed by man with carefully studied information. The result will be smart contracts with errors reduced to zero or almost zero and no bureaucracy.

Note that this is a very high level of human development that poor countries do not have access to. Without proper education and policies, they will not have access to wealth and will be poorer. The result may be a multitude of hungry and desperate people. This may be motivation for wars or invasion of frontiers.

Thus, the typical human–machine interaction will only be positive if richer countries develop policies to help poorer countries get access to work and wealth. Thus, border protection is not through physical structures or obstacles. The borders will be protected with virtual interaction and technological advances.

There is a common perception that the rulers agree with this dynamic relationship by verifying that there is no power without money. Even the hardest rulers and dictators have realized this and invest in diplomatic relations and political, administrative and social infrastructure. War leads to weakening of the economy, and power only matters when correlated to economic power. There is a joint effort to invest in disruptive technologies to strengthen the world economy, thus maintaining security.

The shift in border security, advancing from smart borders to virtual borders, requires significant economic and physical infrastructure investments at or near the border in order to work as envisioned. International cooperation can also reduce the overall costs of necessary infrastructure. However, international cooperation in joint border infrastructure development and joint inspections may be too controversial politically in the immediate future when issues about the minimum existential to people is ignored. The upshot is that significant economic and political barriers to implementing the smart borders concept will bring about the worst consequences or have a rebound effect on sovereignty.

The stability of the citizen is made up of layers that overlap: food, health, legal, social, healthy environment. And economics is the armor that holds this stability because it protects and provides a means of realizing the layers of stability. Politics matters only insofar as it serves to structure and maintain stability.

Physical borders will be protected only when human security is established. Globalization has broadened the border horizon by establishing virtual limits and requires governments to share responsibility for the security of mankind as technology promotes rapid industrial growth and education in developing countries cannot keep pace. Young people in emerging economies are forever playing catch-up as a lack of foundational knowledge means advancing skills knowledge is moving further out of reach; already educated western citizens are able to quickly reskill and work with machines. Thus, partnerships between countries are required to promote equality.

The authors here establish a concept of Worldwide Responsible Security:

> The security of individuals is perhaps not derived from country safety. From the author's point of view, Human Security is not placed just in the hands of the military force, in which case it indicates a late stage and the necessity of emergency action. Human Security is placed in the hands of the economy that can help establish a dignified life and will lead to the reduction of civil and military conflicts because there is no motivation. Safety should be seen in the conditions of everyday life: food, education, housing, employment, health, public safety, etc. This is important because it means all conditions that generate stability and a high level of freedom will play a role in maintaining individual safety. This framework along with a social life will externalize the solidarity in a global chain and lead to the creation of a friendly environment capable of establishing peace. Our concept of human safety was extracted from article III of the Declaration of Human Rights, 1948, as a way to bring together the frameworks of establishing peace in relation to that of the economy.

Blockchain technology combined with *IoT, AI and Cryptocurrency* divided society along new lines. In the past, separation was only that of the wealthy or elites from academic industry, and it was they who disputed the power by the technology. The shift was significant because it brought people closer to feeling a sense of community. These elites are not just the rich but also groups of citizens with transnational interests and identities who often have common points of interest with their peers in other countries, whether industrialized or developing. Physical barriers no longer represent the borders of a sovereign country. Modern sovereignty is maintained by the inclusion of its citizens in the global world to access the wealth and assurance of promoting the same right for people residing outside their borders, giving a sense of global community.

Smart borders are not just a matter of deploying hardware, software and soldiers. They require international cooperation. Existing smart border agreements lay out an agenda for extensive and solid international cooperation, but even more cooperation will be necessary to collect the necessary data for the smart border concept to work in practice.

After all, countries need to agree about *Solidarity Responsibility for Human Security*. Then, the content that the authors have discussed in this text will occur, and it can be concluded that this agreement will go through economic efforts focused on partnerships to developing technology as a Human Right because it will accelerate the economic flow and bring more satisfaction to humanity. If nothing is done in solidarity, the world will collapse long before 2030.

The Search to Solve the Possible Problems to Apply the Legal Doctrine Embodying Other Scientists

Over the development of the research, the lack of real experiments to apply the legal doctrine on a wide scale was observed. Carrying out laboratory tests can bring benefits in terms of shortening the time between the start and end result by providing skillful measures to reduce hunger and poverty and to maximize investments through humanitarian taxation that will improve the economy and lead to sustainable consumption.

However, it is not possible to simulate reality with future socioeconomic behavior in a controlled environment.

The limitations of the research on real-life scenarios during the technological evolutionary cycle can be overcome through laboratory research with tests using Artificial Intelligence to simulate human life and social behavior in the virtual environment without altering the immediate sensory reality.

Laboratory tests will always be better when done in conjunction with surveys to establish statistical data by creating small study groups in at least seven countries.

However, the limitation will be completely overcome when done along with tests with AI in a simulated environment.

As for the future of this research, a reevaluation of the data is needed.

For the authors, the year 2030 is considered the established time frame for a viable reevaluation because these technological challenges need some time to evolve.

The authors selected the year 2030 as a suitable time frame since the 2030 Agenda for Sustainable Development has been established as a global pact.

Thus, it is possible that other scientists can continue and refine the study with similar, complementary techniques.

For the authors, this research can achieve useful results only if the technical community, such as engineers, developers and IT professionals, are included.

Thus, the authors hope to receive a 100% affirmative result which will leave no doubt as to the importance of technology as Sixth Dimension of Human Rights because more mathematical reports will be the outcome.

Also, this represents an opening for the technical community to create new research techniques in response to social outcomes.

The solution suggested by the authors is to Simulate the Social Behavior of the individuals and determine how much this will affect the consumption.

With AI and Big Data, it will be possible to study by simulation the behavior, for example, of groups that suffered aggressions, groups that belong to high and low social classes, men and women, educational qualifications and those living in developed or developing countries.

This will be efficient to know if the results obtained with the tax exception for Smart Economy will generate growth of the Global Economic Flow because human behavior is the unpredictable factor in the legal doctrine presented by the authors.

And if the Smart Economy with Blockchain and Cryptocurrency is increasing the Global Economic Flow, hunger and poverty will come to an end.

Conclusion and the One-Off Discussions

When we are talking about technology it includes not only physical equipment — like infrastructures and installations (so called "artifacts") — but also the knowledge, techniques and skills that surround its deployment and use. These in turn form part of a broader technological "regime" or infrastructure that supports innovation and the ability for one technology to build on or link to another.

Generally, researches who address technology keep the focus on development and technical methods for creating, modifying or improving sharing, use and operativity.

The authors innovated this research methods through a methodological cut using the legal, historical, technical and socioeconomic aspects.

The research sources were useful for extracting data that were analyzed, together forming the structure that makes technological innovation with AI, Big Data and the Digital Economy with Blockchain and Cryptocurrency survive the time to enforce the 2030 Agenda for Sustainable Development (brought out by the United Nations) to end hunger and poverty in the short timespan of 15 years.

The authors concludes that the Annual Participative Budget Plan can maximize the application of taxes, and as the rulers make the annual laws to establish this plan they will improve the citizens wants and needs through putting Fundamental Rights first.

So, after many researches and observation, the authors are assured that the technology is causing the rise of Fundamental Rights from the fifth to the sixth dimension. Thus, this points to technology, specifically AI, Big Data and Digital Economy with Blockchain and Cryptocurrency, taking priority place in the Annual Participative Budget Plan as a means to maximize the application of taxes thanks to its transformative power.

This research is applicable as social, economic and humanitarian policies serve as a doctrine to guide the regulatory world framework by governments, civil society, private companies, agencies and non-governmental organizations.

Since 2008, and to the present day, there is still no inclusive standard of international norms to regulate the digital economy or the use of technologies such as AI, IoT and Big Data for social, humanitarian, environmental or health applications.

For this reason, fees, copyright and royalties still require adjustment laws for the international community.

Have no doubts that Interactions between Humans and Machine mean the Future of Work. Advances in AI, robotics, and deep learning change how we work, and jobs that were once widely viewed as safe are increasingly being automated, increasing migration and forced displacement. It is an augmented labor force that emerges that combines the strength of humans and machines. Localization is developing as additive manufacturing impacts supply chains, immigration and urbanization.

Establishing that human civilization has arrived at the Sixth Dimension of Human Rights goes further than building a humanitarian legal thesis. This means embodying the goals of the Declaration of Human Rights written in 1948 by the United Nations.

This adoption allows us to create a sustainable world along the lines of the 2030 Agenda for Sustainable Development, created by the United Nations.

The authors are addressing technology under the contexts of development, transfer, adoption and dissemination, and they are very thoughtful about the integration of scientific process as an important element of policies and programmes to manage natural resources in an environmentally and economically sustainable and culturally appropriate manner embodying governments, civil societies, private companies and non-governmental organizations to make it possible for developing countries to acquire the benefits from technological innovation. Thus, because of the governmental responsibility for human security, everybody will live in an established sustainable world.

However, laundering of money and frauds are pointed as reasons for the emptying of public coffers, and it makes governments demand increasingly high rates from the people to restore the amount that was taken away illegally. Therefore, these factors are jeopardizing the human survival, thus making people work more and more to pay high taxes.

On the other hand, the population is growing fast every year, leading to a lack of sufficient jobs for all. So, taxes are a real obligation that people cannot escape, and they will pay even when they have not got jobs. In the same way, the need for survival has brought conflict to the territorial borders.

This is the reason to governments share the responsibility for human security. In addition to the gaps associated with the divide between developed and developing countries, other equally important "divides" must be addressed to ensure that technology becomes an effective and equitable means to attain socially and ecologically sustainable development.

For the authors, increasing the economy is an urgent necessity for mankind, and investments in technology can make it faster.

However, governments also need to acquire taxes to manage their activities.

Watching the landscape that the authors report, it gives rise to three problems for humanity's survival:

1. Increasing the economy and creating jobs is an urgent necessity, and it must be done now and fast;
2. High taxes are jeopardizing human survival;
3. Governments must manage the State activities and at the same time they assume responsibility for human security on the global field.

What then is the solution?

Technological innovation is the solution. However, governments need to accept this and apply technological investments focused on improving the economy.

How will the Governments then make it?

The authors conclude that the Annual Participative Budget Plan can maximize the tax applications, and while rulers make the annual law to establish these plans they will improve the level of the citizens' necessities through keeping Fundamental Rights first and as the most vital aspect.

So, after researches and observation, the authors assure that the technology is rising the Fundamental Rights from five to sixth dimension. Thus, it points the technology specially Artificial Intelligence, Big Data and Digital Economy with Blockchain and Cryptocurrency in a priority place to Annual Participative Budget Plan as a form to maximize the taxes application thanks to transformative power.

Besides that, it is part of the democratic system of government the Annual Budget Plan and the Participatory Budget where the governors and citizens define the destination of the money collected with taxes. It means investments in state administration and social programs.

Defining technology as a Human Rights Dimension is to ensure that investments in technology will increase, because it is the fundamental right required for survival. It is the reason why investments in technology may be demanded.

However, the research used a lot of statistical data to conclude that mankind pays too many taxes and that tax that is collected is diluted by corruption and money laundering.

Therefore, establishing a regulatory framework for Smart Economy is urgent because the economy with Blockchain and Cryptocurrency can release mankind from this corrupt cycle and reduce poverty and increase economic flow.

The government's formula for raising taxes to solve the problems of Public Administration is old, does not work and jeopardizes the survival of humanity.

The problems that Smart Economy can control were not ignored by the authors as they believe it is possible to solve the problems through investment in the regulation.

The time is ripe now to maximize tax money and not create more taxes. It will accelerate the growth of humanity, possible only through technology.

But technology will be useless if the rulers do not accept it. Partnerships between civil society, the private sector and governments are a faster way to allow access to education in developing countries.

All the measures that the authors presented create a sustainable, harmonious and safe world.

In parallel, new jobs requiring socio-emotional skills, curiosity and entrepreneurship are emerging.

Thus, AI, Cryptocurrency and Blockchain technology is not a threat to humanity. This brings a better and more dignified way of life. However, the human being will never be able to compete with the machine. Then, we should change the way we educate children and adolescents to develop capacities like communication, partnerships and skills to deal with conflicts and come up with suitable solutions. We should prepare children to acquire principles and ethics.

References

Kofi, A. (2015). Technology Can Improve the State of the World. MIT: Massachusetts. Retrieved from: https://www.kofiannanfoundation.org/annan-work/how-technology-can-improve-the-state-of-the-world/. Accessed on October 10, 2018.

Boden, M. A. (1998). Creativity and Artificial Intelligence. *Artificial Intelligence Journal*, 103, 347–356.

Coelho, F. U. (2007). *Manual de Direito Comercial*: Direito de Empresa. 18. edition. São Paulo: Saraiva.

ESQUERDA NET (2018). EUA: Duas mil crianças migrantes enjauladas e separadas dos seus pais. *Carta Maior*. Retrieved from: https://www.cartamaior.com.br/?/Editoria/Antifascismo/EUA-Duas-mil-criancas-migrantes-enjauladas-e-separadas-dos-seus-pais/47/40655. Accessed on November 22, 2018.

Galligan, D. J. (2012). Does Law have Social Functions? Oxford Scholarship Online. Retrieved from: http://www.oxfordscholarship.com/view/10.1093/acprof:oso/9780199291830.001.0001/acprof-9780199291830-chapter-12. Accessed on October 10, 2018.

Garcia, A. R. (2018a). O desafio tecnológico para o pacto global em 2030: Blockchain, AI e defesa de fronteiras. Presented at the WEBbr 2018 Conference, Sao Paulo: Brazil, October 4, 2018. Retrieved from: https://conferenciaweb.w3c.br/. Accessed on October 14, 2018.

Garcia, A. R. (2018b). IGF 2018: Blockchain for Social and Humanitarian Applications, RAW. Presented on day 2: Salle VII — WS227, at UNESCO, Paris. Retrieved from: Day 2: Salle VII — WS227. Accessed on November 22, 2018.

Goundar, S. (2011). What is the Potential Impact of Using Mobile Devices in Education? Retrieved from: https://www.researchgate.net/publication/268337152_What_is_the_Potential_Impact_of_Using_Mobile_Devices_in_Education. Accessed on October 10, 2018.

Hickel, J. (2017). Aid in Reverse: How Poor Countries Develop Rich Countries. *The Guardian*. Retrieved from: https://www.theguardian.com/global-development-professionals-network/2017/jan/14/aid-in-reverse-how-poor-countries-develop-rich-countries. Accessed on October 14, 2018.

Ingraham, C. (2015). As the Rich Become Super-Rich, they Pay Lower Taxes. For Real. For real. *The Washington Post*. Retrieved from: https://www.washingtonpost.com/news/wonk/wp/2015/06/04/as-the-rich-become-super-rich-they-pay-lower-taxes-for-real/?noredirect=on&utm_term=.a1b0e1e1aaa2. Accessed on October 14, 2018.

ITU-UN (2018). ITU TELECOM WORLD 2018 Conference: Durban, setembro 2018. Retrieved from: https://telecomworld.itu.int/2018-event/smart-abc/. Accessed on October 18, 2018.

Kaddous, K. (2015). *The European Union in International Organisations and Global Governance*. Oxford and Portland: Oregon.

Knight, A., Chynoweth, P. (2008). Advanced Research Methods in the Built Environment: Legal Research. Wiley-Blackwell: United Kingdom.

Lenza, P. (2009). Direito Constitucional esquematizado. 13. ed. rev., atual. e ampl. São Paulo: Saraiva.

Mathew, J. T. (1997). The Power Shift: The Rise of Global Civil Society. *Foreign Affairs*. Retrieved from: https://www.foreignaffairs.com/articles/1997-01-01/power-shift. Accessed on October 10, 2018.

Nguyen, T. (2018). West Virginia to Offer Mobile Blockchain Voting App for Overseas Voters in November Election. *The Washington Post*. Retrieved from: https://www.washingtonpost.com/technology/2018/08/10/west-virginia-pilots-mobile-blockchain-voting-app-overseas-voters-november-election/?utm_term=.e0333d21a489. Accessed on October 10, 2018.

New York Times (2016). Explaining Greece's Debt Crisis. June 17, 2016. Retrieved from: https://www.nytimes.com/interactive/2016/business/international/greece-debt-crisis-euro.html. Accessed on October 14, 2018.

OECD (1948). Retrieved from: http://www.oecd.org/. Accessed on November 23, 2018.

OECD (2018). Multilateral Convention to Implement Tax Treaty Related Measures to Prevent BEPS. Retrieved form: http://www.oecd.org/tax/treaties/multilateral-convention-to-implement-tax-treaty-related-measures-to-prevent-beps.htm. Accessed on October 19, 2018.

Ortiz-Ospina, E., Roser, M. (2018). Taxation. Retrieved from https://ourworldindata.org/taxation. Accessed on October 18, 2018.

Prada, P. (2015). Why Brazil has a Big Appetite for Risky Pesticides. Reuters Investigates. Retrieved from: https://www.reuters.com/investigates/special-report/brazil-pesticides/. Accessed on October 14, 2018.

Rousseau, J.-J. (2008). O Contrato Social. Tradução de Ciro Mioranza. 2.ed. São Paulo: Escala.

Sarma, H. Ch. (2018). Turning the International North-South Corridor into a "Digital Corridor". *Comparative Politics Russia*, 9(4), 124–136. Doi: 10.24411/2221-3279-2018-10008.

Szabo, N. (1994). Formalizing and Securing Relationships on Public Networks. *First Monday*, 2(9).

The World Bank (2018). Financial Inclusion: Financial Inclusion is a Key Enabler to Reducing Poverty and Boosting Prosperity. Retrieved from: https://www.worldbank.org/en/topic/financialinclusion/overview. Accessed on October 18, 2018.

United Nations (1948). Universal Declaration of Human Rights. Retrieved from: http://www.un.org/en/universal-declaration-human-rights/. Accessed on November 23, 2018.

United Nations (2015). Transforming Our World: The 2030 Agenda for Sustainable Development. Retrieved from: https://sustainabledevelopment.un.org/post2015/transformingourworld. Accessed on October 14, 2018.

United Nations (2017). World Population Projected to Reach 9.8 Billion in 2050, and 11.2 Billion in 2100. Retrieved from: https://www.un.org/development/desa/en/news/population/world-population-prospects-2017.html. Accessed on October 18, 2018.

United Nations (2018). World Economic Situation and Prospects 2018. ISBN: 978-92-1-109177-9 e ISBN: 978-92-1-362882-9. Retrieved from: https://www.un.org/development/desa/dpad/wp-content/uploads/sites/45/publication/WESP2018_Full_Web-1.pdf. Accessed on October 18, 2018.

Chapter 4

Autonomous Agriculture Marketing Information System Through Blockchain: A Case Study of e-NAM Adoption in India

Jitendra Yadav*,‡, Madhvendra Misra*,§ and Sam Goundar†,¶

*Indian Institute of Information Technology, Allahabad, India

†The University of the South Pacific, Suva, Fiji

‡rsm2018506@iiita.ac.in

§madvendra@iiita.ac.in

¶sam.goundar@gmail.com

Abstract

The National Agricultural Market, through networking of the APMCs, provides electronic trading for different kinds of agricultural produce. Under e-NAM, all the trading is to be done through a digital platform as prescribed to ensure transparency in the transactions and provide a fair price to the farmers. The study was conducted in three APMCs of Uttar Pradesh to analyze the ground-level practices occurring in these APMCs and to assess the level of adoption of e-NAM. A considerable variation in the arrival and bidding prices obtained from the APMCs was found when compared with the data available on the agriculture market information system (Agmarknet).

In this chapter, we thus propose blockchain-based infrastructure to facilitate a highly transparent and autonomous system to further strengthen the information system and enable the efficient application of government rules and regulations pertaining to agricultural transactions in the APMCs through the utilization of smart contracts.

Introduction

India, being an agrarian economy, has been involved in agricultural activities since ages. The concept of agricultural markets is not new to society. Trade in the agricultural markets bears a high impact of the various socioeconomic factors along with cultural factors. Agricultural markets, like any other marketplace, are the meeting grounds where transactions between buyers and sellers take place with the existence of various intermediaries carrying out a specific task. Agricultural markets may exist as wholesale markets or as derivative markets where the various or singular commodity(ies) is being traded. The exchanges between the buyers and sellers, along with intermediaries in the agricultural market, face various inter-party conflicts such as delivery failures, below-standard-quality product and payment delays. Agricultural produce such as vegetables and fruits suffer from perishability issues, and hence used to be sold by the farmers to nearest available market or sale intermediary at throwaway prices. Keeping in view the losses borne by the farmers, the government introduced the Agricultural Produce Market Committee (APMC) Act. The APMC Act sees that the interest of the farmers is well protected and fair price is being paid for their produce, ensures proper dissemination of the information and sees that these rules are implemented and followed.

APMC markets were made with the pure intention of facilitating a fair pricing scheme for the farmers for their produce by the creation of an open, transparent auction mechanism, but it has been observed that since the past few years these markets have become breeding grounds for exploiting farmers. These markets are controlled by a centralized body which provides limited registration to the traders and commissioners to carry out trade. Since there are multiple farmers to sell their produce to the limited (few) buyers in the form of commission agents and traders, these buyers often tend to form cartels and force the farmers to sell their produce below the minimum support price set by the government. Such markets tend to operate like monopsony markets and control and affect the development of alternate agri-markets such as contract farming in local areas, direct farm to consumer markets and private markets.

To provide fairness to the APMC markets and to preserve the interest of the farmers, the Government of India, in 2016, launched e-National Agriculture Market (e-NAM) which integrated 585 APMC markets and formed an online auction system through unification of the national markets and now serves as a digital platform to facilitate transactions between buyers and sellers. It is a joint contribution of the various agencies such as Small Farmers Agribusiness Consortium (SFAC), central government for framing policies, technical support for assaying facilities from Directorate of Marketing and Inspector (DMI), Nagarjun Fertilizers and Chemicals Limited as a strategic partner for the maintenance of the portal and National Information Centre (NIC) providing the server for hosting the e-NAM website. It is the duty of the state government to provide warehousing for agricultural produce, resolution of the disputes in the APMC and implementation of both physical and online trading in the APMC markets. The e-NAM project is not entirely immune to human intervention and, due to the indulgence of the traders and commission agents, cartels have been formed which collude the bidding process and lower prices for the produce given to the customers and also lead to such malpractices as under-weighment, delay in the payments and making unauthorized deductions in the form of loading–unloading charges and market fees.

This study was conducted to analyze the extent to which the e-NAM framework is being practiced in the APMC markets in Uttar Pradesh. For the pilot study, three APMC markets have been visited, and two most traded commodities from these APMC markets have been taken into consideration for the study. From the study, we have seen a massive difference in the arrival and minimum support prices of the commodities traded in the physical market and reported on e-NAM to the data retrieved from the agriculture market information system (https://agmarknet.gov.in/).

Literature Review

State of agriculture marketing in India

India being an agrarian economy employs about half of the available workforce in agriculture (GOI (Government of India), 2016). NABARD conducted a survey in 2016–2017 which reported that about 48% rural Indian households are solely dependent on agriculture, making a monthly income of INR 3140 from agriculture only and leading to a total earning of INR 107,172 for the year 2015–2016 from cultivation, livestock, non-farming activities and wages/salaries (Nabard, 2018). India has multiple and diverse strengths in agriculture. Geographically, India has the second largest arable land area, and on the supply side, it is the largest producer of milk and holds the global second rank in the production of fish, wheat, rice, vegetables and fruits (Singh, 2017). Agriculture in India has become market-oriented and has become a commercial entity. The output of the food grains to be marketed has increased to 70%, which is twice the proportion of the 30–35% it was in the 1950s (Sharma & Wardhan, 2015). This increase in marketed surplus also led to post-harvest losses of all kinds of produce, for example, losses borne in vegetables and fruits were as high as 30–40%, and according to CIPHET the post-harvest losses incurred by the farmers was estimated to be INR 92,651 crore (Pandey, 2018). The committee on Doubling of Farmers' Income reported that the farmers were unable to sell 34% of vegetables, 44.6% of fruits and 40% of fruits and vegetables combined, and the total estimated loss due to not being able to sell was about INR 63,000 crore (Pandey, 2018). After China, India holds the second position as the largest food producer at the global level, but on the other hand, it holds the 103rd position out of 119 nations in the Global Hunger Index (Global Hunger Index, 2018). Such facts question the efficiency of the current food distribution system and the functioning of the agricultural markets. Multiple researchers tried to identify what role agriculture marketing plays in the regulation of economic development (Pal & Bahl, 1993; Minten *et al.*, 2012), but it was Purohit *et al.* (2017) who found out that there was a positive impact of market regulations, overgrowth of agriculture, expansion of area, adoption of technology, use of fertilizer and area for irrigation.

In India, agriculture is under the purview of the state. Many states have provided a place to make transactions between buyers and sellers of agriculture produce, known as Agriculture Produce and Livestock Market (APMC), under the APMC Act (1963). The purpose of establishing such a marketplace is to facilitate fair trade by providing an open outcry system of auctioning and preventing the intermediaries from forcing farmers to sell their produce at a throwaway price. The agricultural produce must be brought within the boundaries of the market, and following an auction system, the produce must be sold. However, the states failed to adopt the mechanism involved and attract private investment and promote competition. Due to improper application of the APMC Act by the states, traders and merchants indulged in malpractices such as under-weighment, lowered price paid to farmer's produce, payment delays and unauthorized reduction in the produce of up to 10–20% in the form of loading–unloading fee, market fees and involvement of multiple intermediaries (Aggarwal *et al.*, 2017).

Agricultural Produce Marketing Committee (APMC)

Agriculture marketing regulations have deep roots in the history of India since 1886, when the first market place was established at Karanjia by the British rulers under Hyderabad residency order (Paty & Gummagolmath, 2015). The first market regulation for the agricultural commodities was the Berar Cotton, and Grain Law of 1987, which was biased towards the production of cotton to meet the demand of the textile mills established in Manchester, and payments to farmers were made below world price (Rajagopal, 1993). To control the malpractices in the cotton trade, for the first time, the Cotton Market Act 1927 was implemented by the Bombay Government to bring fairness in the marketing practices (Pathy, 2017). Later on, the Ministry of Food and Agriculture, Government of India, enacted the Agricultural Produce Marketing Commission Act in 1938, which was adopted at the state levels also.

The literature review on the regulation of agriculture markets and their actual implementation puts forth two contrasting ideologies. One says that in India agricultural markets are malfunctioning and require intervention by the state government. On the contrary, the other says that the competition within the market has become intense, and there is a need for an infrastructure which is capable enough of meeting the competition (Harriss, 1984). In the 1960s and 1970s, Agricultural Produce Marketing Regulation Act (APMRA) was adopted by many states and put into action. Market yards with fine layouts were constructed and served as trading grounds for the buyers and sellers of the agriculture produce and were governed by the Agricultural Produce Marketing Committee (APMC). Thus, the era of organized marketing of agriculture products came into existence. The Model Agriculture Marketing (Development and Regulation) Act (2003) was circulated to the states, which were directed to amend the existing APMC Acts as per the Model Act. However, after 10 years, it has been observed that the APMC rules and regulations have variations across the states (Subramanian, 2015). The Model Act was framed to eliminate barriers in the agriculture trade and provide a free national market beneficial to both farmers (seller) and consumers (buyers). It also had a measure for efficient dissemination of the agriculture market information and for promoting standardization, assaying, price discovery and transparency to all stakeholders. According to Haque and Jairath (2014), by making use of information technology, redefinition of the intermediary roles and expansion of APMCs, the economic viability of the farmers could be established. To meet the objectives of the APMC Act and provide a common market for the agricultural transactions which cross state boundaries and legal barriers, thus facilitating free circulation of agriculture produce, an electronic platform at the pan-India level — National Agriculture Market (NAM) — was launched that created a unified market for the agricultural products by networking of existing APMCs.

Electronic National Agricultural Market (e-NAM)

The Government of India in 2016 launched the e-National Agriculture Market (e-NAM) portal as a unified national market combining 585 APMC and conducting trade through online auction modes. The online auction mode eliminated physical handling at the various levels of operations and reduced the charges involved in the market. Under e-NAM, electronic trade replaced physical trade in 585 *Mandies* across 14 states as on 28 August 2018 (Reddy & Mehjabeen, 2019). By electronic linking of the markets, traders all over the nation can take part in the bidding process through e-NAM and enjoy price transparency. e-NAM was launched with the vision of unification of the nation-wide agricultural markets, yet it faces many hurdles in implementation. There were 279 million tons of grains produced in the year 2017–2018, but merely 11 million tons of the volume was traded using the e-NAM portal. In monetary terms, the transactions using the e-NAM portal for the period 2017–2018 were recorded to be only INR 29,000 crore, which is very low as compared to the value of India's total agriculture produce which was recorded to be INR 13 lakh crore (Reddy, 2018).

The factors that create a bottleneck in the e-NAM implementation can be broadly characterized as informational, institutional and infrastructure. The informational constraint is explained by the restricted awareness among the farmers about the e-NAM and the involved bidding process. Farmers are also not aware of the existing benefits of the e-NAM, and hence suffer from the low pricing of their products if found to be below sub-standard quality. At the institutional level, it has been found that states refrain from amending their existing APMC Act and hence refrain from developing a single point trading platform, according to e-NAM. It has also been found that there is lack of infrastructure to store the agriculture produce such as inadequate warehousing and availability of cold storage and, apart from these, there is also a lack of backend infrastructures such as inadequate transportation facilities, poor-quality roads, low density of the market, improper assaying facilities and absence of synergy between service providers and the marketing organizations.

For this study, we have selected Uttar Pradesh as it possesses the largest arable land in the country, and is the fourth largest and most populated state. It is the largest food grain producer, accounting for 49.9 million tonnes, which is about 17.83% share in the nation's total agriculture produce for the year 2016–2017, which increased to 51.25 million tonnes in 2017–2018 (IBEF, 2019). Uttar Pradesh meets the four fundamental agricultural contributions as suggested by Kuznet (1964), namely (1) contribution made by the product (2) contribution of the market (3) factor contribution, (4) contribution of the foreign exchange. To verify these fundamental contributors and for the identification of the various antecedents of the agriculture market, a search with the keyword "Agriculture Market Produce" was made, which is represented by a network diagram in Figure 1.

The diagram displays the existence of a trading system which has an association with the regulatory framework and interaction with the farmers and traders. The literature review and network analysis led to the identification of certain important issues such as payment crisis, clearing and settlement disputes, and different forms of commissions and reductions made from the prices paid to the farmers.

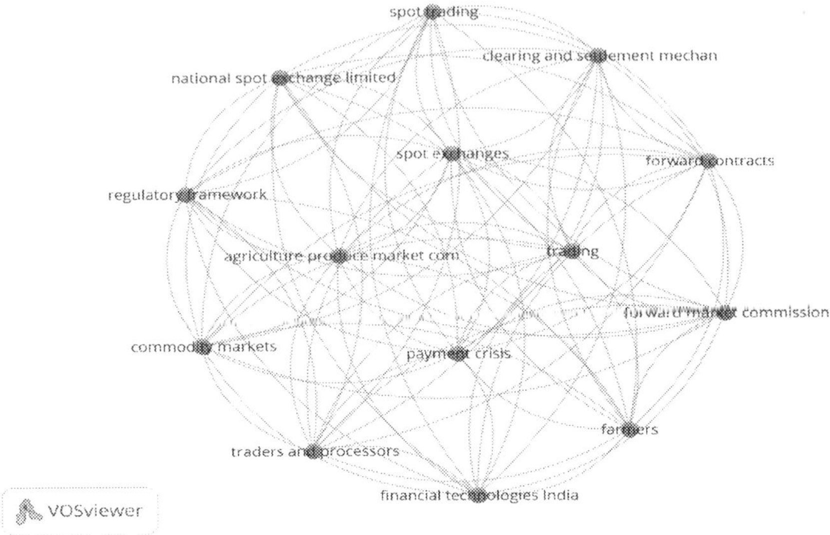

Figure 1: Antecedents of Agricultural Markets

Three APMC markets (*Mandies*) have been selected for the study, and assessment of e-NAM adoption was made. There was no synchronization found in the arrival quantity and sales made through e-NAM, and prices obtained from these APMCs were not in line with data available on Agmarknet (https://agmarknet.gov.in/). For the study, the commodities which are predominately traded in these markets such as onion, potato, wheat and rice were considered. It was found that there exists a need to strengthen the informational infrastructure, and hence the study proposes the use of blockchain technology to empower the existing agricultural marketing information system. A blockchain-based information system for the APMCs has been proposed to provide secure, immutable information to the various stakeholders and effective and efficient implication of the government policies using smart contracts.

Methodology

The methodology adopted for the study is exploratory. Table 1 shows the *Mandies* visited for analyzing the level of the Model APMC Act and

Table 1: APMCs (*Mandies*) and the Commodities Used for the Study

Mandi Name	District	Commodity	Mandi Grade*
Allahabad	Allahabad	Potato, Onion	A+
Ballia	Ballia	Potato, Onion	B
Ajuha	Kaushambi	Paddy, Wheat	B

Source: *Upmandiparishad (2019).

e-NAM along with the commodities traded in these Mandies for the study.

Data Collection

Data was collected in two phases. In the first phase, all three AMPCs were visited, and records related to the sales quantity of the commodity along with the prices paid to the farmers through the e-NAM bidding process were collected. In the second phase, the arrival amount of the commodities and prices paid to the farmers, as mentioned on the Agmarknet website (https://agmarknet.gov.in/), were collected. In both the processes, the data were collected on a monthly basis, for the same commodity and the same APMCs. The selection of the commodities have been made based on their flow rate, that is, these are highly traded in these markets.

Analysis of the APMCs (Mandies)

Allahabad APMC

The commodities at the Allahabad APMC taken for the study were potatoes and onions. The monthly data for the period from August 2017 to August 2018 was collected. The data obtained from the APMC stated that all the transactions were made through online auction using e-NAM. A comparison was made between the data obtained from APMC with the data available on Agmarknet (https://agmarknet.gov.in/). The total quantity of potato sold through e-NAM at the Allahabad APMC was 8397.4 tonnes, which is very low when compared with the total amount that arrived at the

APMC, which was recorded to be 59,198 tonnes. Similarly, the quantity of onion sold through e-NAM was 9892.06 tonnes, whereas the amount that arrived at APMC was recorded to be 23431.5 tonnes (Figure 2).

From Figure 2, it is clear that a fraction of total sales is made through the e-NAM portal. At this APMC, the sales of potatoes and onions have been found to be only 12% and 30%, respectively, and the rest has been sold through other means. The model APMC Act says that all the transactions made within the boundaries of the APMC must be made through online media, yet only a fraction of total sales was made through an online auction. Since both the data sources claim that the sales were made using an online auction, the amount that arrived at the APMC should meet the sales through e-NAM, but the results show a different picture.

The purchase price data obtained from APMC through e-NAM was found to be different from the Agmarknet data. Figures 3 and 4 display the position of the minimum prices paid to the farmers at the APMC and its comparison with the data displayed on Agmarknet.

The minimum price comparison of the commodities shows that there is a slight variation of the prices as obtained from the APMC through e-NAM and Agmarknet. Since the two databases are updated from the same source, their variations raise questions about the information systems' authenticity and creates a dilemma in selection of the right price.

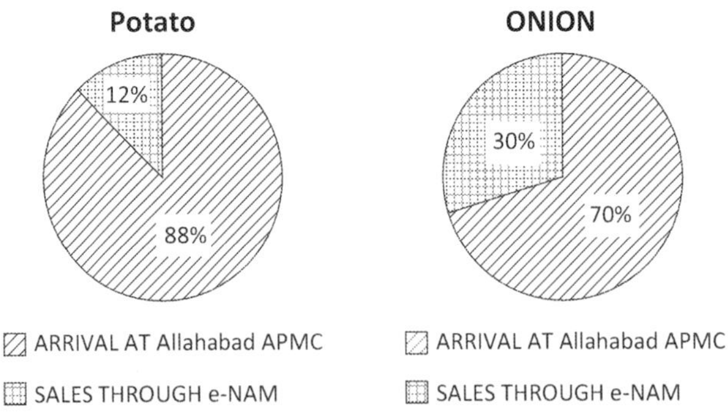

Figure 2: Proportion of Sales Through e-NAM at Allahabad APMC

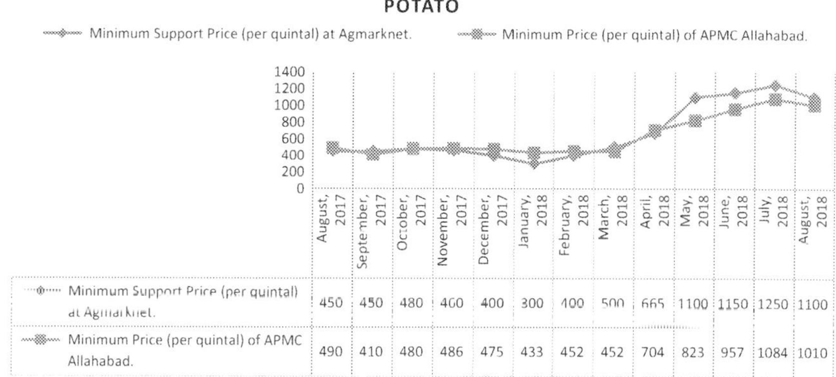

	August, 2017	September, 2017	October, 2017	November, 2017	December, 2017	January, 2018	February, 2018	March, 2018	April, 2018	May, 2018	June, 2018	July, 2018	August, 2018
Minimum Support Price (per quintal) at Agmarknet.	450	450	480	400	400	300	400	500	665	1100	1150	1250	1100
Minimum Price (per quintal) of APMC Allahabad.	490	410	480	486	475	433	452	452	704	823	957	1084	1010

Figure 3: Price Comparison for Potato — Allahabad, India

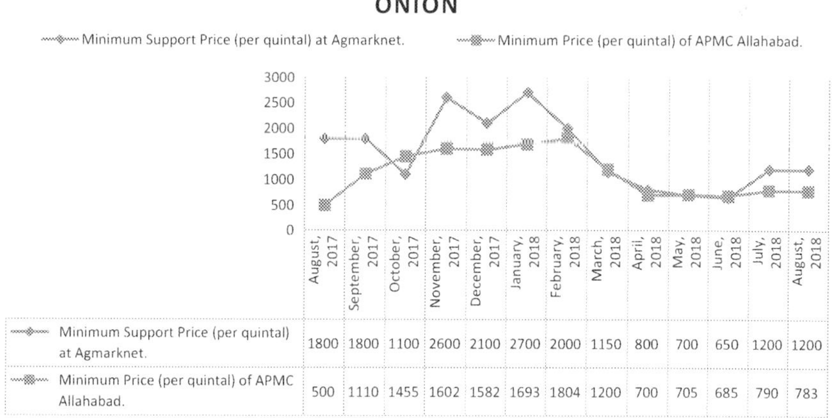

	August, 2017	September, 2017	October, 2017	November, 2017	December, 2017	January, 2018	February, 2018	March, 2018	April, 2018	May, 2018	June, 2018	July, 2018	August, 2018
Minimum Support Price (per quintal) at Agmarknet.	1800	1800	1100	2600	2100	2700	2000	1150	800	700	650	1200	1200
Minimum Price (per quintal) of APMC Allahabad.	500	1110	1455	1602	1582	1693	1804	1200	700	705	685	790	783

Figure 4: Price Comparison for Onion — Allahabad, India

Ballia APMC

The commodities at the Ballia APMC taken for the study were potatoes and onions. The data collection was from August 2017 to March 2019. The sales of potatoes through online auction mode were recorded to be 7513.6 tonnes, which is very low as compared to the amount that arrived at the APMC, which was 51741.5 tonnes. Similarly, for onion, the sales through online auction have been recorded to be 3164 tonnes compared to the arrival amount of 29,843 tonnes at the APMC (Figure 5).

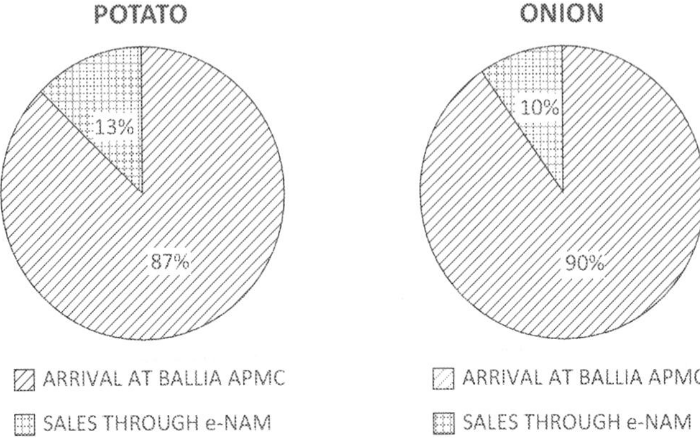

Figure 5: Proportion of Sales through e-NAM at Ballia APMC

From the figure, it is clear that the total sales for potatoes and onions were only 13% and 10%, respectively. There has been a huge variation found in the data obtained from the APMC and that from the Agmarknet. Such a huge variation raises a question on the implementation of the APMC act and practice of e-NAM. Both the data sources claim that the auction was through online mode, which raises another doubt on the security of the data and transparency.

There is huge variation found in the comparison of the minimum prices paid to the farmers for their produce through e-NAM and those communicated over Agmarknet. Price comparison of the two data sources for onion and potato are shown in Figures 6 and 7, respectively.

The analysis of the above two visualizations clearly shows that the minimum price paid to the farmers at the APMC is much less than the minimum price as mentioned on Agmarknet. It is also to be noted that for the period from November 2018 to March 2019, Agmarknet displays that there was trading of the onion, but on the contrary, the APMC record shows that there was no trade at the APMC. This absence of the data (no trade) from one data source raises a question on the proper dissemination of the information as if the commodity is not traded for a certain period, it needs to be communicated to all the public agriculture data sources to inform traders and buyers.

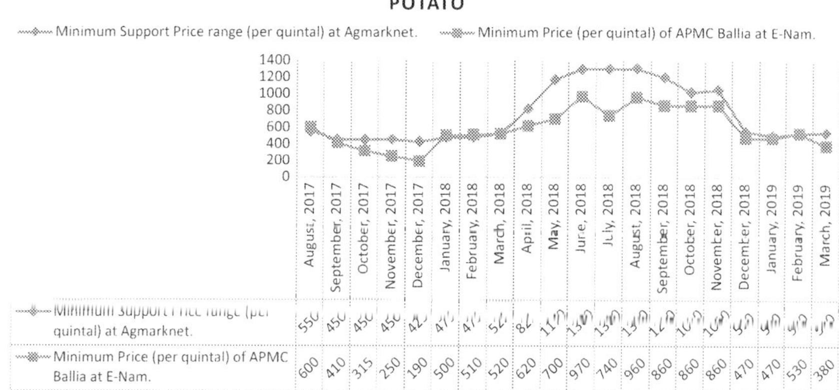

Figure 6: Price Comparison for Potato

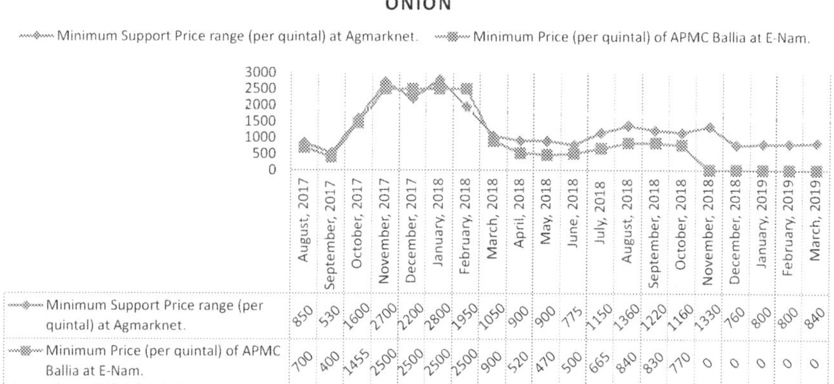

Figure 7: Price Comparison for Onion

Ajuha APMC

The Ajuha APMC is situated in Kaushambi district of Uttar Pradesh. It is a grain market, and to diversify the study Ajuha APMC has been selected to study the commodities of paddy and wheat. The data were collected between July 2017 and March 2019. The paddy sales through online auction were recorded to be 6101.9 tonnes, and the total arrival amount at the APMC was 47251.5 tonnes. The sales of wheat through online auction was 8575.78 tonnes, and total amount that arrived at the APMC was 38462.1 tonnes (Figure 8).

From the figure, it can be seen that the sales percentage through online auction using e-NAM for paddy and wheat was only 11% and 18%, respectively. These results show that improper adoption is not only limited to the vegetable and fruit market but also grain markets.

Comparison of the minimum price for paddy and wheat has also been made between the two data sources. Figure 9 shows the price comparison of paddy, and Figure 10 shows the price comparison of wheat. An assumption was made that the grains can be stored for a longer time; hence, their prices should not vary between the two data sources, and this is proved to be untrue by the outcomes of the study at this APMC.

The prices paid for the paddy and wheat were also lower than those mentioned on Agmarknet, but had less variation as compared to the prices given for the vegetable and fruit market. It is to be noted that for the periods in which no trade has been made at the APMC, Agmarknet displayed a trade price. This means there is no synchronization in the data being updated at the two data generation places.

As a summary of the observations from the three APMCS, we can conclude that the data obtained from the APMC had huge variation from the data posted on Agmarknet. The data were extracted according to the district, mandi, arrival, sales and minimum purchase price. Since the data

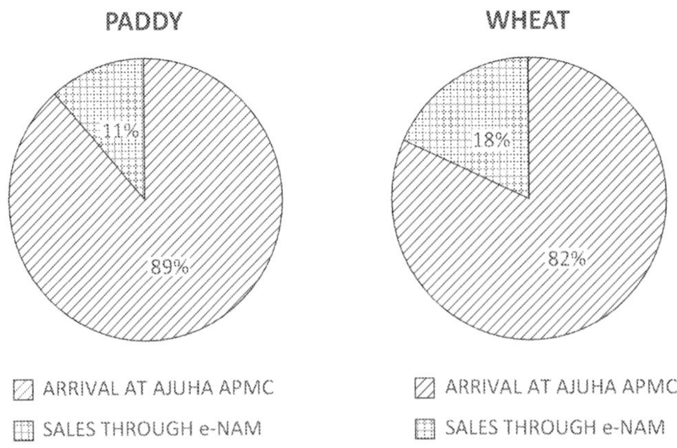

Figure 8: Proportion of Sales Through e-NAM at Ajuha APMC

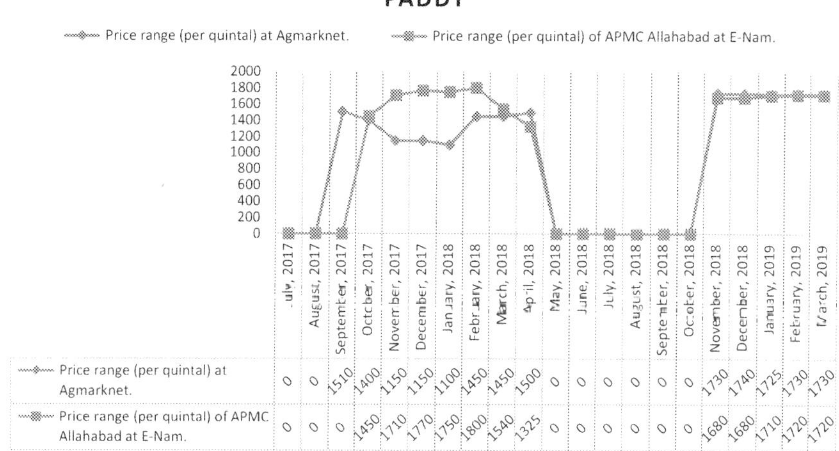

Figure 9: Price Comparison for Paddy

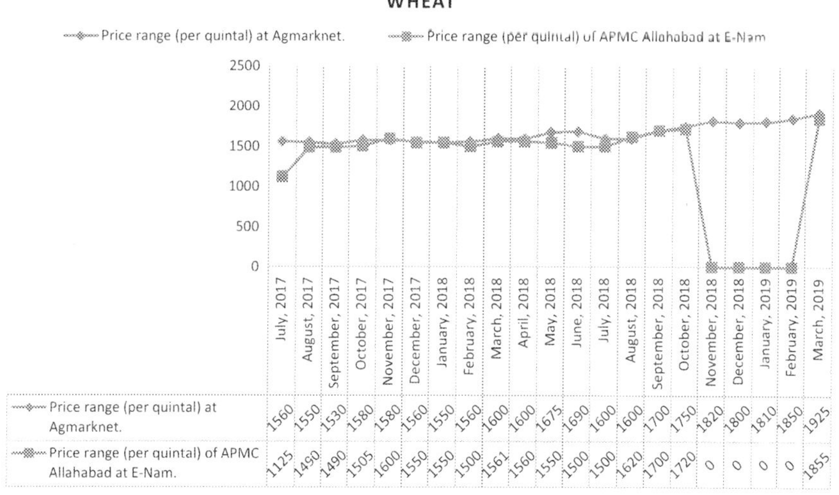

Figure 10: Price Comparison for Wheat

were extracted from the same mandi and maintained monthly, we can assume that the same authority is responsible for the dissemination of the information at both the data sources (APMC and Agmarknet). The variations in the arrival and sales data along with the minimum purchase price

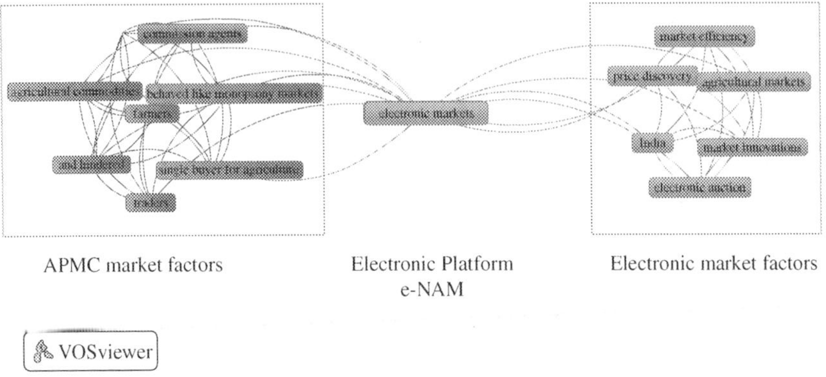

Figure 11: Interaction of the APMC Factors and the Digital Factors

show that the current agriculture market information system is not strong enough to maintain an immutable record and furnish complete transparency in the transactions. It has also been found that the current system is not fully able to adopt the guidelines of the government, which can be seen from the sales of the commodities at prices lower than those decided by the government (CACP, 2019).

The e-NAM platform serves as an intermediary, and it extracts information from the factors of the APMC market and replicates it on the digital platforms to be viewed by all the stakeholders (Figure 11).

Electronic market factors such as price discovery and electronic auction of the agricultural markets lead to the attainment of market efficiency, and hence the data to be translated to the electronic platforms needs to be synchronous, secure and immutable so that transparency and trust can be maintained among the sellers and buyers. To overcome the data security and transparency issues and ensure proper implication of government rules and regulations, we propose a blockchain-based infrastructure which will provide a secure, immutable data record. To provide strength to the government rules and regulations, a special feature of blockchain technology called smart contracts will be used for binding government rules to all transactions.

Blockchain Inclusion to e-NAM

The analysis of the data available from the three APMCs in Uttar Pradesh, when compared with the arrival, sales and price values on agriculture market information network (AGMARKNET), showed the existence of wide variations, raising concerns regarding the authenticity of and transparency in the information system. The study proposes that the existing e-NAM architecture adopt the blockchain technology so as to create a more secure and transparent agriculture market information system. Blockchain is a distributed database of timestamped transaction records shared over a peer-to-peer network and secured through a tamperproof immutable cryptographic algorithm (Nakamoto, 2008). It is a feed forward system of an endless chain of timestamped transaction stored in blocks and verified by the user through a private key. The data once fed to the blocks of the blockchain cannot be altered as the mechanism disables the backward movement, thus providing immutability to the data through hashing. In our architecture, along with various unparalleled features of blockchain technology, the study makes use of smart contracts, which is another important blockchain-based protocol.

The study assumed that the minimum and maximum prices displayed on Agmarknet should tally with APMC's e-NAM database, but there were huge variations found in the two data sets. The variations in the minimum prices paid to the farmers are of utmost importance as they have a direct impact on the sustainability of the farmers. To restrict the dip in the minimum purchase price for the farmer's produce and match it with the decided minimum purchase price of the government, the study suggests making use of smart contracts.

Smart Contracts (Szabo, 1997) can transform the existing administration system of manual verification of the rules and regulations, which are subject to human error, and also serve as a cost-cutting mechanism. Smart contract is an autonomous mechanism of predefined conditions according to which successive processes will take place. The processes which exist outside the boundaries of the predefined conditions will be declined, and such processes need to be modified as per the smart contract in order to pass. The overall possible benefits of blockchain adoption have been explained in Figure 12, with special emphasis on adopting smart contracts in the bidding mechanism to provide a fair price to the farmers and discourage the violation of government standards.

The process (Figure 12) has been designed considering the existing information system and procedures followed by e-NAM. We have integrated the blockchain technology with the existing agriculture market

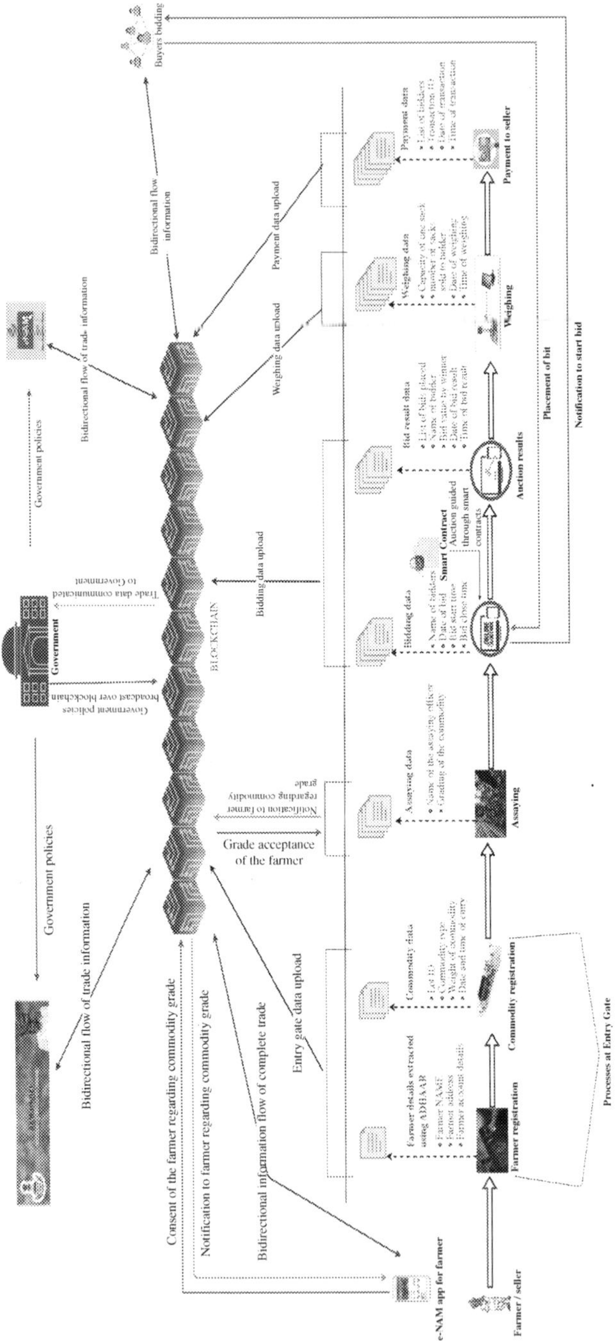

Figure 12: Blockchain-based e-NAM Information Dissemination Architecture

information system. We have segmented the process in Figure 12 into six stages, with explanations provided of how data will be disseminated to various stakeholders in the APMC (*Mandies*).

Registration of the stakeholders

To trade within the boundaries of the APMCs (*Mandies*), all the stakeholders need to be registered on the system. Farmers, being one of the stakeholders in the agriculture trade, also need to be registered. The registration of all the members participating in the trade transactions will be made through ADHAAR. Aadhaar is a 12-digit identification number issued by the Government of India, which contains all the personal details and needs to be updated on a regular basis (Uidai, 2019). Aadhaar not only carries the personal details, but is also connected to bank account details. Use of Aadhaar in the system will provide quick registration and processing of the transactions, such as payments, to farmers.

At the APMC entry gate

To sell the produce, the farmers move to the APMC. At the APMC gate, a biometric scanner will be installed where the farmer needs to sign in using his finger impression. With the sign-in process, the blockchain database will be updated with the information that a farmer has checked in to the APMC to make sales. The vehicle registration number and weight of the produce will be attached to the existing farmer block. The resulting block is assigned a LOT ID with the description of the farmer, type of commodity, registration number of the vehicle, weight of the commodity, and date and time of entry to the APMC.

Assaying

Once the farmer enters the market with his produce, samples are taken from the produce. Quality checking and grading of the agriculture produce is done. The farmer has the liberty to stay during the assay process, or he could relax away from the assaying department. Once assaying of the produce is done, the data will be uploaded to the blockchain and added as a new block. At this stage, we propose the use of a smart contract. A notification will be sent to the farmer's blockchain-based e-NAM application which will ask for the approval to the grading of his produce. Once the farmer gives his consent, a smart contract will allow further trade processes to take place.

Online auction

After grading of the commodity, it will be open for online auction. The commodity will be broken in lots of 25/50 kg weights (or other measurements as suitable), and the lowest bid will start from the minimum price as decided by government and retrieved from Commission for Agricultural Costs & Prices (CACP, 2019). CACP decides the minimum price for commodities such as paddy, wheat, soybean, barley, sugarcane, etc. For vegetables and fruits, individual buyers will bid for the commodity, and the farmer has the liberty to accept the bid as per his choice (highest bid in general). The bidding start and end notifications will be uploaded on the blockchain and also sent to buyers on their e-NAM apps and through web portals. The details of the buyers and bids placed will be updated on the blockchain and visible to all members. At the bidding portal, a smart contract will be used to define the minimum price of the commodity which has been decided by CACP. All bids below the minimum price of CACP will be declined, but there will be no cap for the highest bid. Smart contracts will also be programmed with the bid start time and bid close time. Farmers will be able to view all the bids and sell their produce to the highest bidder based on their discretion after bid close time. Once the whole commodity is sold out, a list of bidders, bid price, commodities and weights allotted to each bidder will be announced over blockchain, and a proper notification will be sent to the bidders that will then be used in the acquisition of commodity.

Weighing

Once auction results are announced, bidders could move to the weighing department and acquire the commodity by displaying their notification at the counter. The weighing machine will be attached to a computer system which will record the commodity, and its weight and will be attached to the buyer's (bidder) block. This data will also be uploaded to the blockchain as a permanent record so that no disputes of acquisition arise in the future.

Payment

With the closure of online auction and announcement of the bid, the winners of the auction need to pay the required amount before the acquisition of the commodity. Payments in cash can be done at the cash counters or payment can also be done through the blockchain-based e-NAM-based app through online banking. The payments made by the bidders will be redirected to the Aadhaar-linked bank account of the farmers for instant payment. The transaction details such as buyer name/ID, transaction ID, and date and time of payment will be uploaded before handing over the commodity. All these details will be uploaded to the blockchain database and communicated to various databases such as Agmarknet.

Discussion and Observations

The blockchain-supported agriculture marketing information system could offer various advantages. It brings transparency in the system and also real-time dissemination of trade information. The proposed infrastructure will enable farmers to the seller their produce without going to the APMC as long as faith is put in the assaying system. The system also enables speedy settlement of the transactions and quick payment. There may be a possibility that the buyer is unable to pay instantly, and in such a case a grace period could be allowed. However, the farmers (sellers) want instant payment for sales made. To tackle such problems, a blockchain-based buffer system can be designed which will act as an escrow and facilitate quick payment to the farmers. The buyers may be asked to deposit some funds prior to the bidding process starts, and these funds will be adjusted to the purchases made by the bidder (if he wins). The registration fee collected by the members of the APMC will also be stored in the buffer system initially to smoothen the payment process. The smart contracts can be widely used at every stage to enable smooth functioning of such tasks as as minimum price decision in the bidding process, warning to the defaulters, assigning a credit score to the buyers and maintaining payment buffer system.

Conclusion

The use of blockchain in the agriculture trade could bring a drastic change in the living standards of the farmers and minimize the farmer suicide rate by enhancing their earning. As the cost of living is increasing and villages have become market grounds for various companies, it has become essential to enable farmers to become financially sound by providing a fair price for their produce. By writing the government rules regarding the agriculture trading in the smart contract and integrating it to the agriculture trading system, there will be a significant reduction in the monitoring burden. The blockchain-facilitated record-keeping of all the transactions made, which are immutable, reduces the auditing burden of the government. We can conclude that the adoption of blockchain technology in the existing agriculture market information system and trading will bring fairness in the system and also reduce the operational costs.

References

Aggarwal, N., Jain, S., Narayanan, S. (2017). The Long Road to Transformation of Agricultural Markets in India: Lessons from Karnataka. *Economic & Political Weekly*, 52(41), 47–55.

APMC ACT (1963). Agricultural Produce Market Committee. Retrieved from: https://macp.gov.in/sites/default/files/user_doc/APMC_Act.pdf.

CACP (2019). *Commission for Agricultural Costs and Prices*. [online] Cacp.dacnet.nic.in. Retrieved from: https://cacp.dacnet.nic.in/. Accessed on June 9, 2019.

Global Hunger Index (2018). *India*. [online] Global Hunger Index — Peer-reviewed Annual Publication Designed to Comprehensively Measure and Track Hunger at the Global, Regional, and Country Levels. Retrieved from: https://www.globalhungerindex.org/india.html.

GOI (Government of India) (2016). *Agricultural Statistics at a Glance 2016*. [online] Retrieved from: https://eands.dacnet.nic.in/PDF/Glance-2016.pdf.

Haque, E., Jairath, A. P. (2014). Why Vadodara APMC is a Hit Among Farmers? *Business Line*, October 13, 2014. Retrieved from: https://www.thehindubusinessline.com/markets/commodities/Why-Vadodara-APMC-is-a-hitamong farmers/article20885834.ece.

Harriss, B. (1984). Agricultural Markets and Intersectoral Resource Transfers: Cases from the Semi-arid Tropics of Southeast India. In *Agricultural Markets in the Semi-Arid Tropics*, p. 279.

IBEF (2019). About Uttar Pradesh: Tourism, Agriculture, Industries, Economy & Geography. Retrieved from: https://www.ibef.org/states/uttar-pradesh.aspx.

Kuznet, S. (1964). Economic Growth and the Contribution of Agriculture. In *Agriculture in Economic Development.* McGraw-Hill: New York.

Minten, B., Vandeplas, A., Swinnen, J. (2012). Regulations, Brokers, and Interlinkages: The Institutional Organization of Wholesale Markets in India. *Journal of Development Studies*, 48(7), 864–886.

Nabard (2018). *NABARD — National Bank For Agriculture And Rural Development*. [online]. Retrieved from: https://www.nabard.org/Press Releases-article.aspx?id=25&cid=554&NID=43.

Nakamoto, S. (2008). Bitcoin: A Peer-to-Peer Electronic Cash System.

Pal, S., Bahl, D. K. (1993). Government Interventions in Foodgrain Markets: The Case of India. *Food Policy*, 18(5), 414–427.

Pandey, K. (2018). *Poor Post-harvest Storage, Transportation Facilities to Cost Farmers Dearly*. [online] at Downtoearth.org.in. Retrieved from: https://www.downtoearth.org.in/news/agriculture/poor-post-harvest-storage-transportation-facilities-to-cost-farmers-dearly-61047.

Pathy, B. (2017). Linking Farmers to Market. Retrieved from: http://www.cips.org.in/documents/2017/july/BKPaty.pdf.

Paty, B. K., Gummagolmath, K. C. (2015). *A Handbook on Agricultural Marketing Extension for Extension Functionaries*. National Institute of Agricultural Extension Management: Hyderabad, India.

Purohit, P., Imai, K. S., Sen, K. (2017). Do Agricultural Marketing Laws Matter for Rural Growth? Evidence from the Indian States. *Discussion Papers*.

Rajagopal (1993). *Indian Rural Marketing*. Rawat Publication: Jaipur, India.

Reddy, A. (2018). Electronic National Agricultural Markets: The Way Forward. *Current Science*, 115(5).

Reddy, A. A., Mehjabeen. (2019). Electronic National Agricultural Markets, Impacts, Problems and Way Forward. *IIM Kozhikode Society & Management Review*, 2277975218807277.

Sharma, V., Wardhan, H. (2015). *Assessment of Marketed and Marketable Surplus of Major Foodgrains in India.* [online] at Iima.ac.in. Retrieved from: https://www.iima.ac.in/c/document_library/get_file?uuid=b8923c25-068d-4455-91a3-4ab7904181ec&groupId=62390.

Singh, S. (2017). *India has One of the Strongest National Agricultural Research Systems in the World.* [online]. Retrieved from: http://pib.nic.in/newsite/PrintRelease.aspx?relid=174109.

Subramanian, A. (2015). *Towards A Pareto Efficient Indian Agricultural Market-with Specific Focus on Rice and Wheat Markets* (No. id: 6625).

Szabo, N. (1997). The Idea of Smart Contracts. *Nick Szabo's Papers and Concise Tutorials*, 6.

Uidai. (2019). *Home.* [online] Unique Identification Authority of India (Government of India). Retrieved from: https://uidai.gov.in/.

Upmandiparishad. (2019). Mandi Details — State Agricultural Produce Markets Board. Retrieved from: http://upmandiparishad.upsdc.gov.in/DynamicPages/MandiDetails.aspx.

Chapter 5

Attack Vectors for Blockchain and Mapping OWASP Vulnerabilities to Smart Contracts

Akashdeep Bhardwaj*,‡ and Sam Goundar†,§

**University of Petroleum & Energy Studies (UPES), Uttarakhand, India*

†The University of South Pacific, Suva, Fiji

‡abhardwaj@ddn.upes.ac.in

§sam.goundar@gmail.com

Abstract

Smart contracts powered by Blockchain render transaction processes more effective, secure and efficient when viewed alongside conventional contacts. Smart Contracts facilitate a trustworthy process and are characterized by time efficiency, cost-effectiveness and transparency, without any necessity for intervention by third-party intermediaries like lawyers. While Blockchains can counter, in a good way, traditional cyber-security attacks on Smart Contract Applications, cyber-criminals keep evolving new mechanisms of threats and attack vectors, capable of hacking Blockchain technologies. The research done in this chapter presents a unique framework to perform Application Security Testing on Blockchain-based Smart Contracts and also compares Manual Penetration Testing with two automated Smart Contract tools to identify critical vulnerabilities on the commercial scale in the Blockchain environment.

Introduction

During the last five years, Blockchain Technology has gained huge momentum in terms of research and implementation by various industries. Blockchain works on peer-to-peer transactions, being distributed with decentralized anonymity and no third party or any centralized control. Smart Contracts (Greenspan, 2018) are digital program scripts of codes stored inside a Blockchain. These programs are tamper-proof, self-verifying, self-executable and self-enforceable (Tsankov, 2018) digital contracts when certain clauses (Wang *et al.*, 2018) with specific predefined conditions are met. Smart Contracts are capable of performing transaction in real time, at low cost, and provide a greater degree of security (Zhang, 2018). The network of Blockchain cryptocurrency nodes executes actions to update the distributed transparent ledger. This update is seen by all nodes and verified (Amani *et al.*, 2018) before acceptance in the network.

As an example, imagine buying a new car. The traditional process starts by going to a car dealer (intermediary third party) and bargaining for your choice of car. Then you go to a bank for a car loan (another third party), and then involve the transport department and insurance companies (more third parties for the paperwork). Once all formalities and payments are completed, there is a waiting period before the car's delivery. This process takes time and involves interactions with multiple other third parties. Now imagine if the car details, ownership, papers and offer are available on the Blockchain with no third party involved. The details are secure and unchangeable and distributed over the Blockchain network. The details are validated by each node on the network, but no one person is in absolute control. Execution of the purchase order is done using the Smart Contract. This system would be secure and payment would be done by using Cryptocurrency in real time. Ownership is transferred immediately as digital identity on the Blockchain Ledger. All nodes update the ledger on the Blockchain network and conclude the transaction (Amani *et al.*, 2018).

A similar process can be followed by banks or other lending organizations for processing loans or receiving automatic payments. Insurance companies can use Blockchain for processing claims. Postal departments can process payment on delivery with Smart Contract systems instead of the traditional transaction process. This concept (Wang, 2018) can be implemented for buying or renting apartments involving two parties only, the tenant and the property owner. Monthly rent or EMIs can be deducted using tokens or cryptocurrencies. So, in effect, performing any transaction can be handled securely and efficiently using Smart Contract systems that are powered by the Blockchain Technology (Chang & Svetinovic, 2019). Global Securities Exchanges in the United States (Australian Securities Exchange, 2018) and Australia (US Securities and Exchange Commission, 2018) have accepted these. However, much like cyber-threats (Zhang, 2018) and attacks on cloud-hosted systems and applications, Blockchain networks also suffer attacks like Denial of Service (DoS) [11], Decentralized Autonomous Organization (DAO) (Siegel, 2018) and Blockchain-specific cyber-attacks, discussed in the subsequent sections in this chapter.

Literature Survey

The authors reviewed research publications since 2016 from IEEE and ACM journals. The reason for concentrating on developments over the past 3 years was that immense growth and changes in the Blockchain Smart Contract domain have happened primarily in the last few years along with latest developments in cyber-security attacks, threat vectors and vulnerabilities discovered and exploited by Cyber-security attackers.

Tonelli *et al.* (2019) implemented Blockchain-based Smart Contract using Micro-Service applications. The authors analyzed and replicated the Smart Contract micro-service architecture in the form of a case study using a set of Smart Contracts. The results displayed the possibility of implementing simple micro-services while maintaining similar paradigms and functionality.

Amoordon & Rocha (2019) proposed a fault-tolerant application promoting awareness about and easing the programing in Blockchain. The authors proposed that one application per Blockchain displayed improved performance and reduced weakness against security attacks. This platform could potentially be an ideal Smart Contract application for Blockchain platforms like Ethereum and Bitcoin.

Yamashita *et al.* (2019) presented a survey on security risks for Blockchains, focusing on the programming languages and development tools. The authors utilized Java and Go language that existed before

Blockchains were created, even though these languages were not designed for writing Smart Contracts. The authors focused on 14 primary risks and observed that existing tools would not cover some risks and so developed a static analysis detecting tool.

Al-Jaroodi *et al.* (2019) surveyed the application of Blockchain technologies and Smart Contracts in various industrial domains (The Energy Web Foundation). The authors observed that deploying Blockchains increased industrial transparency, security, efficiency and traceability even as the cost of deployment and delivery was reduced.

Mohammed *et al.* (2019) discussed the adoption of Blockchain and Smart Contract for industrial sectors, primarily the manufacturing industry. The authors observed that for effective integration with multiple systems and components, there were challenges to overcome. The authors proposed adopting middleware approach in order to effectively utilize Blockchain and use the capabilities to the full extent, leading to smart manufacturing.

Draper *et al.* (2019) reviewed security applications like PGP and ProxyChain and studied the challenges faced by Blockchains. The authors studied the major problems faced and discussed ways of solving problems such as latency, integration, throughput as well as regulatory issues and even provided directions for future research.

Mahmood *et al.* (2019) focused on providing enhanced safety and productivity in logistics operations using Smart Contracts, Big Data and ICT. Implementation of Supply Chain for tracking containers in real time was presented with the help of email and SMS alerting system for customers to help them track international and national delivery of their consignments.

Tateshi *et al.* (2019) presented a unique model to auto-generate executable Smart Contracts in Blockchain-based Hyperledger using a human-written and understandable Contract document. The authors created this using a template with a controlled natural language and evaluated the results using case studies from real-world Smart Contacts in various domains.

Wang *et al.* (2019) proposed a comprehensive overview of Smart Contacts based on Blockchain. The authors introduced the platforms and operating mechanisms of Smart Contracts and the six-layer architecture framework. The authors also reviewed legal and technical challenges

(Hildenbrandt, 2018) and discussed the application security issues as well as provided references for future research.

Ozyilmaz & Yurdakul (2019) designed Blockchain-based Internet of Things using emerging technologies like Swarm, Ethereum and LoRa. The authors addressed the issues of data storage, high availability, mining and denial of service attacks for Smart Contract systems that typically employ trustless nodes in a decentralized manner for distributed storage in Blockchain networks.

Wan *et al.* (2019) focused on industrial IoT nodes to restructure the original architecture and designed a new decentralized model based on Blockchain network. This improved the security and privacy (Knirsch *et al.*, 2018) as compared to traditional architecture as well as optimized application delivery. As the size of the network and the number of nodes increased, the traditional architecture was unable to provide efficient support, and so the proposed architecture emerged as a viable solution.

Suliman *et al.* (2019) utilized the features of Blockchain Smart Contract as a concept for carrying out transactions. The authors discussed the architecture, application logic, entity and the interaction workflow using a decentralized and highly trusted network having no intermediary. This model was based on using live data exchange using Smart Contracts for Ethereum (Wood, 2016).

Attack Vectors on Blockchain Environments

Traditional IT infrastructure and hosted Applications as well as Blockchain environments both face similar Cyber-security threats. In most use cases, the attack vectors are the same; however, the mitigation strategies can vary. While it may seem that the Blockchain is a perfect solution for transactions, the technology still has points of vulnerabilities. The attack vectors are categorized based on Network, Applications, Data Integrity and End User levels, as illustrated in Table 1.

While designing and implementing the Blockchain-based Smart Contract solutions, security threats associated with Smart Contracts can be of various kinds, ranging from source code bugs, virtual machine vulnerability and insecure runtime environment to the Blockchain network itself. These threats are discussed in Table 2.

Table 1: Attack Vectors for Blockchain-Based Smart Contract

Attack Vector	Description
Network Level	• **DoS Attack:** IT infrastructures face denial of service attacks, which typically involve flooding the network pipes and applications with requests. Legitimate users are denied access to the service resources. Blockchain Smart Contracts face service denial attacks when one or more execute and update or when there is creation of new blocks requests that are submitted to the Blockchain in an amount more than what can be handled. Transaction tampering with group routing is another such attacks. Attackers sub-divide the Blockchain network into separate groups. These are not allowed to communicate with each other. Then the transactions are sent to the peer nodes. This makes it impossible for other peers to detect the tampering. Such routing attacks involve partitioning the peer nodes with delays introduced into the network, interfering the message broadcasts being sent on the network. • **Network Efficiency:** Currently in most Blockchain ecosystems, the maximum possible transactions per second is between 3.3 and 7. Credit cards attain around 2,000 transactions per second, while Twitter achieves around 5,000 transactions per second. This low efficiency of transactions often holds back Blockchain adoption for potential clients. This also involves greater processing and throughput efforts inside Blockchain and the miners. As the Blockchain network grows, complexity increases, which in turn interferes with the processing speed and efficiency of the Blockchain network.
Application level	• **Code Vulnerabilities** involve use of multiple iterations of Penetration Testing using secure coding, with manual and automated tools. Smart Contract can be written by any node, which then spreads in the network. Integer Overflow vulnerability was the only major flow detected in Blockchain. • **Points of Failure** involve use of single primary database server or one master backup and can be a glaring vulnerability. IT setups typically use multiple systems and backups and plan for business continuity and disaster recovery. Being a Distributed Ledger with multiple nodes involved in the network, there are no such issues visible in Blockchain.

	• **Timejacking** exploits the Bitcoin timestamp vulnerability; this is done by altering the node time counter or by adding multiple fake peers having erroneous timestamps. This forces the victim node to agree on using another Blockchain network. • **Eclipse Attacks** has the hacker taking control of large number of distributed nodes as network bots. Once the nodes are restarted, outgoing connections are redirected to the attacker's IP address, which is controlled by the attackers. The victim nodes are then unable to obtain their transactions.
Data Integrity Level	• **Wallet Access:** IT Infrastructure manages data security using the CIA triad. This includes backups and implementation of strong security policies and processes with audits. For Blockchain systems, cyber-criminals target user wallet credentials. This involves traditional hacking means like use of phishing emails, dictionary attacks as well as new and sophisticated attacks, which seek vulnerabilities in the cryptographic algorithms. Blockchain utilizes ECDSA Cryptographic algorithm, which automatically generates unique private keys. ECDSA has insufficient entropy vulnerability. This results in the same random value being utilized by more than one signature. • **Fraudulent Modifications** are done by Man-in-the-middle and privilege escalation attacks. These are usually mitigated by security policy, data encryption, salting for IT Infrastructure involving databases. Since Blockchain exists in form of sequential chain of blocks, anyone trying to alter records would have to first alter all transactions leading to that specific transaction, which is complicated. However, attackers can alter transaction ID and broadcast that transaction with modified hash value to the nodes. They would try to get it confirmed before the original transaction completes. The initiator would tend to believe the initial transaction might have failed, even as funds in form of BTCs had been withdrawn from their accounts. This is termed as Transaction Malleability. The attacker tricks the victim into paying twice. In 2014, MtGox Bitcoin Exchange was bankrupt due to such a Malleability attack.

(*Continued*)

Table 1: *(Continued)*

Attack Vector	Description
End User level	• **Endpoint Threats:** Endpoint Security is controlled by enterprise with organization-wise policies and console management for monitoring and detection of end user systems and mobile devices. For Blockchain, the nodes are the endpoints, which can be homogeneous, so a flaw in one node can be exploited as a flaw in Blockchain network systems. • **Intentional Misuse:** Traditional setup faces insider threats by staff and employees who can steal data and affect the setup. In Blockchain, Miners are incentivized for Proof-of-Work, who can group together to take control of the network. Majority attack or 51% Attack occurs in Blockchain network with one group or hacker harnessing enough computing power to compromise the whole network. Hackers can gain control of network hash rates to create alternate forks and then take precedence over existing forks. • **Sybil Attack:** This is performed by controlling multiple nodes as Bots. These surround the victim node with fake nodes transactions or take time verifying the transactions. Victim node thus becomes vulnerable to double-spend attacks, which are difficult to detect and prevent. The attackers use same coins or tokens for multiple different transactions, tricking the Blockchain system to accept the fraud transaction.

Table 2: Threats to Blockchain-based Smart Contract

Threats	Description
Complex Technology	When trying to design and build Smart Contracts from scratch or a localized version, the security vulnerabilities lie with the execution and not the system. Average programmers and developers cannot implement Blockchains. This needs specialized skills.
Inception Vulnerability	For a proper Blockchain to perform, thousands of nodes are required to work in unison. If one node or group of nodes control 51% of the system nodes, then they can control the Blockchain outcome. For a small setup of nodes, it is easily possible.
Government Control	Cryptocurrencies can render the government-controlled currencies less valuable or make them go out of use and destabilize the world's economy. Such authorities would always want some regulation and level of control, which goes against the decentralized concept of Smart contracts.
Third-party Integrations	Use of non-standard third-party platforms can introduce flaws even as Blockchain network maybe secure, e.g. 400 BTCs were hacked from NiceHash Mining marketplace and $60 million stolen as user funds in 2017, BitCoin Gold was hacked in 2018 losing $18 million, while Crypto Exchange Zaif confronted $60 million bitcoin theft.
Security of Keys and Certificate	Dark web has over 60 marketplace portals selling SSL and TLS certificates and related services for $250–$2,000 in March 2019. Blockchain keys and Smart Contracts face yet another set of challenge where Criminals assume identities of trusted machine nodes.
Insecure Source Code	Source code issues Reentrancy attack can lead to passing on the control to untrusted functions of other Smart Contracts, which can have undefined behavior or be used for malicious purposes. Source code bugs in an Ethereum (Wood, 2016) Smart contract cost $80 million in 2016.
Virtual Machine Vulnerabilities	These are low-level attacks using Ethereum Virtual Machine. This has been detected to have immutable defects. Blockchain blocks after creation can be changed or cryptocurrency can be lost during transfer or access control of systems by hackers, which can lead to sensitive functionality access of the Smart Contract.
Mining Pools	Miners unite to combine and create pools of computing power. This helps to mine more blocks and receive more rewards instead of individual miners, which hardly earns any profit or receives any BTCs. Miner Pools (Qin *et al.*, 2018) increase their reward share by delaying the broadcasts of mined blocks to others. Then suddenly all the blocks are released at once. This makes other miners lose their blocks. The largest pool of Bitcoin Miner are AntPool, BTC.com and ViaBTC. Mitigation strategies against such threats are having only trusted miners on the network or modifying the Smart Contract protocols to hide the variance between partial or full proof-of-work inside the Smart Contracts (Gatteschi *et al.*, 2018).

Proposed Framework Architecture

The authors propose the utilization of Static Application Security Analysis at the introductory stage, before execution of the Blockchain code. This includes a custom application code alongside the Runtime stage and incorporates the Blockchain Application Server, Framework and Code Libraries. Regularly, Dynamic Application Security Testing just includes utilization of devices that are necessary for running Blockchain applications. Dynamic Application Security Testing is performed by utilizing and further reproduces focused on assaults or exceptionally made HTTP inputs. By dissecting the HTTP reaction, the vulnerabilities are identified. Be that as it may, DAST, as in Figure 1, is oblivious in regard to what happens inside the application, and gives just restricted inclusion. Like SAST, DAST instruments are moderate, with an average examining procedure taking hours, if not days, to finish.

This performs a full runtime information and control stream examination, combined with static investigation of all the codes, as depicted in Figure 1, while likewise dissecting all the inbound and outbound HTTP traffic produced amid typical testing of the application. This permits performing dynamic investigations more powerful than DAST, without requiring any devoted security tests, misuse of the objective application, or security specialists to be associated with the testing procedure.

Since the evaluation works from inside the application, this enables more precise testing than customary Penetration (Pen) Testing

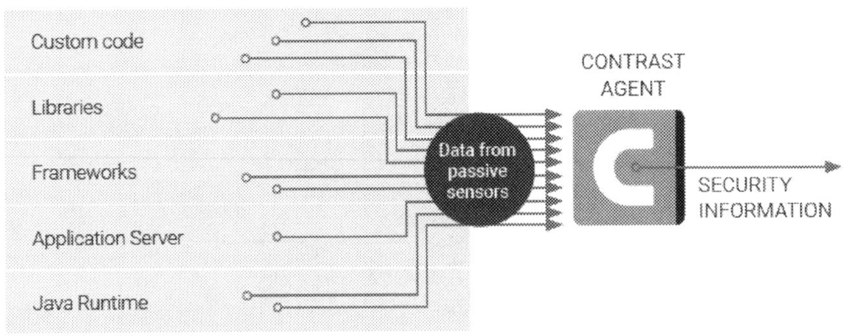

Figure 1: Deep Level Application Security Test

Source: Brucker & Sodan (2014).

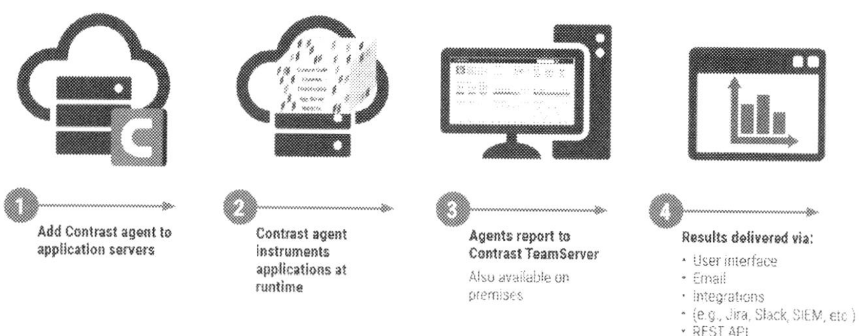

Figure 2: Proposed Architecture

apparatuses. Furthermore, this is not at all like either SAST or DAST items. The creators ran a Software Composition Analysis (SCA) to assemble a stock of all outsider segments (for example libraries, structures and so on), including open source programming (OSS), that are utilized by the application. This distinguishes known and obscure vulnerabilities over a whole application, including every one of those parts.

The proposed engineering includes two principle segments — one to provide more information regarding an operator that keeps running near the application on the application server. This also performs weakness evaluation utilizing latent sensors. The second segment is the centralized administration server that gathers and reports on vulnerabilities recognized by the operators and controls the organization's local mix with different instruments like IDEs and CI/CDs, supporting highlights for announcing warnings and get to procedure with RESTful API for custom integrations as in Figure 2.

Evaluation Performed

Cyber-criminals have been abusing Blockchains by requesting ransoms in different types of digital currencies and by initiating ransomware assaults. In any case, presently, the attacks focus on Blockchain Smart Contract vulnerabilities, which form the primary wellspring of income, for their assaults. The setup included facilitating on Amazon Web Services M5 General Purpose Instance (Figure 3) running RHEL 5.8 Kernel from

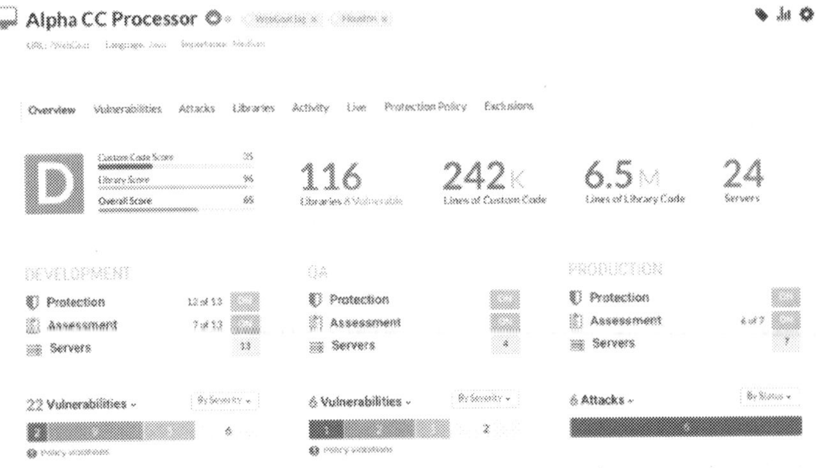

Figure 3: AWS System Setup Console for the Smart Contract Blockchain

Source: www.amazon.com.

2.6.18 working framework. The nodes have been designed to run the Smart Contract application on m5.4xlarge with 16 vCPU, 64GB Memory, with 2 × 300 GB SSD drives. The system has 3500Mbps of committed EBS transmission capacity, with extension up to 10Gbps.

The authors performed Penetration Testing on Blockchain application running in the pre-production environment, and the critical vulnerabilities are mentioned in the following. These vulnerabilities map the critical vulnerabilities found and are mapped to OWASP Top10 for the Blockchain Smart Contracts.

Vulnerability type: Injection

Threat Level: High

Process: Validated strings with white listing before the Database SQL query as in Table 3.
Issue: Buffer-out-of-Bound issue detected on system in the Smart Contract Parsing module. This poor sensitization of input allowed authentication to be bypassed and unauthorized commands to be executed. This vulnerability on the Sandbox launched a reverse shell on the infected nodes in the network. The authors found three functions in the Data

Table 3: Detailed Report for Database SQL Query Injection Vulnerability

data/Query-Builder.java: Lines 61, 65, 72, 75, 81, 182, 187, 202
data/App-Provider.java: Lines 166, 745, 761, 802, 958, 981, 1032, 1078
data/TempApk-Provider.java: Lines 72, 86, 91
data/Apk-Provider.java: Lines 305, 748, 652
data/Fdroid-Provider.java: Lines 24, 88, 201, 451

sub-directory code that were using string concatenation query for performing Database operations on package-supplied parameters.

Vulnerability type: Broken authentication

Threat Level: High

Process: Design issues in LISK Cryptocurrency do not bind short addresses immediately to Public Keys. Attackers can overtake any unclaimed account.
Issue: Incorrect implementation of Near-Swap feature makes it prone to different attacks. Best option is not opening Web server access for everyone. There should be some level of authentication in place. The application's feature for Near-Swap allows a third person to snoop into the communication and download files from either of the two user's devices, without their permission.

Vulnerability type: Transaction routing attack

Threat Level: High

Process: Hack peer nodes to change the state of transactions before they are committed on the network.
Issue: Divide the Smart network into groups, in order to delay the transactions, tamper the propagating messages sent on the network and even divert the Blockchain traffic as illustrated in Figure 4.

To demonstrate the advantages of using the manual penetration testing approach against the automated scanner, the authors compared the manual results against two state-of-the-art Penetration Testing analyzers. For the sake of confidentiality, names cannot be revealed. One of the tools is

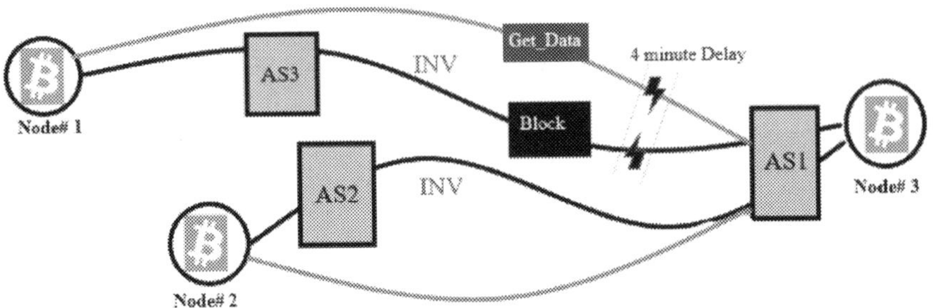

Figure 4: Blockchain Node Transaction Delays

Source: Brucker & Sodan (2014).

Table 4: Comparing Manual and Automated Benchmarks Reported for Project Effectiveness

Vulnerability Types	Manual V Automated	Manual – Automated	Automated – Manual
Timestamp Value	522	671	103
Reentrancy Routine	15	129	17

based on Symbolic Execution, while the other is based on dynamic random testing.

For comparison with the first tool, Smart Contract is taken as input and checked for any match for concrete traces in the tools' predefined security properties. This is compared to the manual Penetration Testing results obtained. The authors performed two comparisons that analyze relieving the vulnerabilities discovered using the Penetration Tests for the Smart Contract. Right off the bat, the viability of this present reality's vulnerabilities were resolved and, furthermore, computerized Penetration Testing apparatuses were looked at which are used in the business for Smart Contracts Penetration Testing. The creators included more than 30,000 Smart Contracts, with the most extreme assault program size set to three and having a delay timeout of 15 minutes for each Smart Contract. So as to comprehend the adequacy of the Manual Static Penetration Testing performed, correlation was done utilizing computerized dynamic Penetration Testing apparatuses. The outcomes are displayed in Tables 4 and 5.

Table 5: Analysis of Resulting Rates After Complete Penetration Testing for 55 Random Samples

Benchmark	Manual FP Rate (%)	Manual FN Rate (%)	Automated FP Rate (%)	Automated FN Rate (%)
Timestamp	6	11	39	31
Reentrancy	15	8	44	39

Conclusions

The authors compared manual Penetration Testing with two Application Security Testing tools for automated synthesis of Smart Contracts that can exploit the vulnerabilities of victim nodes. To ensure that the synthesis was tractable, summary-based symbolic evaluation was introduced. This reduced the number of data paths that tools needs to traverse and explore while maintaining the precision of the vulnerability queries. By building on the summary-based symbolic evaluation, manual Penetration Testing further introduced optimizations that enabled parallel exploration and other forms of cyber-attacks. The authors encoded known Smart Contact vulnerabilities in the search query and also evaluated the entire data set with over 25,000 Smart Contracts. The experimental results show manual Pen Testing significantly outperformed the automated Smart Contract tools in terms of execution time, precision and soundness of issues detected. Also manual Penetration Testing uncovered over 20 previously unknown instances with the Batch Overflow vulnerability.

Even though Blockchain technology for Smart Contract applications is relatively new, this holds huge promise for the future of contracts. The Blockchain attack vectors which can exploit the vulnerabilities can perform cyber-security attacks on the Blockchain networks. This can in turn slow down the adoption process. Most of the attack vectors at end user or data integrity level can easily be avoided by creating awareness among Blockchain implementation users, but other Network and Application levels can only be mitigated with professional expertise. OWASP Top10 vulnerabilities are mapped to threats and attacks on Blockchain, which also illustrates that most cyber-security attacks can be performed on both cloud-hosted applications and Blockchain-based Smart Contract applications.

References

Al-Jaroodi, J., Mohamed, N. (2019). Industrial Applications of Blockchain. In *2019 IEEE 9th Annual Computing and Communication Workshop and Conference (CCWC)*, Las Vegas, NV, USA. Doi: 10.1109/CCWC.2019.8666530

Amani, S., Bégel, M., Bortin, M., Staples, M. (2018). Towards verifying Ethereum Smart Contract Bytecode in Isabelle/HOL. In *Proceedings of 7th ACM SIGPLAN International Conference for Certified Program Proofs (CPP)*, Los Angeles, CA, USA, pp. 66–77.

Amoordon, A., Rocha, H. (2019). Presenting Tendermint: Idiosyncrasies, Weaknesses, and Good Practices. In *2019 IEEE International Workshop on Blockchain Oriented Software Engineering (IWBOSE)*, Hangzhou, China. Doi: 10.1109/IWBOSE.2019.8666541

Australian Securities Exchange (2018). CHESS Replacement. Retrieved from: https://www.asx.com.au/services/chess-replacement.htm. Accessed on February 15, 2019.

Brucker, A., Sodan, U. (2014). Deploying Static Application Security Testing on a Large Scale. Sicherheit 2014 — Sicherheit, Schutz und Zuverlässigkeit.

Chang, T. H., Svetinovic, D. (2018). Improving Bitcoin Ownership Identification using Transaction Patterns Analysis. *IEEE Transaction on Systems, Man, and Cybernetics: Systems*.

Draper, A., Familrouhani, A., Cao, D., Heng, T., Han, W. (2019). Security Applications and Challenges in Blockchain. In *IEEE International Conference on Consumer Electronics (ICCE)*, Las Vegas, NV, USA. Doi: 10.1109/ICCE.2019.8661914

Greenspan, G. (2018). Why Many Smart Contract Use Cases Are Simply Impossible. Retrieved from: https://www.coindesk.com/three-smart-contract-misconceptions. Accessed on March 10, 2019.

Gatteschi, V., Lamberti, F., Demartini, C., Pranteda, C., Santamaria, V. (2018). Blockchain and Smart Contracts for Insurance: Is the Technology Mature Enough? *IEEE Future Internet*, 10(2), 20–26.

Hildenbrandt, E. (2018). KEVM: A Complete Formal Semantics of the Ethereum Virtual Machine. In *IEEE 31st Computer Security Foundation Symposium (CSF)*, pp. 204–217.

Knirsch, F., Unterweger, A., Engel, D. (2018). Privacy-Preserving Blockchain-Based Electric Vehicle Charging with Dynamic Tariff Decisions. *Computer Science — Research and Development*, 33(1–2), 71–79.

Mahmood, S., Hasan, R., Ullah, A., Sarker, U. (2019). SMART Security Alert System for Monitoring and Controlling Container Transportation. In *2019*

4th MEC International Conference on Big Data and Smart City (ICBDSC), Muscat, Oman. Doi: 10.1109/ICBDSC.2019.8645574

Ozyilmaz, R., Yurdakul, A. (2019). Designing a Blockchain-based IoT with Ethereum, Swarm, and LoRa: The software solution to create high availability with minimal security risks. *IEEE Consumer Electron Mag*, 8(2), 28–34. Doi: 10.1109/MCE.2018.2880806

Qin, R., Yuan, Y., Wang, Y. (2018). Research on the selection strategies of blockchain mining pools. *IEEE Transactions Computer Society*, 5(3), 748–757.

Siegel, D. (2018). Understanding the DAO Attack. Retrieved from: https://www.coindesk.com/understanding-dao-hackjournalists. Accessed on January 19, 2019.

Suliman, A., Husain, Z., Abououf, M., Alblooshi, M., Salah, K. (2019). Monetization of IoT data using smart contracts. *IET Networks*, 8(1), 32–37. Doi: 10.1049/iet-net.2018.5026

The Energy Web Foundation (2018). Promising Blockchain Applications for Energy: Separating the Signal from the Noise. Retrieved from: http://www.coinsay.com/wp-content/uploads/2018/07/Energy-Futures-Initiative-Promising-Blockchain-Applications-for-Energy.pdf. Accessed on January 2, 2019.

Tonelli, R., Lunesu, M., Pinna, A., Taibi, D., Marchesi, M. (2019). Implementing a microservices system with Blockchain smart contracts. In *2019 IEEE International Workshop on Blockchain Oriented Software Engineering (IWBOSE)*, Hangzhou, China. Doi: 10.1109/IWBOSE.2019.8666520

Tsankov, P. (2018). Securify: Practical Security Analysis of Smart Contracts. ArXiv Preprint, arXiv:1806.01143v2.

US Securities and Exchange Commission (2018). Investor Bulletin: Initial Coin Offerings. Retrieved from: https://www.sec.gov/oiea/investor-alerts-and-bulletins/ib_coinofferings. Accessed on February 5, 2019.

Wan, J., Li, J., Imran, M., Li, M., Fazal, A. (2019). A Blockchain-based solution for enhancing security and privacy in smart factory. *IEEE Transact Industrial Inform*. Doi: 10.1109/TII.2019.2894573

Wang, F., Yuan, Y., Rong, C., Zhang, J. (2018). Parallel Blockchain: An architecture for CPSS-based smart societies. *IEEE Transactions Computer Society*, 5(2), 303–310.

Wang, S. (2018). A preliminary research of prediction markets based on Blockchain powered smart contracts. In *Proceedings of IEEE International Conference of Blockchain*, pp. 1287–1293.

Wang, S., Ouyang, L., Yuan, Y., Ni, X., Han, X., Wang, F. (2019). Blockchain-Enabled Smart Contracts: Architecture, Applications, and Future Trends.

IEEE Transactions on Systems, Man, and Cybernetics: Systems Doi: 10.1109/TSMC.2019.2895123

Wood, G., Dr. (2016). Ethereum: A Secure Decentralized Generalized Transaction Ledger. Retrieved from: https://ethereum.github.io/yellowpaper/paper.pdf. Accessed on March 15, 2019.

Yamashita, K., Nomura, Y., Zhou, F., Pi, B., Jun, S. (2019). Potential Risks of Hyperledger Fabric Smart Contracts. In *2019 IEEE International Workshop on Blockchain Oriented Software Engineering (IWBOSE)*, Hangzhou, China. Doi: 10.1109/IWBOSE.2019.8666486

Zhang, J. (2018). Cyber Physical Social Systems: The State of the Art and Perspectives. *IEEE Transactions Computer Society*, 5(3), 829–840.

Zhang, Y. (2018). Smart Contract-based Access Control for Internet of Things (IoT). ArXiv Preprint, arXiv:1802.04410.

Chapter 6

Blockchain Application in Fiji's Aviation Industry

Sam Goundar*,§, Elvis Chandra*,¶, Divesh Anuj*,‖, Bharath Bhushan†,** and Kennedy Okafor‡,††

*The University of the South Pacific, Suva, Fiji

†Sree Vidyanikethan Engineering College, Tirupathi, India

‡Federal University of Technology, Owerri, Nigeria

§sam.goundar@gmail.com

¶elvis.chandra@ats.com.fj

‖anujdivesh8@gmail.com

**bharath.bhushan4@gmail.com

††kennedy.okafor@futo.edu.ng

Abstract

In today's high-technological era, organizations have accelerated the use of blockchain technology to enhance their business processes. Blockchain is a somewhat updated version of a database, which is a powerful technology in terms of managing data when compared to normal SQL databases. In Fiji, flight information is a mission critical system as a large number of stakeholders depend on it, such as, hotels, airlines, airports, ground handlers and even the general public. Current flight information is meeting day-to-day organizational needs, but there is evidence of information technology problems associated with it, such as inconsistent information, data silos, availability, etc. With the introduction of blockchain technology, the aviation industry can become more powerful in terms of providing high-quality flight data to all its stakeholders. By the end of the research, we should be able to build a conceptual model that solves the flight data problem in Fiji.

Introduction

Blockchain came into the picture after the success of Bitcoins; it has a number of benefits such as persistency, decentralization, auditability and anonymity (Friedlmaier *et al.*, 2016). Blockchain is used in a wide range of applications such as finance, internet of things, risk management, etc. We are realizing the need for this powerful technology to establish a "single source of truth" for flight data across the air transport industry. The current manual process of passing data and manual input of information into Flight Information systems leads to inefficient, inaccurate and inconsistent data being used by the industry stakeholders. Flight information in Fiji is categorized as a mission critical system, where data should be of highest quality and available when required. Any inconsistent or incorrect data in Aviation industry could mean a heavy price for the organization to bear. This chapter presents a way in which blockchain technology could provide true flight information across distributed parties.

Methodology

For the purpose of this research project, a qualitative research method was used, which is also sometimes called exploratory research. This was used to gain understanding of the organizations' underlying problems, reasons and options and provide motivation. Issues and problems of the organizations were studied in-depth, and underlying trends and loopholes in the current system were identified. Unstructured and semi-structured techniques were used to gather data, i.e. group discussions, questionnaires, interviews and observations.

By then end of the research, we will be proposing a model (conceptual framework) (Adom *et al.*, 2018) that should be used by the aviation industry in Fiji to enhance their business processes relating to flight information. As there are a huge number of people relying on critical flight data, the proposed blockchain model ensures that there is accurate, consistent and timely information available.

Flight Information in Fiji

Flight information is very critical to the aviation industry in Fiji. The major stakeholders that require critical flight information are the airports, ground handlers, security firms and regulatory bodies, government agencies, airlines and passengers. In Fiji, the major entities managing the only international airport have their own separate flight information systems.

These three entities are Fiji Airports Limited, Air Terminal Services Limited and Fiji Airways.

Fiji Airports Limited is a fully state-owned enterprise which looks after all the airports in Fiji. Air Terminal Services PTE Limited is the only Ground Handler for Nadi International Airport. Air Terminal Services is another State-owned enterprise which looks after the Catering for all local and regional airlines going out of Nadi International airport, provides Cargo & Ramp services, Technical services and passenger services at the Nadi International Airport (ATS, 2018). Fiji Airways is 51% owned by the state and is the International carrier for Fiji Islands. Seventy percent of the flights from Fiji are from Fiji Airways, which is therefore the main source of flight information.

Apart from Fiji Airways, there are other Airlines that route passengers to and from Fiji. These airlines are Air New Zealand, Virgin Airlines, Jetstar, Solomon Airlines, Air Nauru, Air Niugini and other private jets and Fix-based operational flights. All these airlines provide a source of information known as flight movement summary to Air Terminal Services Ltd. The Flight operation team inputs the data into the Flight Information System, updates any changes, allocates gates and sends a copy of flight movement summary to all the stakeholders. The stakeholders then update their respective database or applications based on the data received from Air Terminal Services Limited. The flow of information today is a manual process that leads to untimely and inconsistent information and even communication breakdown at times, with lack of availability of data to all stakeholders.

Flight Information Problems and Challenges in Fiji

There are basically three organizations in Fiji that are interested in critical flight information, i.e. Fiji Airways, Air Terminal Services and the Airport itself. Air Terminal Services are the first party to receive flight information in Fiji. They receive flight data and process it on their system first, before distributing it to other organizations such as Fiji Airports Limited and Fiji Airways. Each of the organizations has its own way of processing and displaying data. The major problem here is inconsistent flow of Flight Information data.

These organizations are working on different information platforms with no links to each other's system and, because of this, it does not confirm if the flight information available is same for all. Air Terminal Services play a vital role in distributing flight information; any error caused by ATS will lead the other organizations into problems. If Air Terminal Services delays forwarding flight information to other parties which is normally done through emails, then there will be inconsistency in flight information. For instance, if ATS forgets to send out flight delay details of a particular flight, then only ATS will have the flight delay information, and the other organization will assume the flight will arrive as scheduled. This results in different flight information displayed on the screens, even at the airport; this is due to improper flow of information from one stakeholder to the other. This further leads to misguiding the passengers about flight information. We cannot afford to give all the power of flight information to ATS — all the participating organizations needs to work collectively to have the correct flight information.

Figure 1 shows the flight information made available through the Air Terminal Services website. Figure 2 shows flight information available from the Fiji Airports Limited website. Both figures were taken on October 23, 2018, and we can notice that there is inconsistent information made available by the two organizations.

Finally, the challenge that now remains in Fiji's Aviation industry is how the major stakeholders can share accurate, timely, consistent information of mission critical systems online, which will lead to better decision-making and assist regular airline customers.

Today's International Arrivals & Departures at Nadi Airport

Tuesday, 23 October 2018 04:40:34 PM

Arrival Log

*STA: Scheduled Time Arrival | *ETA: Estimated Time Arrival

Flight No	Aircraft	STA	ETA	Origin	Gate	Status
FJ960	B73H	04:35	04:30	ADL	4	Landed
FJ811	A332	05:50	05:20	LAX	7	Landed
FJ930	B73H	06:30	06:45	MEL	5	Landed
FJ302	A330	07:05	07:00	HKG	3	Landed
FJ360	A330	11:00	10:55	SIN	8	Landed
FJ914	B73H	11:20	11:20	SYD	5	Landed
NZ52	B773	11:45	11:33	AKL	7	Landed
VA181	B73H	13:35	13:32	SYD	4	Landed
VA185	B73H	14:35	14:34	MEL	5	Landed
VA175	B73H	14:55	14:35	BNE	4	Landed
FJ410	B73H	16:00	16:00	AKL	5	Landed
FJ920	B73H	17:00	16:45	BNE	7	Normal
FJ450	B73W	18:25	18:05	CHC	3	Normal
FJ910	A333	18:50		SYD		
FJ210	ATR 72	20:10		TBU		

Figure 1: Air Terminal Services Flight Information Displayed on Website

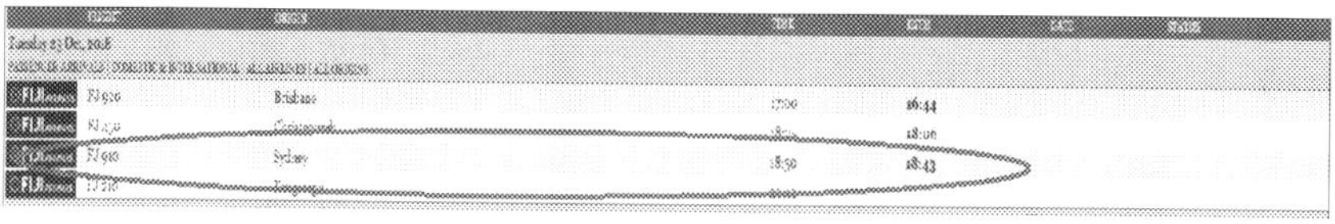

Figure 2: Fiji Airports Limited Flight Information Displayed on Website

Related Work — Literature Review

Société Internationale de Télécommunications Aéronautiques (SITA) is an IT technology firm that proposed the idea of blockchain in flight data; they called this "FlightChain" (SITA, 2017). The research was carried out in Heathrow Airport, Geneva Airport, Miami Airport and British Airways. The firm built a private blockchain and also deployed smart contracts on each node of the network. The idea was to have a single source of true flight data across the mentioned organizations.

According to the author, blockchain is defined as a digital database, the records of which are shared between parties. Data are stored on blocks and are accessible by the participants across the network, and the ledger is immutable. Flight information was used by the company to test the capabilities of the blockchain technology as it did not contain sensitive information and airports and airlines were comfortable sharing the data.

The company Société Internationale de Télécommunications Aéronautiques (SITA) created a private blockchain among the participants, which included three airports and British Airways. The goal of the project was to demonstrate how blockchain would create correct flight data that can be used by the aviation industry. During the project, more than two million flight instances of data were processed by smart contracts and stored on blockchain ledger. The project was implemented using Ethereum and Hyper ledger fabrics (McLaughlin, 2017). These technologies were chosen because they supported smart contracts with private permissioned blockchain.

The paper's key lessons are regarding governance of blockchain, use of smart contracts, system performance and overall security. It was also pointed out by the author that blockchain is a new technology and that it is too early to make recommendations.

Why Blockchain?

A normal SQL database which is used by most organization could have been used to solve the problem of flight data; this holds true if only one organization is involved. In our case, there were a number of organizations involved, i.e. Air terminal services, Fiji Airports Limited, Fiji Airways and other airline companies. Blockchain was used because of the following reasons (Lin & Liao, 2017):

- Blockchain provides a cryptographically immutable ledger that is shared on a network among a number of participants. All participants have agreed on the records in the ledger, and therefore it is legit.
- Allowed parties can update a common dataset.

- Use of smart contracts allows organizations to have business rules defined across the network, to have a shared control over the data.
- Impossible to change records in the distributed ledger.

Key Requirements Building the Conceptual Model

- Private blockchain will be created among the participating organizations.
- Smart contract will be running on each node to validate flight data.
- Source of flight data from airlines, ground handlers, etc.

Private Blockchain

Private blockchain is usually used by a few number of participants, not everyone. It is usually set up by an individual or an organization, and participants join through invitations. Different participants have different levels of access, which include read, write and update. Private blockchain network can be considered a not truly distributed network as governance is required (Reijers *et al.*, 2016). This governance is required to ensure that there is no compromise of integrity of the blockchain. In our case, air terminal services will play the role of the governing body, the roles of which include the following:

- Define permission levels;
- Upgrading smart contracts;
- Adding nodes;
- Sending invitations.

Smart Contract

Smart contracts simply help exchange anything of value in a transparent, conflict-free way, and also avoid middleman services (Christidis & Devetsikiotis, 2016). Smart contract puts rules, agreements or business rules which are defined on paper in automatically. In blockchain, when a transaction occurs, smart contracts are executed on multiple nodes across the network. If all nodes agree on the output produced, only then is the transaction committed on the blockchain ledger. Smart contracts will also help in deciding which party can update a particular flight data, for instance, Fiji Airways will not be able to update flight data of Air New Zealand airlines, and vice versa.

Conceptual Model

To build the conceptual model for Fiji's Aviation Industry, there will be a private blockchain created and smart contracts used to verify transactions on the digital ledger. Air terminal services are the first point of contact of flight information; currently, they will act as the governing body of the blockchain network. They will be allowed to manage the entire blockchain, add nodes on the network, give invitations and control the permissions. There will be three nodes created initially: Fiji Airways, Air Terminal Services and Fiji Airports Limited. Each will have a local copy of the entire blockchain whereby data integrity is maintained. Each node will also have a smart contract running, defined by the organizations collectively.

To start with, ATS, which is the governing body, will give invitations to airline companies to provide flight data. The airline company will have to verify itself to ATS using Public Key Infrastructure (Gorssbart, 2012); then, a cryptographic key will be issued by ATS to the airline company so they can write data on the shared blockchain ledger. Figure 3 is the screenshot after the airline company has written data on the blockchain.

```
"chain": [
    {
        "previousHash": "0",
        "timestamp": [illegible],
        "transactions": [],
        "hash": "[illegible]",
        "nonce": 0
    }
],
"pendingTransactions": [
    {
        "airlinename": "fijiairways",
        "flightno": "[illegible]",
        "origin": "Sydney",
        "STA": "[illegible]",
        "delay_min": "0"
    },
    {
        "airlinename": "fijiairways",
        "flightno": "[illegible]",
        "origin": "Brisbane",
        "STA": "[illegible]",
        "delay_min": "0"
    }
]
```


Figure 3: Sample JavaScript Code for a Block

The data provided by airlines will not be committed on the block ledger immediately, as we can see above, the data is sitting on pending transactions waiting for it to be processed. Now, the smart contracts that are sitting on each node of the network will run on the transaction to verify the transaction. Each node produces an output; the results produced from each node should be same for all the nodes (consensus achieved) in order to successfully commit the transaction on the blockchain ledger (Baliga, 2017). Smart contract is usually built on Ethereum platform (Beck *et al.*, 2016). Each airline will have a list of transactions about their flights, such as flight number, estimated time of arrival, delays, etc. As we can see here, we have used smart contracts to validate transactions; this is because we are using a private blockchain. If a public blockchain was set up, there would be different clients who will be mining (solving mathematical problems) to validate a particular transaction and finally updating it to the blockchain ledger [12]. By using private blockchain and smart contracts, we have saved a great deal of computing processing power as computers in Fiji are usually of low-to-medium specifications. Figure 4 shows the committed transactions.

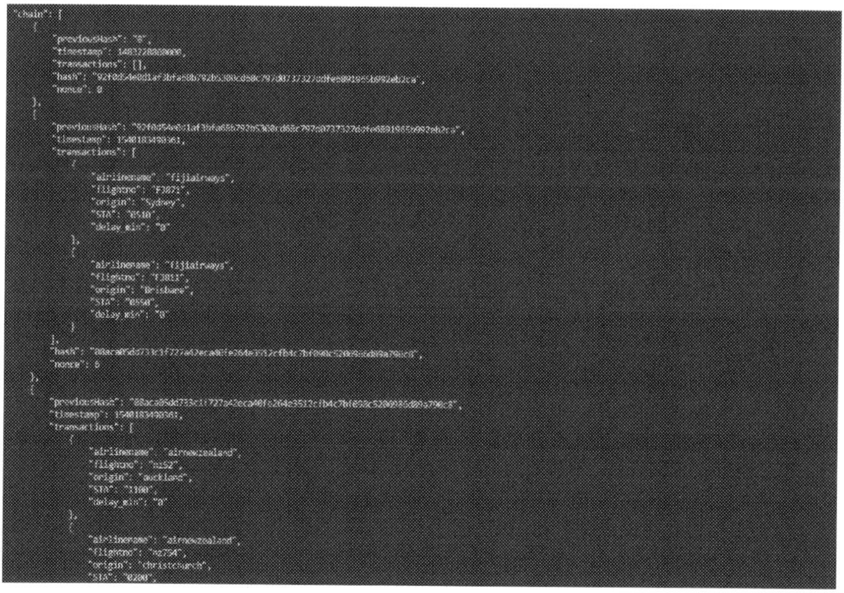

Figure 4: JavaScript Environment — Coding Blockchain

Figure 5: Sample Block of Code in JavaScript

Once the flight departs the origin airport, the airline companies will again have the privilege to write on the blockchain stating if a particular flight has been delayed or not. Figure 5 depicts this.

All the data which are entered in the blockchain ledger are shared between the three major organizations, Fiji Airports Limited, Air Terminal Services and Fiji Airways. There is a single database that is accessed by the organizations participating, enabling distribution of true flight information around Fiji.

Benefits of the Model

With the use of blockchain technology, there will be a single copy of flight data kept across the participating organizations (Swan, 2017). There will be good decisions made by the organizations, and they will agree on each other's decisions as the initial data they are using is the same for all. There will be early detection of flight delays, and customers can be notified in a timely manner; this will reduce chaos at the airport. The information shared across the organizations will be of high integrity, and data silo problem will be solved. Everyone on the network will be given the latest information on flight updates, and flow of information will be consistent so that stakeholders can be provided with true flight information.

Future of Blockchain in Flight Data

Once we have blockchain fully functional and adopted across the organizations in Fiji, Web3.js technology could be explored and we can set up clients that can access data on the blockchain network. As all nodes in the network have same information, so we will be using JSON RPC (Remote procedure call protocol) (Gregory, 2018), which will act like an API to request information from a particular node in the blockchain network and display the information on web browsers. Here we can use any node to request information, as all nodes in the network have the same copy of information. Web3.js technology can be used by Fiji Airports Limited and Air Terminal Services (Fiji) Limited to show real-time flight data on their website in an efficient manner. This is because in the current era, people are relying more on web media as there are a huge number of benefits associated with it.

Conclusion

Flight Information is critical to the aviation industry and its stakeholders in Fiji. Accurate data will lead to more informed decision-making in determining the future of the aviation industry. The blockchain concept can play a more critical role in developing a more precise and accurate Flight information system that can assist the industry in decision-making. More awareness and research work needs to be carried out on the Blockchain concept in the near future.

References

Adom, D., Hussein, E., Agyem, J. (2018). Theoretical and Conceptual Framework: Mandatory Ingredients of a Quality Research. Retrieved from: https://www.researchgate.net/publication/322204158_theoretical_and_conceptual_framework_mandatory_ingredients_of_a_quality_research.

ATS (2018). About us. Retrieved from: https://www.ats.com.fj/About-Us.

Baliga, A. (2017). Understanding Blockchain Consensus Models, 1–14. Retrieved from: https://pdfs.semanticscholar.org/da8a/37b10bc1521a4d3de925d7ebc44bb606d740.pdf.

Beck, R., Czepluch, J., Lollike, N., Malone, S. (2016). Blockchain — The Gate Way to Trust-Free Cryptographic Transactions, 1–15. Retrieved from: https://pdfs.semanticscholar.org/ee1e/fd77e8b6287438d312b244177bb143f7a072.pdf.

Christidis, K., Devetsikiotis, M. (2016). Blockchains and Smart Contracts for the Internet of Things. *IEEE Journals & Magazines*. Retrieved from: https://ieeexplore.ieee.org/abstract/document/7467408.

Friedlmaier, M., Tumasjan, A., Welpe, I. (2016). Disrupting Industries With Blockchain: The Industry, Venture Capital Funding, and Regional Distribution of Blockchain Ventures. *SSRN Electronic Journal.* Doi: 10.2139/ssrn.2854756

Gregory (2018). Intro to Web3.js · Ethereum Blockchain Developer Crash Course, Dapp University. Retrieved from: http://www.dappuniversity.com/articles/web3-js-intro.

Lin, I., Liao, T. (2017). A Survey of Blockchain Security Issues and Challenges. Retrieved from: https://pdfs.semanticscholar.org/f61e/db500c023c4c4ef665b-d7ed2423170773340.pdf.

McLaughlin, B. (2017). Let's Collaborate to Explore Blockchain: SITA's "Aviation Blockchain Sandbox", SITA. Retrieved from: https://www.sita.aero/resources/blog/lets-collaborate-to-explore-blockchain-sitas-aviation-blockchain-sandbox.

Reijers, W., O'Brolcháin, F., Haynes, P. (2016). Governance in Blockchain Technologies & Social Contract Theories. Retrieved from: http://www.ledgerjournal.org/ojs/index.php/ledger/article/view/62.

SITA (2017). Research into the Usability and Practicalities of Blockchain Technology for the Air Transport Industry, pp. 1–20. Retrieved from: https://blockchain-x.eu/wp-content/uploads/2018/02/flightchain-hitepaper.pdf.

Swan, M. (2017). Anticipating the Economic Benefits of Blockchain, pp. 1–11. Retrieved from: https://timreview.ca/sites/default/files/Issue_PDF/TIMReview_October2017.pdf#page=6.

Chapter 7

Blockchain-based e-Voting Application

Sam Goundar*,‡, Rukshar Khan*,§, Kunal Chand*,¶, Emmenual Reddy*,|| and S. P. Raja†,**

**The University of the South Pacific, Suva, Fiji*

†Vel Tech Institute of Science and Technology, Chennai, India

‡sam.goundar@gmail.com

§khan.rukzzz@gmail.com

¶kunalkrishneel@gmail.com

||emmenual.reddy@usp.ac.fj

***avemariaraja@gmail.com*

Abstract

Voting has been a fundamental part of the democratic system as it allows individuals to voice their opinions. Over the past few years, voting turnout has diminished as concerns regarding security, privacy, accessibility and integrity have been escalated.

In order to address these issues, e-voting was introduced; however, only a few countries managed to use the application due to cost and central authority approvals. Hence, blockchain technology is an emerging platform as it allows decentralization through the use of distributed technology, expanding industries and processes.

In this chapter, the researchers will discuss the significance of blockchain e-voting applications as well as provide details of the issues faced by current blockchain technologies. A comparative analysis of existing mechanisms is also provided in order to understand and mitigate the gaps before fully adopting blockchain technologies for e-voting applications.

Thus, this chapter will be a kind of roadmap for blockchain-based e-voting applications to improve the current voting practices and processes.

Introduction

Commensurate with the increase in the number of technological interventions, traditional systems are now adopting modern technologies to ease business processes. Likewise, many countries' election processes have also moved from traditional paper-based voting to electronic voting (e-voting).

Wu (2017) states that electronic voting assists in casting and counting of votes in an election, and it also reduces the number of errors that could be made. The application is normally environmental- and user-friendly as it was introduced to attract the younger generations to vote, as the younger generations prefer online applications rather than the traditional paper-based systems.

Moreover, e-voting has been widely used in such countries such as Estonia, Canada, Australia, Brazil, United Kingdom and Japan (Paatey, 2011). Estonia was the first country in the world to introduce electric voting in 2005.

On the other hand, Kumar *et al.* (2014) state that Germany abandoned the e-voting system due to its insufficient security and vulnerability. Some of the e-voting systems have been analyzed for security issues and flaws identified by researchers, such as vulnerability to hacking and cyber-attacks (Ling & Wang, 2017). Thus, such issues can be exploited and undermine trust in an election.

Koc *et al.* (2017) state that an individual with physical access to such machines can sabotage the machine, thus affecting all the casted votes. The e-voting application has failed in such areas as electoral fraud, posing threat to voters and in cases of vote buying, which is one of the most common problems in a democratic society (Paatey, 2011).

In addition, in order to ensure fair and free election, Cabuk *et al.* (2018) suggested that blockchain technologies can address the existing issues faced with e-voting application and can make e-voting cheaper, easier and much more secure to implement. Blockchain has been considered as a new paradigm that can help to form a decentralized system and assure availability, data integrity and fault tolerance (Hjálmarsson & Hreiðarsson, 2017).

The motivation for using blockchain is that it can make it easier for the citizens, it is reliable, and is trusted and distributed. The importance of blockchain in an election process would be to ensure a free and fair election for the citizens of a democratic country.

However, various issues within blockchain need to be overcome in order to conduct complete block-chain-based elections. Thus, the research in this chapter will provide an overview of the existing issues within blockchain technologies. In addition, it will recommend potential solutions or mechanisms to solve the issues faced by blockchain.

Background

In today's society, due to mistrust towards the government and interference by other external bodies, the democratic process of voting is now even more critical compared to the past. Many democratic countries have experienced dictatorial regimes, which has introduced widespread terror among the people. This has led to human rights violation and freedom of expression being taken away (Koc *et al.*, 2017).

In such scenarios, having a fair and transparent election plays the critical role of constructing a democratic society. According to Evertt *et al.* (2008) the current voting system offers anonymity to the voter, but the vote counting process is not transparent. Citizens of the country are supposed to trust the election commission, which provides the result, thus making the process of counting a major vulnerability in the current scenario.

Furthermore, though the issues of traditional system, such as ballot stuffing and booth capturing, are phasing out, the major issue of voter fraud still exists in the current electronic voting system. This is due to lack of distinction between the actual votes and votes without authorization (Kumar & Walia, 2011). As for the electronic voting system, it has to ensure a proper election scenario and provide utmost security and anonymity during application. Hacking activities have been one of the major headlines, and for many bigger elections this hacking has been blamed on foreign governments or agencies owing to their interest in home and abroad.

In addition, Hjálmarsson & Hreiðarsson (2017) state that blockchain technology tends to shine after entry into the field and wide acceptance of the bitcoin, which was the first cryptocurrency in people's everyday life. Early on, blockchains were only used for monetary transactions and trade, but Ling & Wang (2017) now suggest that it can be used in election process due to its transparency.

Hence, before blockchain becomes the ultimate solution, the existing issues with blockchain need to be addressed. This will ensure that the same issues will not be repeated as was observed in the transition process from traditional systems to e-voting applications. Due to lack of proper research and mechanism of action, security, verification and fraud issues still exist in e-voting application.

Lastly, before the application is run on a national scale, it would be better to run it on a small scale in smaller elections and find the issues before any major issues are created.

Problem statement

There is a tremendous need for a suitable technology to address the existing problems in the current voting system. As stated by Okediran (2011), having a proper election application will ensure free and fair voting process. A fair and free voting process allows the citizens of a country to elect a deserving candidate, as this process impacts the welfare and economy of the country.

Moreover, the application of this technology continues to struggle with issues of security and data integrity; the following are some common problems faced by existing e-voting applications: (Khan *et al.*, 2017)

- High initial setup cost
- Increased security problems such as cyberattacks
- Lack of transparency and trust
- Voting delay and inefficiencies in remote voting.

However, apart from these problems, blockchain also faces some further issues in the election context, which are as follows:

- Verification and anonymity
- Scalability
- Protocols.

Like any other emerging technologies, blockchain will need to solve all the existing issues of the current applications. If the issues of anonymity and verification are solved by blockchain, then it can provide the benefits of locking down data and ensuring no tampering of data.

Thus, there is a need for a better understanding of existing issues for block chain to ensure an error-free election.

Project objectives

The objective of this research is to provide a comprehensive analysis of the problems faced by blockchain currently and outline recommendations (solutions or mechanisms for a well-structured block chain technology) for successful use in elections.

The study also has the following subobjectives:

1. To provide a comprehensive review of issues typically found in blockchain technologies
2. To review current research mechanisms in regard to e-voting based on blockchain technology
3. To compare and contrast research findings on e-voting based on blockchain technology.

The result of this study will be valuable to industries, electronic commissions as well as software providers to help in developing a better practiced and well-suited protocol for e-voting application based on blockchain technology.

Literature Review

A democracy is the form of government in which the power is given to the people to elect the leader under a free electoral system. An election is a process in which voters choose their representatives. This election and democracy has been running for more than 2500 years; however, in recent years, technology has always influenced and shaped the elections.

According to Okediran (2011), the traditional systems have been accused of violence, ballot stuffing, intimidation, underage and multiple voting, complicity of security agencies, counting error and absence or late arrival of election material.

In addition, with the significant development in information technology, nations all over the world have started replacing the traditional systems with electronic voting systems (e-voting). As stated by Okediran (2011), the major aim of this system was to increase voter participation and speed up the results process. Statistics show that the voting system in India, which has one of the largest populations, has eliminated the occurrence of invalid votes during election (Hjálmarsson & Hreiðarsson, 2017). The system also tallied the results within 3–4 hours compared to previous systems that required 30–40 hours (Khan *et al.*, 2017).

In UK, the application was used in various forms such as through the Internet, kiosks, interactive voice recognition via telephone and by post. This application managed to count all the ballots within 6 minutes (Koc *et al.*, 2017).

On the other hand, where there are inventions, there are always pros and cons to those. Likewise, e-voting was noted to have issues with confidentiality, integrity, reliability and availability. As stated by Ayed (2017), there are still criteria that are difficult to satisfy.

As stated by Navya *et al.* (2017), one of the major issues seen with digital voting is the accessibility of Internet in remote polling areas and lack of knowledge of technology in order to use those voting applications. However, according to Khan *et al.* (2017), digital voting has managed to bridge the gap between the high and lower socioeconomic classes. Wang *et al.* (2018) claim that digital voting is also prone to security attacks such as data hacking. Countries like Netherlands and Germany have stopped using digital voting systems after it was demonstrated to be unreliable.

Cabuk *et al.* (2018), in their research, highlight some of the major issues of the existing system such as mining centralization, cyber-security hacks and scalability. Ayed (2017) also claims that through blockchain's authorization, authentication and data credentials, these issues can be solved.

In addition, Ayed (2017) states further drawbacks of the existing systems, which had been raised by Estonian and Norwegian authorities based on their electronic systems. One of the issues was that having a centralized server makes it more vulnerable to DDOS attack, which would jeopardize the entire election process. It is also noted that centralization leads to high cost of infrastructure and maintenance (Kumar & Walia, 2011). These systems have been questioned by researchers on issues such as transparency, vulnerability and security.

According to Navya *et al.* (2017), the blockchain will help to store the cast ballots, acting as a transparent ballot box. With blockchain being a part of electronic voting, it allows groups of people to maintain a public database, thus eliminating the centralized voting of data.

As stated by Ayed (2017), blockchain technology will make voting more open and fault-tolerant. The technology will allow voters to verify their votes and catch any missing or invalid votes before the election is over.

On the other hand, as stated by Wu (2017), there are a vast number of utilizations for blockchain technology, such as e-voting, but these protocols lack proper documentation. Table 1 shows the overview of the most well-documented and most used blockchain technologies.

Table 1: Commercial e-Voting Blockchain Protocols

	Protocols		
Properties	**Bitcongress**	**Follow My Vote**	**TIVI**
Fairness	No	No	No
Eligibility	No (One Bit-coin addr. one vote)	Yes	Yes (Unclear how)
Privacy	Yes	Yes	Yes
Individual Verifiability	Yes	Yes	Yes
Universal Verifiability	Yes	Yes	Yes
Forgiveness	No	Yes (Unclear how)	Yes (Unclear how)

As there exist blockchain technologies for digital voting, many researchers are suggesting the use of POA consensus algorithm. As stated by Koc *et al.* (2017), consensus algorithm enables to set restrictions on a set of selected entities in order to validate, certify and censor the transactions on blockchain. Previous applications on blockchain have used miners on public blockchain, which uses proof-of-work consensus algorithm.

Thus, instead of employing mining fees for public blockchains, using permissioned blockchain allows the validators to get paid for the service of validation provided in the system. Thus, by using a private network it also limits the eavesdroppers' monitoring of the traffic or reading of incoming data. Thus, this feature will help to fulfill the rights of the voters as their identity or data need to be protected from leakage.

Lastly, from the literature review, it can be seen that there is a suggestion, with a high probability, for blockchain technology to solve the existing problems of the current system. However, there is lack of research on problems faced or to be faced by blockchain as part of an election system. There is a need to understand the current problems before committing a new change, which can cause further problems to the voters. For instance, with the introduction of e-voting the problem of security and fraud is still a major concern. The researchers have also failed to consider the weakness of using e-voting on block chain technologies. Thus, there is thus far only an indication of the positive side, failing to showcase the negative influences.

Research Methodology

The primary research method for this study is literature review and conceptual modeling. This will allow the researchers to compare and contrast the existing e-voting application based on blockchain and find the weakness and strength of the existing e-voting-based block chain systems.

In addition, this research will first review various issues of blockchain from journals and other articles. Based on the findings, the researchers will construct a SWOT analysis to highlight the strengths and weaknesses of e-voting application based on blockchain technology.

The following research questions would be focused on during the research:

1. What are the new success measures for voting applications?

2. What are the major issues of blockchain technologies?
3. What are the current mechanisms or protocols for e-voting application based on blockchain technology?

Discussion

Current issues which can be eliminated through the use of blockchain-based e-voting application

The introduction of blockchain-based e-voting system will provide the following benefits and opportunities.

First, the security concerns of data tampering in the existing electronic and online voting platforms would be mitigated through the use of block chain, as block chain decentralization makes attacking difficult. In addition, Hardwick *et al.* (2018) looked at voter tampering, which is also addressed by blockchain as it generates cryptographically secure voting records (Ayed, 2017). Through the use of cryptographic methods, voters are recorded accurately, securely and transparently. This avoids attackers from modifying or manipulating data or votes.

Second, blockchain promotes a greater level of transparency and clarity to the voters. For instance, Jun (2018) states that there are around 23 countries that have adopted online voting practice. Though there needs to be further support for users as the current online processes are complicated for some users due to lack of knowledge of technology, one of the major concerns in the current paradigm is the casting of vote which is whether a vote was counted or intended. Blockchain also allows results to be audited by the public (Evertt *et al.*, 2008).

Third, the current systems face issues with identity verification and slow election process. For instance, the federal court in Texas registered around 608,470 voters who lacked verification identification, and around 11% of US citizens do not have government-issued photo identification. Blockchain-improved identity verification can help to increase the access and participation level of users (Wang *et al.*, 2018).

In addition, it can also increase the speed of voting tallies. For example, Agora managed to publish election results 5 days before the official manual counts ended. Likewise, blockchain can eliminate ambiguities. For instance, Jun (2018) states that the 2017 Virginia House of Delegates

Setting	The context	Remarks
The city of Moscow's Active Citizen program	In December 2017, the program started using a blockchain for voting and to make the voting results publicly auditable. Each question discussed by the community and put up for voting is moved to the e-voting system using a blockchain. After the voting is complete, the results are listed on a ledger containing all the previous polls.	The most popular polls were reported to have 137,000 to 220,000 participants.[10] In one such case on the Ethereum platform, citizens indicated their preferences for temporary relocation if the building in which they were living would be demolished and replaced by a better building. The platform reached a peak of approximately 1,000 transactions per minute. It's not clear whether the platform can handle the volume if a higher proportion of Moscow's 12 million citizens participate in the voting.
The South Korean province of Gyeonggi-do's community projects	The province used a blockchain-based voting system to gather votes on community projects. 9,000 residents voted.	The Korean financial-technology startup Block developed the blockchain platform.
The annual general meeting of the Estonian tech company LVH Group	Shareholders can log in using their verified national online ID and vote at the meeting.	The voting system issues voting-right assets and voting-token assets to shareholders. A user can spend voting tokens to vote on meeting agenda items if that user owns the related voting-right asset. Nasdaq designed the system.
Sierra Leone's March 2018 general elections	Swiss startup Agora carried out tallying in two districts. After the voting, a team of accredited observers from different locations manually entered approximately 400,000 ballots into Agora's blockchain system.	This test was considered a partial deployment of a blockchain.[11] The elections were only verified by blockchain, not blockchain powered. Agora provided an independent vote count, which was compared with the main tally.

Figure 1: Blockchain-based Solutions

Source: Kshetri *et al.* (2018).

election was chosen from paper ballots and one vote was initially not counted due to confusing marks on the ballot. Hence, such ambiguity issues are less likely to arise in blockchain-based e-voting application (Wu, 2017).

Lastly, through the use of blockchain, Figure 1, individual votes will be publicly available while the voter identity will be encrypted, thus ensuring a greater deal of data privacy and security when compared with traditional ballot boxes.

Risks and current issues of blockchain technologies

Though there are significant advantages to having e-voting application on blockchain, there are still areas of risks and dangers that need to be hindered before adopting a new technology for election processes. Thus, this section will discuss some of the potential risks and dangers of blockchain technologies.

Manipulation of data consensus

As stated by Harris (2018), in undeveloped countries the government has the incentives to manipulate transactions or voter consensus through the introduction of delays in the validation process, thus allowing early timestamps for manipulating data. On the other hand, Wang *et al.* (2018) state that a DDoS attack, which has a possibility of 51% as being the choice weapon of hackers, can likely cause damage or manipulation of voter entries, thus providing vague results. These issues mostly occur when private or a semi-private blockchains are implemented, thus limiting the effectiveness of blockchain transparency.

For data confidentiality, it is suggested to use permissioned blockchain as it is more flexible with potential solutions for access control.

Privacy and anonymity issues

Privacy of data is always a concern, and for election process confidentiality of data is a major concern for e-voting applications based on blockchain. Rahardijo (2017) states that for blockchain, a set of parameters need to be set out as not all data should be shown on a public ledger for everyone to see. Especially for election data, there needs to be an extra challenge as this data can be used by political parties to hinder and alter voter's perspectives (Ayed, 2017).

Although, in private block chain the privacy issues have the tendency of improvement, in semiprivate and public block chains the pseudonymous and not anonymous can be identified with enough data (Rahardijo, 2017). This becomes a major concern as voters who cast votes to a particular party can be revealed, which would create issues for them as it is a violation of free voting practice.

Scalability and storage issues

One of the biggest concerns is size of the blockchain ledgers and storage of data. As blockchain grows over time and requires an effective record management, it will be a concern for public blockchains. This will lead to data centralization issues, reflecting the government's regulations (Zhang *et al.*, 2018).

Storage will also be a hurdle; although blockchain eliminates the need for having a central services to store data, the data must be stored on the nodes. Limitation of node access will need to be regulated by government to ensure reliability of data on the blockchain nodes.

Concusses in the block chain

Moreover, as block chain has the feature of decentralized system, the problem of concusses can occur. Concusses happen when different voters cast their votes at approximately the same time. In blockchain when a voter casts a vote, that vote is linked to the previous vote in order to create a chain that is not corruptible or changeable (Rahardijo, 2017).

As stated by Hjálmarsson *et al.* (2018), in order to overcome this issue, the longest chain rule can be used, as it is used in bitcoin to resolve the simultaneous fielding issues in ledgers.

Lastly, as the traditional voting system emphasizes authority of the state, blockchain-based e-voting application emphasizes voter transparency, decentralization and a bottom-up approach. This system might not function well in societies where culture and values exhibit low compatibility. The application will also shift the power away from central and electoral authorities and government agencies; thus, the technology might face resistance from political leaders who benefit from the traditional voting systems.

Hence, blockchain will reduce the cost of paper-based elections, increase voter participation and ensure free and safer elections.

Comparative analysis of current mechanism and protocols

A comparative analysis will highlight the strengths and weaknesses of existing mechanisms and point out protocols that should be considered before implementing blockchain-based e-voting applications.

Type	Description	Strengths	Weakness	Paper
Blind Signatures with Hash functions	These blind signatures are used for signing encrypted messages with no decryption technique	Used to preserve voters' choices during election. Voter's privacy is protected	Potential of security risks and forgery A blind signature is secured if only it satisfies two key properties, unforgeability (that is cannot produce more signatures) and blindness	(Ling & Wang, 2017)

(*Continued*)

Type	Description	Strengths	Weakness	Paper
			(cannot link particular signature to a signing instance)	
Consensus algorithm using Delegated Proof of Stake (DPOS)	It ensures consistency of data in a distributed computing system Used for smart contracts	Cheap transactions Scalable Energy efficient Miners can collaborate to make blocks unlike PoW and PoS Faster compared to other consensus algorithm Suitable for large-scale transaction Ensures integrity of the data recorded on blockchain	Partially centralized	(Wang *et al.*, 2018)
Unlinkable signatures	Allows users to publish an address that is not traded by multiple transactions	Address is unique No issue to design address reuse Protect the receiver of transaction anonymity	Slow process Security issues as two signatures are linkable Will need another algorithm to protect sender's information	(Wang *et al.*, 2018)
Ring signatures	Special signature with no trusting center or group establishment process Contains four algorithm, GEN, SIG, VER and LNK	To protect the anonymity in the voting based on blockchain Help to keep the anonymity of sender Provide higher level of privacy	Security issues still exist	(Wang *et al.*, 2018) (Wu, 2017)

Success measures for e-voting applications

There need to be measures to determine whether an application is meeting all the criteria or not. Thus, this section will discuss some of the success measures that should be considered for e-voting applications.

Privacy

The system should ensure that a level of voter privacy should be maintained throughout the election process. Hence, through the cryptographic properties of blockchain, the privacy of a voter can be achieved. According to Kumar *et al.* (2014), blockchain-based e-voting applications will generate a voter hash upon voter registration, which will have a unique identifier of a voter, thus protecting the user from collision resistance property. Thus, blockchain ensures that that traceability of the voter is non-trivial (Harris, 2018).

Eligibility

As per the government requirements, eligible users must register and have a unique identifier. Thus in case of blockchain, it has to have a strong authentication mechanism, such as using fingerprinting technology, to allow only authorized users to vote through the system.

Receipt freeness

The system should allow the voters to vote as per their choices. In blockchain applications, the system creates a cryptographic hash for each event or transaction, and this is to achieve verifiability.

On the other hand, using the hash does not allow the user to extract information about how the voting was done.

Convenience

The system should be user-friendly, with an interactive web-based interface and requiring minimal input from the user. Through blockchain, the fingerprint should allow authentic users to proceed to vote in a seamless manner (Ayed, 2017).

Verifiability

The system should allow users to verify if their voting was included for tallying. Through blockchain, after the user has successfully voted, a unique transaction ID in the form of a cryptographic hash is provided

(Wu, 2017). This ID can be used by user track if their vote was included in the tallying process. However, the hash does not enable the user to view how they voted in order to avoid threats.

The above analysis presents the success measures for an e-voting application. The researchers have also included the characteristics for each measure in order to achieve an efficient block chain-based e-voting system. Hence, this information presented can make significant contribu tions to the existing knowledge in terms of blockchain technology in order to achieve a secure electronic voting system.

Conceptual modeling of blockchain based e-voting application

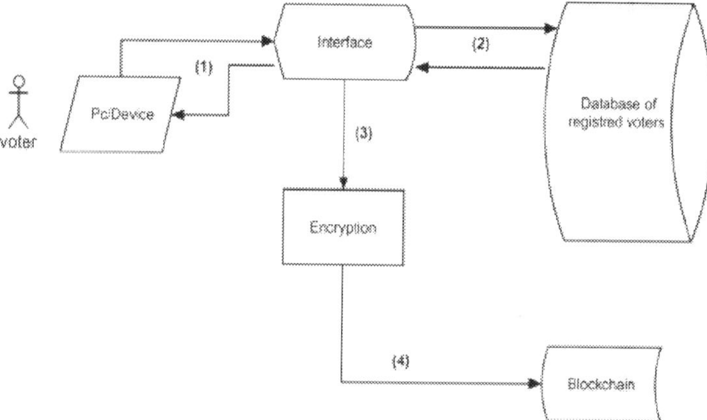

Figure 2: Conceptual Model of Blockchain-based e-Voting Application
Source: Ayed (2017).

Requesting allows to vote

The user logs in into the system through the use of biometrics. Upon successful authentication, the user moves to the voting screen.

Casting vote

Upon seeing the list of candidates, the user casts a vote for their selected candidates. A transaction ID is created which users can use to track their vote for tallying purpose.

Encrypted votes

Before the transaction ID is generated, the vote casted is encrypted using the hash functions.

Vote added to blockchain

After successful completing of casting, the users vote is the transaction that is added to the chain of the blockchain and gets linked to the previous vote casted.

SWOT Analysis of election systems

	Blockchain-based E-voting	Naive E-voting Systems	Traditional Paper-based Elections
Strength	• Transparent and provides privacy • It is cheaper for the long run • Results are instant • Maintains anonymity • Faster process for voting and processing compared to traditional elections • Promotes free election • User friendly • Record deletion is impossible, thus it has immutable records • Allows users to trace whether vote was tallied or not	• Cheaper for long run • It allows elastic elections, that is for customizable, condition, durations and target groups	• As long as the paper-based voting and counting is transparent, people trust it • Does not require internet, thus works well in remote areas
Weakness	• Scalability issues as it is a new technology • Developer and tester are not adequate • Initial deployment costs are higher but lower than naïve solutions	• The initial deployment costs are high • Privacy and trust issues • Uses non-scalable databases, thus less transparent	• Paper wastage • Expensive for long run • Long queues for casting votes • Presence of physical security requirement • Transparency issues

(Continued)

	Block Chain Based E-voting	Naive E-voting Systems	Traditional Paper Based Elections
Weakness	• Requires internet access, thus issue for remote areas	• Process and casting is also less transparent • Attacks can result in disruption	• Miscounting issues during final process • Traceability issues
Opportunities	• New model to improve voting privacy and allow transparency • Secure storage of records • Allows people to select a democratic government	• New model to improve voting privacy and allow transparency • Secure remote participation	• Easier for elderly and disabled people
Threats	• In case the cryptographic keys fail, the attackers can misuse the system • Type of blockchain for implementation should be chosen wisely • Consensus protocol to be chosen depending on the type of blockchain to avoid risk of attackers	• It can create a single point of failure due to centralized processing • Easier for attacks due to centralization structure	• Humans can create errors while casting or counting • Physical attacks • Ballot damages • Stolen ballots • Replacing ballots for political benefits

PESTEL Analysis for blockchain based e-voting application

Factor	Drivers	Drawbacks
Political	Transparency The public blockchain can be viewed by public but cannot be altered	Government regulations If the government has the control of voting process, then transparency can be comprised if private or semi-private blockchains are used

(Continued)

(*Continued*)

Factor	Drivers	Drawbacks
Economic	Costs It has the ability to automate functions, thus reducing third-party cost, and the processing completion is also faster compared to current practices	Security For additional layers of security, cost can increase
Social	User control The application has the ability to monitor transaction or records in one single location	Privacy and security Due to the public blockchain ability to showcase information publicly, many users limit the adoption
Technology	Quality Allows greater protection against fraud Reliable and durable	Innovation It is a solution of fast processing of records privacy and ability to integrate within existing networks
Environment	Environment friendly Reduces paper wastage Reduces environment pollution	Difficulty for elders Have to educate non-technical users on usage
Legal	Legal regulations Allows for legal regulation bodies to regulate process Regulations on privacy and security concerns	Government regulations If the government has control of regulatory bodies, voting process transparency can be comprised if private or semi-private blockchains are used

Conclusions

A block-chain-based e-voting system as discussed in this chapter is a potential solution to replace the existing traditional and online e-voting systems. Blockchain-based e-voting system is more transparent and ensures privacy of records. The main purpose of this research was to investigate the areas of weakness in block chain technologies in order to comprehensively understand the technologies. Some of the major issues discussed are manipulation of data consensus and privacy, that is, if it is using private or semi-private blockchain technologies. It was also found that using permissible blockchain technologies could help to avoid the abovementioned issues.

In addition, a comparative analysis of current mechanism was identified, with strengths and weakness, in order to allow researchers to understand the possible mechanisms to use to avoid issues.

The chapter also discussed the success measure for e-voting applications in order to establish a guideline for a well-structured blockchain-based e-voting application. Hence, SWOT and PESTEL analyses were constructed to highlight the importance of moving to new technology.

Lastly, as technology is revolutionizing a lot of processes, one effort in the core blockchain technology would be to improve the voting process.

References

Ayed, A. B. (2017). A Conceptual Secure Blockchain Based Electronic Voting System. *International Journal of Network Security and its Applications*, 9(3), 1–9.

Cabuk, U. C., Adiguzel, E., Karaarslan, E. (2018). A Survey on Feasibility and Suitability of Blockchain Techniques for the E-Voting Systems. *International Journal of Advanced Research in Computer Science and Software Engineering*, 7(3), 1–12.

Evertt, S., Greene, K., Byre, M., Wallach, D., Derr, K., Torous, D. S. (2008). Electronic Voting Machines versus Traditional Methods: Improved Preference, Similar Performance. In *CHI 2008 Proceedings on Measuring Business and Voting*, Rice University, Florence, pp. 883–892.

Harris, C. G. (2018). The Risks and Dangers of Relying on Blockchain Technology in Underdeveloped Countries. *IEEE*, 1–4.

Hardwick, F. S., Gioulis, A., Akram, R. N., Markantonakis, K. (2018). E-Voting with Blockchain: An E-Voting Protocol with Decentralisation and Voter Privacy. *Semantic Scholar*, 1–7.

Hjálmarsson, F. Þ., Hreiðarsson, G. K. (2017). Blockchain-Based E-Voting System. *IEEE*, 1–10.

Hjálmarsson, F. Þ., Hreiðarsson, G. K., Hamdaqa, M., Hjálmtýsson, G. (2018). Blockchain-Based E-Voting System. *IEEE*, 1–4.

Jun, M. S. (2018). Blockchain Government — A Next Form of Infrastructure for the Twenty First Century. *Journal of Open Innovation Technology, Market and Complexity*, 4, 1–12.

Khan, K., Arhsad, J., Khan, M. (2017). *Secure Digital Voting System Based on Blockchain Technology.* University of West London: London.

Koc, A. K., Cabuk, U. C., Yavuz, E., Dalkilic, G. (2017). Towards Secure E-Voting using Ethereum Blockchain. *IEEE*, 1–7.

Kshetri, N., Antoniol, G., Laplante, P., Counsell, S. (2018). Blockchain Enabled Evoting. *IEEE*, 1–5.

Kumar, S., Walia, E. (2011). Analysis of Electronic Voting System in Various Countries. *International Journal of Computer Science Engineering*, 3(5), 1–6.

Kumar, V., Batham, S., Jain, M., Sharma, S. (2014). An Approach to Electronic Voting System using UIDAI. In *2014 International Conference on Electronics and Communication Systems,* ICECE, India, pp. 1–5.

Ling, Y., Wang, Q. (2017). An E-voting Protocol Based on Blockchain. *IACR Cyptology ePrint Archive*, 1–11.

Navya, Roopini, Sai, Prabhu. (2017). Electronic Voting Machine Based on Blockchain Technology and Aadhar Verification. *International Journal Advanced Research Ideas and Innovation Technology*, 3(3), 1178–1182.

Okediran, O. (2011). A Framework for a Multifaceted Electronic Voting System. *International Journal Applied Science and Technology*, 1(4), 135–142.

Paatey, G. O. (2011). The Design of an Electronic Voting System. *Research Journal of Information Technology*, 3(2), 91–98.

Rahardijo, R. H. (2017). Blockchain Based Evoting Recording System Design. *IEEE*, 1–6.

Wang, B., Sun, J., He, Y., Pang, D. (2018). Large Scale Election Based on Blockchain. *Prodecia Computer Science*, 129, 234–237.

Wu, Y. (2017). *An E-Voting System Based on Blockchain and Ring Signature.* University of Birmingham: Birmingham.

Zhang, P., Jiang, H., Zheng, Z., Hu, P., Xu, Q. (2018). A New Post Quantum Blind Signature from Lattice Assumptions. *IEEE*, 1–8.

Chapter 8

Blockchains for Supply Chain Management Networks

Sam Goundar[*,‡], Sheenal Chand[*,§], Pranesh Chand[*,¶], Nizam Khan[*,||], Asneel Raj[*,**] and Rajiv Pandey[†,††]

The University of the South Pacific, Suva, Fiji

[†]*Amity University, Lucknow, India*

[‡]*sam.goundar@gmail.com*

[§]*S11107869@student.usp.ac.fj*

[¶]*S11085228@student.usp.ac.fj*

[||]*S95008116@student.usp.ac.fj*

[**]*S11096861@student.usp.ac.fj*

[††]*rpandey@lko.amity.edu*

Abstract

Blockchain is a distributed and digital ledger which has transformed supply chains in various ways. In this chapter, we will investigate how blockchain can add value to the supply chain management system. This chapter will further investigate the influence of integrating blockchain technology to the current supply chain system and discuss its long-term implications. In essence, research has been carried out to verify if blockchain technology is capable of providing the transparency and the accountability the current Supply Chain Management (SCM) system lacks. The chapter looks at advantages and disadvantages of such integration and provides feedback and recommendations on the same. The research findings aim to provide better insight into current practices used by large logistic and supply industries and what the future holds for such companies using the SCM system.

Introduction

Blockchain is a public distributed digital ledger that records and tracks transactions in series of blocks. By using math and cryptography, blockchain provides an open, decentralized database of any transaction involving value, such as money, goods, property, work or even those creating a record whose authenticity can be verified by the entire community. Many organizations today are showing interest in integrating the blockchain technology into their current Enterprise Resources Planning (ERP) system as this could mean enhancing productivity and efficiency. While implementation of supply chain alone has moved companies into a more profitable position, there is still need for further transparency and accountability within the supply chain. The need for verification and authenticity of a product we consume on a daily basis is still a matter of concern that we still have not overcome with the current supply chain system.

Blockchain technology is challenging the status quo in a radical way. Blockchain may change the way all major logistic companies operate using supply chain in future. Because of the multifaceted nature of these industries and the absence of transparency within their current supply chain system, there is a growing interest as to how blockchains may change the supply chain and logistic industries (Marr, 2018). For larger logistic companies, their supply chain can span several hundreds of stages depending on the product and services offered. In addition, dealing with several geographical locations and working with a multitude of invoices and payments, we may see that the supply chain and logistics domain will evolve into one of the most active sectors for blockchain take-up (O'Byrne, 2017).

The contribution of this chapter is twofold: we will first examine the benefits and second, the impacts of blockchain evolvement with the supply chain industry. We will also examine the impact of the blockchain ledger on supply chain management. This chapter is of interest as, "the authors yet to date are not aware of any at-scale applications to the supply chain, raising an essential question: Can blockchain technology add value to supply chains?" (McKinsey, 2019). This chapter will give insights into and also inspire companies to evaluate the potential of adopting blockchain as a new technology for the supply chain industry. In particular, academic literature has supported studies that relate to Bitcoin and digital cryptocurrency. Some logistics experts in the transport and logistics industry are also of the opinion that blockchain technology has the potential to transform the supply chain (Friedlmaier *et al.*, 2018). This chapter will aim to provide knowledge about blockchain and how blockchain-based applications such as supply chain can transform the industry. This chapter tries to fill the gap of limited (academic) knowledge on potential benefits and impacts of blockchain in this sector. It will address four specific research questions. For this, we use systematic mapping process to derive meaningful outcomes in the area of blockchain in relation to the supply chain industry. This chapter is structured as follows: First, it provides the introduction and background on Blockchain Technology (BCT) and SCM, followed by a literature review. Research methodology will be addressed next and will contain four Research Questions (RQ). This chapter then highlights results and discussions. The last part of the chapter will discuss the limitations, conclusions and recommendations.

Literature Review

Blockchain

Blockchain may be seen as a distributed register that contains transaction records in an immutable manner, validated with the aid and agreement of the majority of users and then shared among peers. Blockchain technology manages transactions and statistics in a decentralized manner. "Blockchain, mostly known as the technology running the Bitcoin cryptocurrency, is a public ledger system maintaining the integrity of transaction data" (Swan, 2015). An asymmetric encryption cryptography protocol is used for blockchain security, wherein the keys used for encrypting and decrypting messages are separate. "Blockchain advocates claim transparency, speed, accessibility and non-falsifiability as the cornerstones of this new paradigm" (Aptea & Petrovskyb, 2016).

Valuable attributes such as data integrity, security and anonymity without third-party agents taking control of transactions are major causes of interest in blockchain technology. "The interest in Blockchain technology has been increasing since the idea was coined in 2008" (Yli-Huumo *et al.*, 2016). There are multiple applications for Blockchain technology. "Blockchain technology is finding applications in a wide range of areas; both financial and non-financial" (Crosby *et al.*, 2016). One such area of application is Supply Chain Management, which enables it to capture the journey of a product throughout the supply chain.

Research has shown that blockchain technology for supply chains potentially helps organizations transform their business process. With the help of blockchains, supply chain participants are able to connect in real time. "Blockchains can facilitate supply chain network information management providing real-time tracking, verifiability, and security" (Zhu & Kouhizadeh, 2019). This feature is then utilized by the organizations to track their products and transactions. "The supply chain and logistics domain can take advantage of blockchain technology for product tracking, product tracing, or to trace related financial transactions" (Swan, 2015).

Benefits of blockchain in supply chain management

Blockchain promotes transparency — "blockchain is well suited for use in supply chains in part because the technology has the potential to provide an unprecedented level of transparency" (Boschia *et al.*, 2018). This is well suited for SCM as it allows the different parties to build trust in each other.

All parties have the obligation to transfer their data and information about a particular item. "Blockchain technology can help remove middlemen from transactions" (Zhu & Kouhizadeh, 2019). A computerized collection of exact information improves accountability and trust between partners. Blockchain shows the updates of a product in real time, so all the associates know the exact status of a product at all times. For example, "using the publicly available records on the Blockchain, a potential buyer can clearly determine if the seller is the actual owner of the diamond and can also make sure he is not buying a fake" (Hackius, 2017).

"Blockchain technology offers swift implementations of automated transaction management with comparatively little coding effort" (Risius & Spohrer, 2017). Automation significantly benefits SCM as it helps reduce manual effort and increases efficiency. Blockchain technology can potentially increase the efficiency of the SCM and settlement processes through dispute unravelling and automation. "Automations of processes are done through smart contracts, these contracts can automate commercial processes the moment that agreed conditions are met" (Heutger & Kückelhaus, 2018). It is designed in such a way that the "payment by the sender is only released once the shipping company confirms the delivery. This allows for a transaction to be automated, yet documented and controlled" (Hackius, 2017).

Limitations of blockchain in supply chain management

Theoretically, blockchain technology is very workable, but SCM are not easy to alter and adjust to. "Plans for blockchain implementation should be handled in incremental stages, starting with the most immediate impact" (Al Barghuthi *et al.*, 2018). Blockchain has limitations and faces challenges in areas such as anonymity, data integrity, throughput, latency, size, bandwidth and security attributes and also in regard to scalability of the system. "As blockchain is growing, data becomes bigger and bigger, the loading, storing and computing will also be getting harder and harder" (Lin & Liao, 2017). Due to issues in data integrity and anonymity, researches suggest "data chosen to be stored on the blockchain should not be sensitive nor detrimental to the source if publicly viewed" (Kim *et al.*, 2018).

As the communication becomes more vigorous between the parties in a supply chain, throughput issues will arise. "When the frequency of transactions in Blockchain increases, the throughput of the Blockchain network needs to be improved" (Yli-Huumo, 2016). Studies have revealed that fraud on SCM has increased in the past couple of years and is a major risk for SCM; however, there are small signs that blockchain may change this in the near future. "Even though blockchain systems are designed to prevent reporting errors or fraud by a single party, some systems could be vulnerable to fraud executed through collision among a significant number of participants in the system" (Yeoh, 2017).

There are also concerns related to the complexity of the implementation of blockchain, similar to the issues observed during the launch of the Internet, and some researchers have also questioned the longevity of blockchains projects. "There are very few Blockchain projects with high longevity" (Perboli *et al.*, 2018). However, researchers have also pointed out that employees do not essentially need to comprehend all details of the technology as long as the applications are intuitive, appropriate for use and trustable; however, lack of understanding may cause some backlash for the companies associated. "Some companies have put in years refining Supply Chains and it will not be easy to insert new technologies inside already established supply chains" (Mougayar & Buterin, 2016). Other researchers have also pointed out that there is a lot of room for improvement despite all the strengths possessed by blockchain technology and that it should not be rushed. "Any plans for blockchain implementation should be handled in incremental stages, starting with the most immediate impact".

Future of the relationship of blockchain with supply chain management

Blockchain technology has seen several evolutions since its inception, but in the past couple of years combining BCT with SCM has become a trend due to its numerous advantages. There are two facets to the current research: the first is to restructure the entire blockchain system so it can meet the requirements of SCM, and the second is to use the existing architecture to solve key problem areas in SCM. Furthermore, digitization is predicted to be a major force for the currently evolving modern society in the coming years. Due to its positive performance and effectiveness of the programmable methods, digitalization has been tipped to reform even expertise-intensive industries and services. "Due to its potential pervasiveness, especially blockchain technology represents a potent driver of digitalization" (Risius & Spohrer, 2017).

BCT has been attracting a lot of interest from researchers and experts. While there has been swift advancement on research in some areas (e.g. payments, cryptocurrencies), a broader know-how concerning relations of applications and scenarios is normally lacking. "Blockchain possesses a great potential in empowering the citizens of the developing countries if widely adopted by e-governance applications for identity management, asset ownership transfers of precious commodities" (Miraz & Ali, 2018). The evolution of blockchain in the past few years has been monumental. From a technological perspective, it has pushed new boundaries, but that doesn't mean it is still out of the infant stage. When compared with other technologies out there, it still has a lot to grow.

Research Methodology

In this chapter, we have used the systematic mapping process as our research methodology. The goal of using such an approach was to provide an overview of our research area and to establish if there were any comparative research evidence which existed, and quantify the amount of evidence. This has further helped us follow the SMS process, as described by Petersen, to explore the existing studies related to blockchain and Supply Chain Management (Petersen *et al.*, 2008). We also use the guidelines provided by Kitchenham and Charters for a systematic literature review (SLR) and search for relevant papers that cover the literature for the past 10 years (Kitchenham & Charters, 2007). The results of the SMS process helped us identify and map research areas related to BCT-based SCM and analyze whether Blockchain Technology will impact supply chain management. The supply chain process is depicted in Figure 1 and consists of five process steps and outcomes (Youness *et al.*, 2018).

We will carry out Quantitative Research based on the research conducted 2009 to 2019 on Blockchain and supply chain management. We designed the following four RQ that formed the basis for our research analysis:

- **RQ1: What research topics have been addressed in existing research on SCM and BCT in the last 10 years?**

The core research question of this systematic review is to gain knowledge on existing studies on topics based on SCM and BCT. A scientific database was used to collect the relevant papers. This helped us create the understanding that existed between blockchain technologies and supply

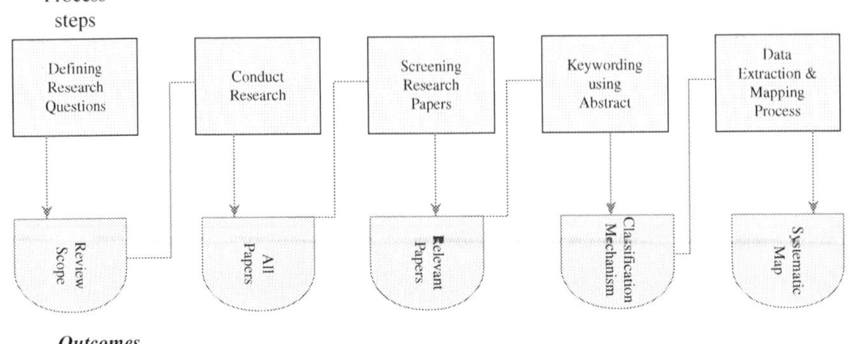

Figure 1: Systematic Mapping Process

chain management. Mapping this analysis done on SCM and BCT can facilitate other researchers to realize higher knowledge and understanding on the current research topic, which is then able to cater to the research analysis on SCM and BCT.

- **RQ2: What are the limitations of blockchain evolvement with supply chain management?**

As with most new technologies, there are restrictions and therefore considerations that need to be accounted for, and this research effort identifies the limitations of Blockchains on SCM. It is important to identify the current limitations of BCT in SCM as it helps the experts in this area determine the flaws BCT has in SCM.

- **RQ3: What are the positive impacts Blockchain technology brings to solve the existing problems in supply chain management?**

Blockchain has an extraordinary impact of transferring things of value to each other. This will be beneficial in answering the research question as it would bring out the positive impacts of blockchains in supply chain management. Finding research points about positive impacts of blockchain will help find out how BCT technologies can influence SCM positively.

- **RQ4: Will blockchain become a new platform for Supply Chain Operating Networks?**

Having knowledge or predicting the future of BCT that will drive or will be a required as a feature of SCM networks, RQ1–RQ3 are to be analyzed. Responding to this RQ is beneficial when choosing how the examination on BCT and SCM innovation ought to be guided and what problems should be solved.

Screening of related and relevant work

There are many systematic reviews in the literature on different topics of blockchain technologies. All papers reviewed were not related to the research questions directly. Hence, they needed to be assessed for their actual relevance (Yli *et al.*, 2016). For reviewing papers, we utilized a process that was influenced by Dybannd Dingsoyr. In the first phase of screening the research papers, we reviewed the journal articles and papers related to Blockchain in general and its relevance to other fields such as Internet of Things, Security, and its implication in the fields of Accounting and Finance. This had different conceptual overviews that were clearly beyond the scope of this mapping study; hence, we have validated it to be excluded from the research screening process. However, in other cases it was difficult to assess the relevance of the research papers based on their titles. Thus, in this process, the research review was moved to the second phase of further reading and analysis. This phase consisted of the authors reading and referring to the abstract of every research paper that was passed down from the first phase.

Search strategy

We now present our search on scientific and electronic databases that was utilized to gather the findings presented in this chapter. The search strategy combines the key concepts of designed research questions to retrieve accurate results (University of Leeds, 2019). The electronic databases included high-impact-factor conference proceedings, standards, journals and magazines, early-access articles, courses and books. The following

Table 1: Selected Digital Library

Digital Database	URL
Science direct	https://www.sciencedirect.com
IEEE	https://ieeexplore.ieee.org
ACM	https://dl.acm.org
Springer	https://link.springer.com
ProQuest	https://search.proquest.com
Google Scholar	https://scholar.google.com/
Scopus	https://www.scopus.com

digital libraries listed in Table 1 were used in the automated search process for this study.

Reference search string

The main aim of the search string is to capture all the relevant results that relate to blockchain and assess their impact on Supply Chain Management. The research is of much importance and is of relevance in this day because blockchain technologies have become a new technical paradigm that is driving change across all sectors that creates a digital ledger of transactions to be shared among a distributed network of computers, removing the need for a trusted authority. The search string used in all seven (7) digital library databases is:

> *Application OR Impact* OR Implementation OR Influence** and *Blockchain Technology or Blockchain in Supply Chain Management*

Though our search string uses explicit keywords, our research study was not limited to those keywords only. We intended to discover every dimension of the blockchain technology and its emergence in the field of supply chain management.

Inclusion & exclusion criteria

We utilized certain inclusion and exclusion criteria to screen each paper. It was decided to exclude (1) publication of those papers after 2009 since our research was based on the 10 years till 2009, (2) conference, book reviews, editorials, surveys and notes, (3) certain papers on search engines like IEEE, Springer, ScienceDirect & Scopus that required to be purchased or had a subscription fee, (4) papers that had some other titles related to blockchains. In addition, (5) all papers that were not primarily in English were also excluded.

After application of inclusion and exclusion criteria, all the papers that were screened and found to be duplicates with other search engine results were removed as well. All papers considered were based on Blockchain and supply chain management, and it was decided to move these to the next stage of screening.

Key wording using abstracts

The next stage in the systematic mapping study after screening and finding the relevant studies was through abstract key wording. For this stage, we utilized the procedure that was defined by Petersen (Petersen *et al.*, 2008). Abstract key wording was done in two stages. The first, initial stage comprised of reading the abstract and identifying the keywords and ideas that mirrored the contribution of the paper. In the second step, a higher level of understanding was built up depending on the keywords. We utilized keywords that were clustered and formed categories that mapped the investigations of the study. Once all categories had been grouped, we read all the selected papers. Once, the reading was done, the categories were updated accordingly, and new ones were created to verify if the paper unveiled anything new. Hence, this resulted in a systematic map consisting of clustered categories that formed the basis of all the relevant papers on the mentioned research topic (Figure 2).

Results

The results of the data extracted based on our research are presented in Figure 3. Using the search string "Blockchain Technology", a total of 261,840 papers were retrieved from the selected scientific database. This search also included the papers that were published in the past 10 years. The second criterion limited the search results to those articles titled "Blockchain in Supply Chain Management". The paper titles were

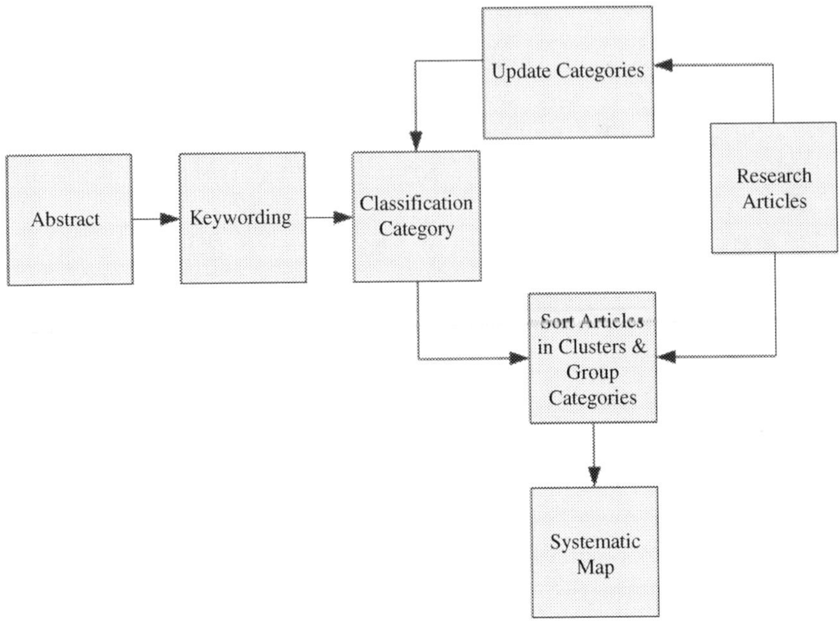

Figure 2: Building the Classification Scheme

scrutinized by four authors, which resulted in the final selection of papers totaling 871. The final criterion used for selection of papers was inclusion of those that were open source, inclusion of journal articles only and exclusion of papers that were not in English (as their main language). Finally, all papers that were screened and found to be duplicates were also removed. This led to a final count of 73 papers.

The abstracts from these papers were reviewed and analyzed by the four authors; however, no papers were excluded as the abstracts had content related to blockchain and SCM.

However, the authors decided to filter some unclear papers in the next round of selection, which was done by reading the entire paper (in-depth analysis). In the final stage of paper selection, four authors scrutinized the entirety of all papers. A total of 56 primary papers were selected by this process.

These 56 primary papers were selected for this research were those that were published between 2010 and 2019. A detailed explanation of this is shown in Figure 4. Interestingly, after analysis, it was found that BCT and SCM technologies have become hot topics of research since

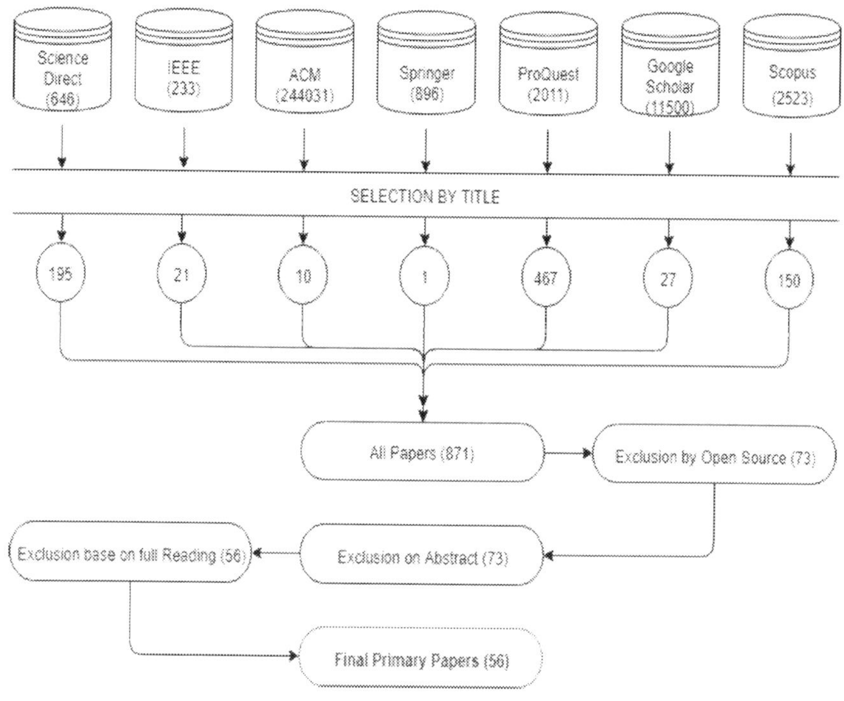

Figure 3: Search/Selection Steps Towards the Paper

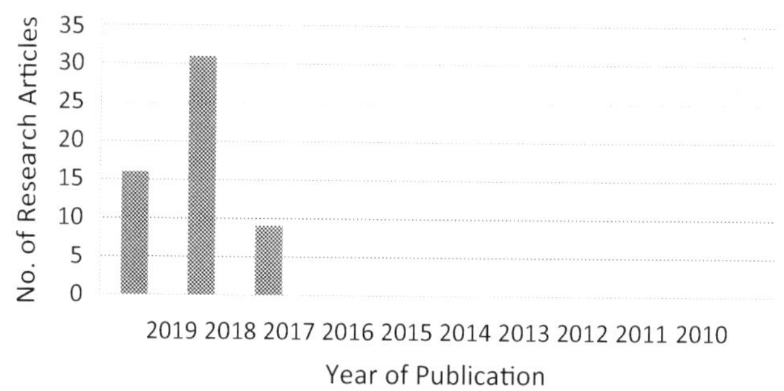

Figure 4: Year of Publication for Selected Research Papers

2017. This shows that BCT and SCM are modern and valuable areas of research. Upon further scrutiny of the publication year, 16 of the papers (28.6%) were published before May 2019 while 31 (55.4%) were published in 2018 and 9 (16.1%) in 2017; from 2010 to 2016, there was no publication on BCT and SCM.

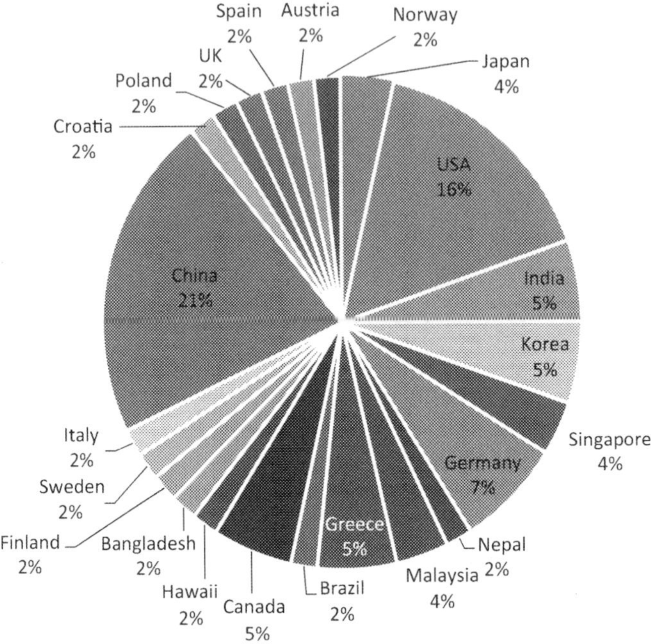

Figure 5: Geographical Distribution of the Selected Papers

The geographical distribution of the selected papers is shown in the Figure 5. The largest number of papers was published in 2018 in China (a total of 21% (12 papers)). On closer analysis, 16% (9) of the papers on Blockchain and Supply chain management were from the USA; 4% (6) of the papers were from Japan, Singapore and Malaysia, respectively. As can be seen from the figure, which shows the distributed percentage for the 23 countries, 13 countries had a segmented percentage of 2% (13 papers) per the analysis. This implies that blockchain has gained interest in recent years. Overall, from 2% to 21%, there was a slight increase in the growing levels of positive impact causing more studies to be carried out on BCT and SCM technologies. This implies that Blockchain and Supply Chain research areas are open, and further studies can still be carried out as these are very recent and new areas of research.

Studies on BCT and SCM made up 74% (32 papers) of the total research articles chosen for the study, showing a positive impact in this field. However, concentrating on the 19% (8) papers, it was found out that

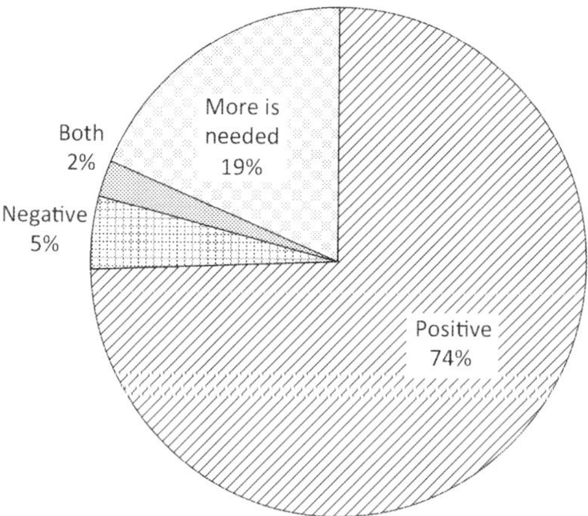

Figure 6: Outcome of the Selected Papers

authors emphasized that although Blockchain technology has been a recent revolution, there must be more research done to ensure that BCT is studied in an in-depth manner and it was also emphasized that it is too early to comment on the positive and negative aspects of BCT. Our results also showed that in 5% (2) of the papers, the authors pointed out that BCT would have a negative impact and may be hard to manage, and hence this technology can also create job loss. In 1 paper (2%), the author discussed both sides, that is, BCT and SCM technologies (Figure 6). These results as a whole gave a good understanding that BCT has positive impacts; however, it is also too early to conclude; hence, more research is required on the negative impacts, and the content of the research study must cover both aspects of the BCT technology as there are fewer publications on this topic.

Furthermore, Table 2 shows the relevant databases and the related papers selected from those databases. This also shows the area or field of research.

The systematic mapping mechanism is presented in the bar graph (Figure 7); the vertical axis represents the area/organization of the study and the horizontal one represents the number of publications.

While looking at the area/organization the publication is based on, 28 papers (50%) are on random topics or are not based on any organization or specific area. This shows that the researchers are more focused on the

Table 2: Primary Research Papers from All Databases

Count	Title	Publication Type	Area
	Science Direct		
1	"Fit-for-purpose?" — Challenges and opportunities for applications of blockchain technology in the future of healthcare	Journal	General
	IEEE		
1	Ultralightweight Mutual Authentication RFID Protocol for Blockchain-enabled Supply Chains	Journal	IT Industry
2	A Novel Blockchain-based Product Ownership Management System (POMS) for Anti-Counterfeits in the Post Supply Chain	Journal	e-Commerce
3	Security, Performance, and Applications of Smart Contracts: A Systematic Survey	Journal	General
4	Blockchain in Industries: A Survey	Journal	General
5	Blockchain in Logistics and Supply Chain: A Lean Approach for Designing Real-world Use Cases	Journal	Logistics
6	Food Safety Traceability System based on Blockchain and EPCIS	Journal	Agriculture
7	Blockchain Applications Usage in Different Domains	Journal	General
8	Autonomous Resource Request Transaction Framework based on Blockchain in Social Network	Journal	General
9	DL-Tags: DLT and Smart Tags for Decentralized, Privacy-preserving and Verifiable Supply Chain Management	Journal	IT Industry
10	When Intrusion Detection Meets Blockchain Technology: A Review	Journal	IT Industry
	Google Scholar		
1	A Novel Blockchain-based Product Ownership Management System (POMS) for Anti-counterfeits in the Post Supply Chain	Journal	General
2	Leveraging Blockchain Technology to Enhance Supply Chain Management in Healthcare	Journal	Health care

Table 2: (*Continued*)

Count	Title	Publication Type	Area
	Google Scholar		
3	A Framework for Blockchain Technology in Rice Supply Chain Management	Journal	Agriculture
4	A Study on the Transparent Price Tracing System in Supply Chain Management based on Blockchain	Journal	General
5	A Blockchain Aided Metric for Predictive Delivery Performance in Supply Chain Management	Journal	General
6	Examples from Blockchain Implementations in Logistics and Supply Chain Management: Exploring the Mindful Use of a New Technology	Journal	Logistics
7	Blockchain in Handicraft Supply-chain Management	Journal	Handicraft
8	The Role of Blockchain Technology Applications in Supply Chain Management	Journal	IT Industry
9	Traceability Decentralization in Supply Chain Management Using Blockchain Technologies	Journal	General
10	An Exploration of Blockchain Technology in Supply Chain Management	Journal	Logistics
11	Blockchain Implementation in Supply Chain Management. Case Study on an e-Commerce Food Retailer	Journal	e-Commerce
12	The Blockchain Application in Supply Chain Management: Opportunities, Challenges and Outlook	Journal	General
13	Blockchain Technology in Supply Chain Management: An Application Perspective	Journal	General
14	Supply Chain Management for Garments Industries Using Blockchain in Bangladesh	Journal	Garment Industry
15	Potential and Barriers to the Implementation of Blockchain Technology in Supply Chain Management	Journal	General
16	The Potential of Blockchain Technology in Solving Green Supply Chain Management Challenges	Journal	General

(*Continued*)

Table 2: (*Continued*)

Count	Title	Publication Type	Area
17	Blockchains, the New Fashion in Supply Chains? — The compatibility of blockchain configurations in supply chain management in the fast fashion industry	Journal	Garment Industry
18	Review of Blockchain Technology & Its Potential in Supply Chain Management	Journal	General
19	A Framework for Blockchain Technology Applications in Supply Chain Management	Journal	IT Industry
	ACM		
1	Block-Supply Chain: A New Anti-counterfeiting Supply Chain Using NFC and Blockchain	Journal	IT Industry
2	Antecedents to the Success of Block Chain Technology Adoption in Manufacturing Supply Chains	Journal	Manufacturing
	Springer		
1	Analysis of Blockchain Technology: Pros, Cons and SWOT	Journal	General
	ProQuest		
1	A Fully Observable Supply Chain Management System Using Block Chain and IOT	Journal	IT Industry
2	Information Sharing for Supply Chain Management based on Block Chain Technology	Journal	Manufacturing
3	Analysis of Coordination Mechanism of Supply Chain Management Information System from the Perspective of Blockchain	Journal	General
4	Easysight Supply Chain Management Co., Ltd. — Announcement on Progress in Investing in Establishing Block Chain Investment Fund	Journal	General
5	Easysight Supply Chain Management Co., Ltd. — Announcement on Plan of Investment in Establishing Block Chain Investment Fund	Journal	General

Table 2: (*Continued*)

Count	Title	Publication Type	Area
	ProQuest		
6	YTO Express Group Co., Ltd. — Notice of Transferring Convertible Corporate Bonds to Zhejiang Cainiao Supply Chain Management Co., Ltd. through Block Trading by Controlling Shareholders	Journal	Banking
	Scopus		
1	"Fit-for-purpose?" — Challenges and opportunities for applications of blockchain technology in the future of healthcare	Journal	Health care
2	Information Technology Outsourcing Chain: Literature Review and Implications for Development of Distributed Coordination	Journal	IT Industry
3	Big Production Enterprise Supply Chain Endogenous Risk Management based on Blockchain	Journal	General
4	Food Safety Traceability System based on Blockchain and EPCIS	Journal	Agriculture
5	Applications of Blockchain Technology to Logistics Management in Integrated Casinos and Entertainment	Journal	Logistics
6	A Study on the Transparent Price Tracing System in Supply Chain Management based on Blockchain	Journal	General
7	Blockchain Practices, Potentials and Perspectives in Greening Supply Chains	Journal	General
8	The Impact of the Blockchain on the Supply Chain: A Theory-based Research Framework and a Call for Action	Journal	General
9	Credit Evaluation System based on Blockchain for Multiple Stakeholders in the Food Supply Chain	Journal	General
10	Applying Blockchain Technology: Evidence from Norwegian Companies	Journal	General
11	Governance on the Drug Supply Chain via G-coin Blockchain	Journal	Health care

(*Continued*)

Table 2: (*Continued*)

Count	Title	Publication Type	Area
12	A Sustainable Home Energy Prosumer-chain Methodology with Energy Tags over the Blockchain	Journal	Energy
13	When Intrusion Detection Meets Blockchain Technology: A Review	Journal	General
14	Permissioned Blockchain Technologies for Academic Publishing	Journal	Publishing
15	A Distributed Ledger for Supply Chain Physical Distribution Visibility	Journal	General
16	A Novel Blockchain-based Product Ownership Management System (POMS) for Anti-counterfeits in the Post Supply Chain	Journal	General

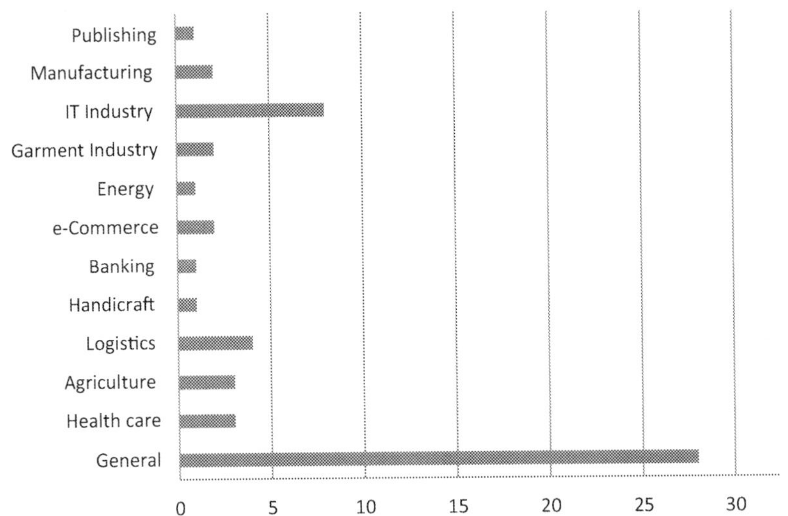

Figure 7: Systematic Map in the Form of a Bar Graph

content that will impact all the organizations rather than limiting their research to one specific industry. The research based on the IT industry stood second out of the 56 primary papers. A total of 8 papers (14.3%) were based on IT-related backgrounds, which again shows that BCT and

SCM research is carried out well in the IT industries. The logistics industry had 4 papers (7.1%) published.

Furthermore, Healthcare and Agricultural sectors are also open areas for research. A total of 3 (5.4%) papers were published in each sector. Other industries such as Handicraft, Banking, e-Commerce, Manufacturing, Energy and Publishing had published 1 (1.8%) and 2 (3.6) papers, respectively.

Discussion

This chapter presents the systematic mapping results of how blockchain technology can influence Supply Chain Management. The systematic mapping study has shown that a majority of the research results that were focused on the positive impacts of BCT in Supply Chain Management. These results were quite sentient because blockchain has greater potential to transform the traditional supply chain. First, the data were retrieved from 7 digital databases and it was identified that a total of 56 papers focused on BCT and SCM. We present early evidence on the areas and topics for research is illustrated in Figure 8.

The novelty of this chapter lies on the relationship between blockchain and supply chain management. However, only 5% (2) of the papers discussed the negative impact of blockchains. We have summarized the negative impacts of blockchains based on the study by Treiblmaier (2018)

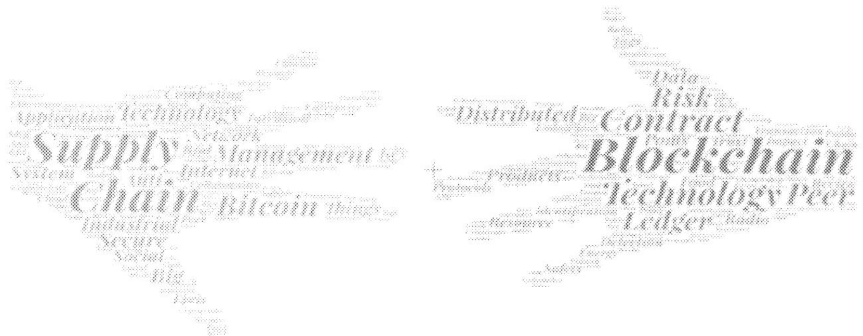

Figure 8: Taxonomy on Research Topics

who said that from a technological point of view that although blockchains have been gradually developed over the recent years, the technology does not significantly represent a single monolithic artifact. Hence, it becomes crucial for future researchers to clearly address and specify the type of blockchain they are particularly investigating. Furthermore, the adoption of Blockchain technology with SCM also influences transaction costs. This refers to the internal and external costs and can thus lead to the shrinking and expansion of the company boundaries. The study does have an interdisciplinary nature where systematic mapping is applied; however, the potential business impacts of blockchain remain undiscovered and underresearched.

The traditional supply chains inherently suffer from single point failure issue. This chapter presents the evidences and results obtained from 32 out of the 56 papers, accounting for 74% of the positive impact results from the selected publications. As the arrival of blockchain technology is set to significantly transform the supply chain activities, it was found that scholars have begun to research more on the positive impacts of BCT and SCM rather than the negative impacts. This result analyzed presents the topic facet that blockchains have globally become an area of growing interest within the 23 countries analyzed and it is likely to be a topic of interest for research in other countries as well. According to the research by Yoo (2018), blockchain technology enhances security of the data management systems. It was also found that blockchain technology enables the working of the operation process in a transparent manner (Meng & Qian, 2018a). The positive aspect of BCT technology has been actively researched as several papers classified blockchains as cutting-edge information technology. The traditional supply chain management has been transformed with the potential benefits of blockchain technologies. For instance, early evidences showed that the link of blockchain with supply chain management activities will most likely increase transparency and accountability. It was also retrieved from several positive papers that the SCM management objectives are impacted by the potential of blockchain. Some of the SCM objectives include the cost, speed, quality, sustainability, flexibility and dependability. It is further underlined that the incorporation of blockchains into supply chain management can have several advantages if established with the traditional centralized supply chain.

Academic and professional discourse researchers have identified a wide spectrum in the current SCM, and this can be potentially solved through BCT technologies. The study that was carried out connected the three research questions in proposing blockchain as a new platform for the supply chain management system. Approximately 74% of the positive results obtained from the selected publications were useful in choosing the innovation of BCT on SCM. "Blockchain was proposed generally as a system that guarantees transparency in product distribution for SCM systems" (Yoo and Won, 2018). In addition, the developed blockchain technology can fulfil the gap existing in SCM by a new platform for the operating networks.

Limitations

Publication bias, misclassification of papers, biased selection of papers and inaccurate extraction of data are some of the limitations of this chapter. Publication bias refers to the issue of some papers being omitted as there is a greater tendency to publish positive papers. Misinterpretation of the selection criteria used leads to a biased selection of papers due to the inclusion and exclusion criteria applied during the search process. Inaccurate extraction of data and misclassification of papers is possible due to the threat that the authors may have gone off track while collecting data. Furthermore, some papers were also left out after the initial search as they were not available for public access.

Conclusions

In this chapter, we propose blockchain to be a new platform for the supply chain operating network. Blockchain approaches can help improve the current supply chain network. The study conducted in this chapter was focused on the impacts of BCT and its potential to improve supply chain management effectively. The results were obtained through the Systematic Mapping Process that was followed on each aspect of refining the data to get the best results relating to the research topic that was chosen. The research was further guided through the 4 specific research questions.

A total of 56 papers were selected, with 2018 being the latest year of publication. The results analyzed demonstrated that 5% of the papers focused on the negative impacts of blockchain, 74% on the positive impacts, 19% on the areas where more research was required and, finally, 2% of the papers discussed both the positive and negative impact. This implied that blockchain technology is a recent area of study that is seeing advances in many sectors.

Recommendations and Future Research

After conducting this study, it is seen that the search result is positively skewed, accounting for 74% of the papers; hence, there is a possibility of papers that were written from a neutral or negative perspective being missed out. Therefore, for the results to be normally distributed it is recommended that more research needs to be done in terms of balancing the positive and negative papers. Targeting more databases as a source for identifying relevant research with more rigorous exclusion and inclusion criteria can help get better results for more accurate analysis. From this study, it is very evident that there is a gap in knowledge on the shortcomings of BCT in SCM, and therefore it is highly recommended to conduct further research in this area.

Furthermore, additional research needs to be carried out in terms of ascertaining blockchain as a new platform for supply chain. Researchers can also use this study to conduct further research on how exactly blockchains can be used as a new platform for supply chain.

References

Al Barghuthi, N. B., Mohamed, H. J., Said, H. E. (2018). Blockchain in Supply Chain Trading. In *2018 Fifth HCT Information Technology Trends (ITT) IEEE*, pp. 336–341.

Aptea, S., Petrovskyb, N. (2016). Will Blockchain Technology Revolutionize Excipient Supply Chain Management? *Journal of Excipients and Food Chemicals*, 76–78.

Boschia, A. A., Borina, R., Raimundob, J. C., Batocchio, A. (2018). *22nd Cambridge International Manufacturing Symposium*. University of Cambridge: Brazil, 2(6–10), 71

Crosby, M., Nachiappan, P., Verma, S., Kalyanaraman, V. (2016). BlockChain Technology: Beyond Bitcoin. *Applied Innovation Review*, 6–19.

Friedlmaier, M., Tumasjan, A., Welpe, I. (2018). Disrupting Industries with Blockchain: The Industry, Venture Capital Funding, and Regional Distribution of Blockchain Ventures. *In Proceedings of the 51st Hawaii International Conference System Sciences*, Waikoloa Village, HI, USA, pp. 3–6.

Hackius, M. P. (2017). Blockchain in Logistics and Supply Chain: Trick or Treat? *Digitalization in Supply Chain Management and Logistics*, 23, pp. 3–18.

Heutger, M., Kückelhaus, M. (2018). *Perspectives on the Upcoming Impact of Blockchain*. DHL Customer Solutions & Innovation: Troisdorf.

Kim, M., Hilton, B., Burks, Z., Reyes, J. (2018). Integrating Blockchain, Smart Contract-Tokens, and IoT to Design a Food Traceability Solution. In the *2018 IEEE 9th Annual Information Technology, Electronics and Mobile Communication Conference (IEMCON)*, pp. 335–340.

Kitchenham, B., Charters, S. (2007). Guidelines for Performing Systematic Literature Reviews in Software Engineering. *The Journal of Systems and Software*.

Lin, I.-C., Liao, T.-C. (2017). A Survey of Blockchain Security Issues and Challenges. *International Journal of Network Security*, 6533 6539.

Marr, B. (2018). How Blockchain Will Transform The Supply Chain And Logistics Industry. *BlockChain*. Retrieved from: https://www.forbes.com/sites/bernardmarr/2018/03/23/how-blockchain-will-transform-the-supply-chain-and-logistics-industry/#2a5842805fec.

McKinsey (2019). Blockchain Technology for Supply Chains — A must or a maybe? *Business Function*. Retrieved from: https://www.mckinsey.com/business-functions/operations/our-insights/blockchain-technology-for-supply-chainsa-must-or-a-maybe. Accessed on March 6, 2019.

Meng, M. H., Qian, Y. (2018a). *The Blockchain Application in Supply Chain Management: Opportunities, Challenges and Outlook* (No. 596). EasyChair.

Meng, M. H., Qian, Y. (2018b). A Blockchain Aided Metric for Predictive Delivery Performance in Supply Chain Management. In the *2018 IEEE International Conference on Service Operations and Logistics, and Informatics (SOLI)*, Singapore, pp. 285–290.

Miraz, M., Ali, M. (2018). Applications of Blockchain Technology Beyond Cryptocurrency. *Annals of Emerging Technologies in Computing*, 1–6.

Mougayar, W., Buterin, V. (2016). *The Business Blockchain: Promise, Practice, and Application of the Next Internet Technology*. John Wiley & Sons, Inc.: New Jersey.

O'Byrne, R (2017). How blockchain can transform the supply chain. Logistics Bureau.

Perboli, G., Musso, S., Rosano, M. (2018). Blockchain in Logistics and Supply Chain: A Lean Approach for Designing Real-World Use Cases. *IEEE Access*, 6, 62018–62028.

Petersen, O., & Jansson, F. (2017). Blockchain Technology in Supply Chain Traceability Systems.

Risius, M., & Spohrer, K. (2017). A Blockchain Research Framework. *Business & Information Systems Engineering*, 59(6), 385–409.

Swan, M. (2015). Blockchain: Blueprint for a New Economy. "O'Reilly Media, Inc.".

Treiblmaier, H. (2018). The Impact of the Blockchain on the Supply Chain: A Theory-Based Research Framework and a Call for Action. *Supply Chain Management*, 23(6), 545–559. doi:10.1108/SCM-01-2018-0029

University of Leeds (2019). *Literature Searching Explained*. Retrieved from Library Leeds: https://library.leeds.ac.uk/info/1404/literature_searching/14/literature_searching_explained/4.

Yeoh, P. (2017). Regulatory Issues in Blockchain Technology. *Journal of Financial Regulation and Compliance*.

Yli-Huumo, J., Ko, D., Choi, S., Park, S., & Smolander, K. (2016). Where is Current Research on Blockchain Technology? — A systematic review. PloS one, 11(10), e0163477.

Yoo, M., Won, Y. (2018). A Study On The Transparent Price Tracing System in Supply Chain Management Based on Blockchain. *Sustainability (Switzerland)*, 10(11). doi:10.3390/su10114037.

Younes, G. (2018). The GDPR-Blockchain Paradox: A Work Around. In Proceedings of the 1st Workshop on GDPR Compliant Systems, Co-located with 19th ACM International Middleware Conference.

Zhu, Q., & Kouhizadeh, M. (2019). Blockchain Technology, Supply Chain Information, and Strategic Product Deletion Management. *IEEE Engineering Management Review*, 47(1), 36–44.

Chapter 9

Comparison of Three Different Darknet Cryptocurrencies in e-Commerce in Our Digital Era

Sam Goundar*, Rahul Chand†, Fariha Tafsil‡, Reema Mala§ and Reshma Nath¶

The University of the South Pacific, Suva, Fiji

**sam.goundar@gmail.com*

†s11098227@student.usp.ac.fj

‡tafsilfariha@gmail.com

§s11031131@student.usp.ac.fj

¶s11091515@student.usp.ac.fj

Abstract

The emergence of the Internet has opened a world of possibilities to connect and interact through web portals and to exchange information over the network. In the past decade, buying and selling of goods and services online has become more common through e-commerce. With the advent of Cryptocurrencies, the possibilities of e-commerce have reached new heights for all web users who see potential in this technology. Cryptocurrencies have opened new dimensions based on a Blockchain technology for e-commerce through decentralization; increased privacy and digitalization of coins allow users to anonymously trade online. This has become more common in the Darknet, which is simply the unindexed side of the Internet. This chapter compares the three Cryptocurrencies, namely bitcoin, ethereum and monero, used for e-commerce in the Darknet.

Introduction

There will be a continuous increase in the overall usage of e-commerce as Internet becomes easily available even in the most remote places through networking technologies (Yazdanifard, 2011). Global e-commerce insights (2022) have forecasted that the decrease in the overall price of mobile devices has made it easier to connect to the Internet (Statista Global, 2018). This will allow accessibility to e-commerce websites from anywhere in the world, and this will surpass the trade market by 2022. This unprecedented growth will allow traders to dive into Cryptocurrencies to effectively and efficiently buy and sell without the concern of any third-party organizations handling the money. Cryptocurrencies have shaped the e-commerce market to allow traders to explore the depth of the web, more commonly known as the Darknet, through possibilities like never-before-seen capacities of security privileges when buying and selling online anonymously. This has led to an increase of e-commerce activity in the Darknet for end-users to explore an emerging Blockchain technology.

Blockchain technology is a revolutionary paradigm in Cryptocurrencies. As the digitalization of trade grows, more organizations head towards the increasingly popular marvel of Blockchain technologies for efficiency and to create value towards the exchange of goods and services online. Blockchain creates the foundation on which cryptocurrencies work by simply decentralizing the transaction through interconnected blocks, built upon several algorithms to protect the transaction. To date, the Blockchain algorithm used in cryptocurrency has never been compromised due to its sophisticated methodology in storing the transaction (Severeijns, 2017). This feature used in cryptocurrencies gives users the upper hand in Darknet when using the e-commerce by addressing some of the issues faced when dealing with fiat currencies, that is the money used every day for buying goods and services.

Traditional e-commerce deals with flat currencies, which are still used, in the Darknet but with the added risk of being hacked or exposed easily, especially if the user prefers anonymity. Flat currencies are unable to satisfy the abovementioned requirements. The transactions that occur in the Darknet deal with many risks, especially the capacity of hackers to sabotage entire transactions. These hacking issues are more common in the Darknet since it becomes easier for hackers to sniff open ports and alter protocols due to the lack of a legal statutory body behind Darknet (Kurtz, 2017). Cryptocurrencies promise a swarm of computational technologies to specifically solve the issues faced in Darknet e-commerce. This involves the use of distributed Blockchain Ledger technology to uphold the true power that cryptocurrency promises. For the purpose of the research done in this chapter, the three different cryptocurrencies selected are Bitcoins, Ethereum and Monero, from the other thousands of choices. These three cryptocurrencies selected have different algorithms to support their uniqueness. To be successful, these cryptocurrencies will need to measure the best option of Darknet e-commerce using the following essential factors:

- **Security:** One of the biggest factors to consider in cryptocurrencies when dealing with e-commerce on the Darknet is the security issues that cryptocurrencies face. Darknet has been surrounded by a higher level of risk when compared to normal e-commerce used in the surface web. Thus, there have been a number of security concerns with each of the cryptocurrencies.
- **Market Trend:** Each cryptocurrency has its own unique market analytics based on price. The transaction cost and the speed of each transaction depends on the algorithms and features it promises, which keep upgrading overtime. Different users have different usability requirements and, based on that information, a particular cryptocurrency can be selected.
- **Legality:** Cryptocurrencies are more popular due to their attached legal issues. Based on that data, users can predict how safe or vulnerable each transaction will be as it goes through online. None of the regulating bodies support Cryptocurrencies, which makes it more of a threat to the flat currencies. Flat currencies are those in control by the government, which makes it a more reliable option for many, thus making cryptocurrencies very vulnerable to legal issues.

- **Market Force:** Users are also influenced by the demand and supply of each cryptocurrency. The demand and supply chain creates a guiding structure to predict the market share and forecast its worth.
- **Internal Competition:** Based on the abovementioned factors, these give a clear insight to users on how each cryptocurrency is performing individually through rapid competition with the others. Most cryptocurrencies are formed through the same concept used by the pioneers, but, with slight alterations or tweaks to improve the performance.

Cryptocurrency Technology in the Darknet

The use of cryptocurrencies has given added security in the Darknet. Users find it more efficient to use cryptocurrencies in the Darknet.

Bitcoin (BTC)

In 2009, an unidentified hacker or a group of hackers under the name Satoshi Nakamoto created a peer-to-peer and decentralized financial system called "Bitcoin" and published it as a whitepaper (Kaushal *et al.*, 2017). Since its creation, it is by far the most successful one although numerous private cryptocurrencies have been introduced. According to Michalik (2015), bitcoin is a powerful and successful digital currency; based on cryptography and a decentralized ledger, it has simultaneously been heralded as the future of finance and a gateway to the criminal underworld. It has been getting a lot of media attention, and its total market value has reached US$20 billion in March 2017. More importantly, a number of central banks have recently started to explore the adoption of cryptocurrency and Blockchain technologies for retail and large-value payments. For instance, the People's Bank of China aims to develop a nationwide digital currency based on Blockchain technology (Figure 1). Figure 1 depicts blockchain data structure, whereby each block is identified by a hash generated using the cryptographic hash algorithm. It is an ordered back-linked list of blocks of transactions that can be stored in simple database or as a flat file.

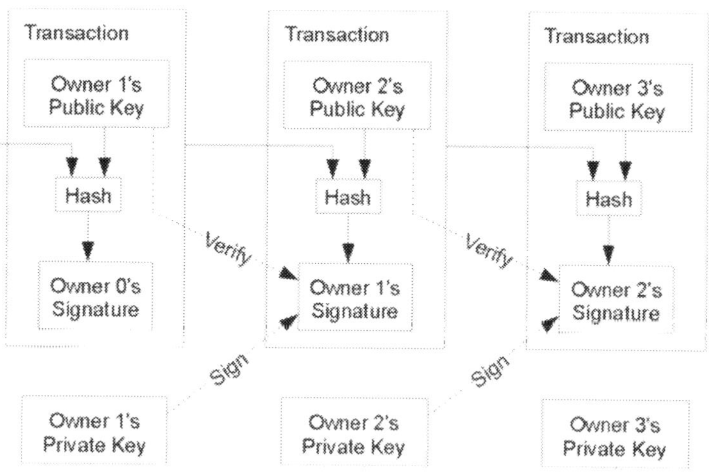

Figure 1: Simple Structure of Bitcoin Transactions (Liu *et al.*, 2018)

Ethereum (ETC)

According to Orcutt (2018), Ethereum was launched in 2015 with a market value of $70 billion.

Ethereum uses its own coin known as ether (Etheruem, 2020). When we look at cryptocurrencies, our mind focuses on the payment methods they have been created for, but Ethereum is different from the other cryptocurrencies. Ethereum serves as a payment method and also as a computing platform, as mentioned by Dika (2017). Ethereum is powered by Blockchain technology allowing full transparency, without a mediator to control. Most of the cryptocurrencies are working with Blockchain technology, so what makes Ethereum stand out is the contract method that it uses.

Figure 2 shows clearly how Ethereum platform works with contracts. There are two types of contracts: external or smart contract that makes Ethereum different and more secure in comparison with others. The moment an Ethereum smart contract code executes, the code executes on every single node on the Blockchain and must reach the same result at the end of the execution of the code on each node for the transaction to be considered valid, thus making it a more secure process (Bacina, 2018).

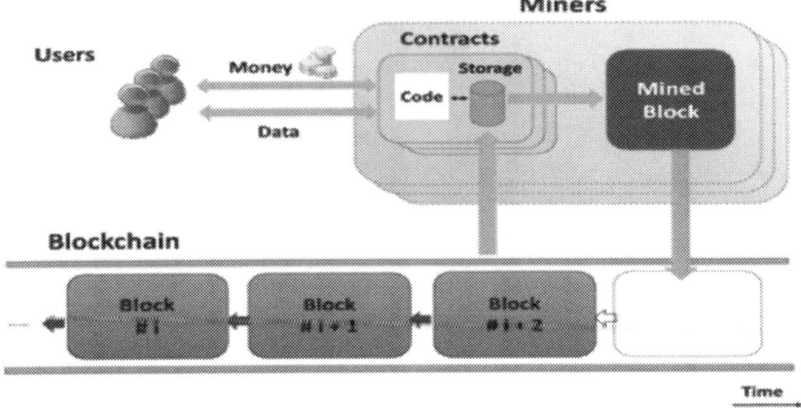

Figure 2: Semantics of a Blockchain Platform with Smart Contracts (Dika, 2017)

Monero (XMR)

Similar to the above cryptocurrencies in terms of having a Blockchain platform, Monero goes an extra mile to provide highly secured transactions that are untraceable and private. This allows users to send and receive payments with complete anonymity. Not only in terms of security, but the cryptocurrency also gives confidence to users who value total privacy, especially in Darknet e-commerce for the financial transactions (Coin Checkup Organization, 2018).

The original team of Monero comprised 30 core developers, and later it was owned and controlled by a big community. The algorithm behind Monero keeps upgrading, similar to Ethereum, to provide better efficiency to its users (Saberhagen, 2013). This cryptocurrency was initially created by Nicolas Van Saberhagen in April 2014.

The technology behind Monero (Figure 3) is the use of minimum ring signature; this is what actually gives the privacy feature that automatically hides all transactions. Having the untraceable feature, another technology used is the ring signature, which mixes up the address of the payer and payee with their transaction, thus making it harder to find the exact location.

Apart from being open source, Monero can work in any major operating system such as Windows, Mac and Linux. The processing power is far less compared to bitcoin. A simple low-end CPU is capable enough to mine Monero, which also has less electricity consumption.

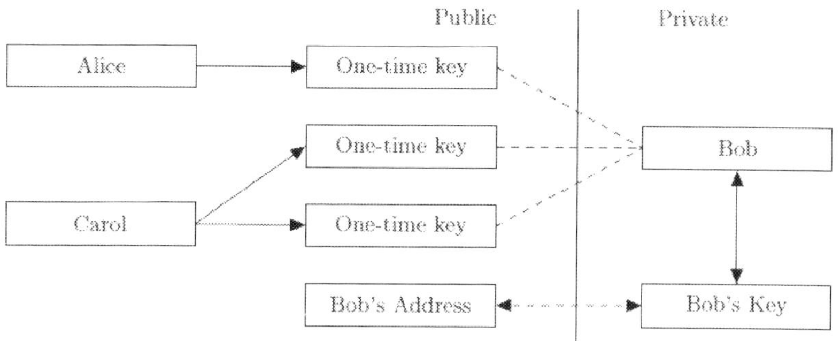

Figure 3: Semantics of Monero Cryptonote Keys (Kumar *et al.*, 2018)

Literature Survey

For the purpose of this research, the authors were able to identify 42 research papers published from 2011 to 2019 on cryptocurrencies and Darknet e-commerce. After sorting the research papers, a total 32 were found to be relevant to the research.

Market force

Cryptocurrencies have their own reasons for existence. The first ever cryptocurrency created was the Bitcoin. Bitcoin was incepted in the year 2009, and is gaining popularity. However, Urquhart concluded his 2016 paper by stating that Bitcoin is not weakly efficient (Brauneis & Mestel, 2018).

The idea for Ethereum was conceived from bitcoin by looking at the vulnerabilities of bitcoin in 2013. Ether was launched in 2015, and it became very popular in a short time. The lifetime of Ethereum in the market is very short, so it is still a baby compared with the other cryptocurrencies. It slowly started growing, but then in 2016 there was a security breach in which an organization called the Decentralized Autonomous Organization (DAO) was sitting on 7.9 million units of ether, or roughly $132.7 million at the time, when it was hit with a devastating attack.

Unidentified hackers exploited vulnerabilities in the Ethereum system and stole around $50 million worth of ether from the DOA (Coin Bundle Team, 2018). This was covered by the media, and market force withdrew from ether; thus, a big drop was noted. Ethereum developers did not give up and secured the ether by creating a better version of ether [ETC] with smart contracts (Romano & Schmid, 2017), visible to everyone in the market since media coverage continued, and thus the new ether picked up very quickly as this was a new and improved version of cryptocurrency (Dika, 2017).

The market force is a factor that affects the price and the growth of any cryptocurrency. Market forces determined the ether's (ETC) trend and the fluctuation in value. Its popularity was determined by the market forces as well.

Internal competition

Competition exists everywhere, whether it be the local currencies or the digital coin, i.e. Cryptocurrencies.

As stated by Hanna (2014), "winner takes all" applies to our cryptocurrency rates that are in competition. The digital coins that are in competition will have a winner if they hold the maximum market value. After its inception in the year 2009, Bitcoin ranks the highest to date; however, its value is decreasing with the growing number of other cryptocurrencies.

The year 2017 was a good year for Ethereum. Due to a lot of security issues with other cryptocurrencies, Ethereum gained much more popularity that year, and this allowed Ethereum to be second in line behind bitcoin. Ethereum is still trending in the competition as its smart contracts have provided a much more secure method of operation (Hanna, 2014).

Internal competition has certain factors that allow a particular cryptocurrency to stand out. These include the security of the cryptocurrency and market value of the cryptocurrency in comparison with others, and all this leads to one winner in the internal competition among the cryptocurrencies.

Security

According to Demchenko, when it comes to bitcoins, it is considered an investment itself and not just as instrument of investment, considering its ever changing value. The role of bitcoins in the financial instruments market is limited to future contracts and investment activity; it cannot be considered as security (Demchenko, 2017). The U.S. Securities and Exchange Commission (SEC) issued two orders BZX and NYSE Arca Order to not allow securities with bitcoin, as their concern is that bitcoin markets are unregulated and susceptible to manipulation (Hu *et al.*, 2017).

According to Gurgaon (2017), SER is the first ECM vendor to cleverly incorporate ECM and Blockchain technology that acts as a security guard for all parties concerned and eliminates the possible distrust against the owner of the collaboration platform.

Toyoda *et al.* (2017) also states that Ethereum security works on Blockchain-based decentralized cryptocurrency where any code execution is possible. Toyoda explains in depth in his paper how Blockchain technology works best for Ethereum.

NandarAugun (2017) has mentioned smart contract being introduced in the blockchain method to improve security. He explains that the Ethereum Blockchain consists of two types of accounts: externally owned account and contract account to specify an authorized person of SH (SuperHash). During the installation, an externally owned account has been automatically created as a default. A contract account can be set up with the policies for handling transactions, which is known as smart contract. A smart contract is a legal agreement between parties for carrying out operations.

Rauhani (2017) agrees with Yu Nandar, whereby smart contract is more favored, as this improves the security system of Ethereum.

Market value

The market value keeps on fluctuating every minute based on the activities of the users, which then causes a shift in the supply and demand of the cryptocurrencies.

As Orcutt (2018) has mentioned, all crypto currencies are not equal. It is evident from the graph that it all started with its initial market value and then later on it either trended up or moved down the graph, showing a reduction in the value. Bitcoin started with a market value as in Figure 4 of $163 billion, and its current market capitalization is $112,298,682,388 (CoinLore). Ethereum started with a market value of $70 billion and currently stands at $20,796,583,911, a reduction of $203.17 per ether (Etherscan).

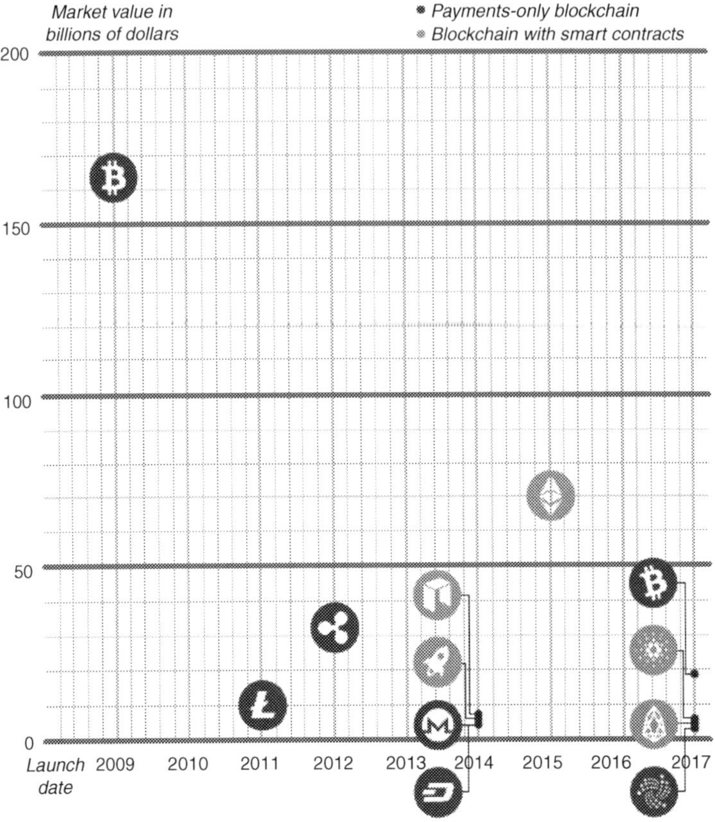

Figure 4: Market Value of Cryptocurrencies

Legality

Bitcoin has faced legal issues that have been taken to court. Bitcoin creators had no intention of illegal and criminal activities; however, individuals use it illegally. Individuals do so since bitcoin characteristics such as anonymity and no requirement of personal identity information tend to be advantageous in these cases. Bitcoin allows for easy money laundering (international transfers) without supervision, and as it is peer-to-peer, it requires just Internet access — hence use in illegal activities is rampant as its infrastructure is spread across the globe and is difficult to intercept individual transactions (Ciaian *et al.*, 2016).

Considering the role of Bitcoin in investment activity, its involvement in future contracts, in a particular case the U.S. Securities and Exchange Commission charged a man from Texas and his company for defrauding investors in a Ponzi scheme involving bitcoins (an investment scam that involves the payment of purported returns to existing investors from funds contributed by new investors). The defendant was sentenced to 18 months in prison (Demchenko, 2017).

Ethereum has not faced any legal issues yet. The smart contracts are more like legal agreements that bind things together, but if there are violations of the smart contracts then legal issues would arise. In the span of 4 years from its birth in the year 2015 till 2019, no legal issues have arisen.

Ethereum is based on open-source software, but license issues will slowly arise since, according to Savare (2017), the Ethereum Foundation currently utilizes a variety of open-source licenses for Ethereum's different components. To make matters more complicated, the body has indicated that it has not yet selected a final open-source license on which the core of Ethereum will be made available in the future.

Results Obtained

Our results were obtained through our research questions. The answers to these are provided in the following.

Is cryptocurrency the future of money? If yes, how?

Yes, cryptocurrency is the future of money.

Cryptocurrency has almost eliminated physical and card money and is well established in the market. Though it has security concerns for some and there are other issues for the others, it has already made a mark, and slowly the code developers are trying to eliminate errors and are succeeding.

Cryptocurrency has shown its advantages, which far outweigh the disadvantages. It has proven to be worthy; so, yes, cryptocurrency is the future of money.

Is using cryptocurrencies in the darkweb legal?

Using cryptocurrencies in the darkweb is legal. So far, most of the sites are using cryptocurrencies. If exchange of goods and services are for illegal purposes, then the activity becomes illegal, but the cryptocurrency remains legal. Most of the illegal activities use such cryptocurrencies where it cannot be traced back so as to evade being caught doing illegal exchanges, e.g. buying drugs etc, if illegal in the country.

Which type of cryptocurrency is better for e-commerce?

The selected three cryptocurrencies for the study showed their own benefits in different ways that cannot be compared directly. Bitcoin, Ethereum [ETC] and Monero are all in the top trending cryptocurrency. **Monero** is selected to be the best cryptocurrency for e-commerce even though it ranks fifth because of privacy features that benefit both Darknet and the surface web (Table 1). Other benefits that added to the decision of selecting Monero were looking at its security and the fact that it uses a new private key in every transaction, which is decomposed after the transaction, thus making it impossible to trace back. Monero also attracts more people because of its anonymity feature and cheap transactions.

Table 1: Comparison of Three Darknet Cryptocurrencies

	Bitcoin (BTC)	Ethereum (ETC)	Monero (EMR)
Internal competition	First place	Second place	Fifth place
Security	Not considered secure enough	Is excellent due to smart contracts	Uses unique composite public key in every transaction
Market value [2018]	Fluctuating [better than ethereum]	Fluctuating $20,796,583,911 $203.17 per ether	It has been increasing due to its privacy feature
Legality	Few issues, bitcoin is considered legal; however, usage of it depends on carelessness on cryptocurrency owners	No major issues seen. Possible, can arise due to licensing issues	Prime choice for hackers due to its untraceable trait

Table 1: (*Continued*)

	Bitcoin (BTC)	**Ethereum (ETC)**	**Monero (EMR)**
Market force	Ranks first from its inception; however, its value is diminishing with the evolution of other cryptocurrencies	Allowed Ethereum to remain in market with the new improved version (ETC)	High demand due to its anonymity feature and cheap transaction, especially common in Darknet

Conclusions

Upon thorough literature review of Bitcoin, Ethereum and Monero, it was noted that all cryptocurrencies are best in their own ways. Direct comparison could not be made with values, but trends were noted, and this was used to answer the research questions that were formulated.

Cryptocurrency is trending in the market, and many researchers have discussed in their papers that cryptocurrency is here to stay. Looking at Bitcoin, Ethereum and Monero, Ethereum ranks 2nd to bitcoin at the moment, but will slowly overtake all other cryptocurrencies, whereas Monero will lead in the Darknet.

Cryptocurrencies are being used in the Darknet as a medium of exchange for things such as illegal drugs, weapons, child trafficking, etc.

e-commerce, being introduced in today's technical environment, has led to the changes we see today as the medium of exchange. The changes are that from Physical money to card and to cryptocurrency, which is here to stay. Cryptocurrency will further improve in the near future in terms of security, since that is what it currently lacks. Out of the three cryptocurrencies, Monero is the cryptocurrency that will lead the market of e-commerce since it outshines the others in terms of security, and the best feature that it carries with it is that it is untraceable at the moment.

References

Aung, Y. N. and Tantidham, T. (2017). Review of Ethereum: Smart home case study. In 2017 2nd International Conference on Information Technology (INCIT), IEEE, pp. 1–4.

Bacina, M. (2018). When Two Worlds Collide: Smart Contracts and the Australian Legal System. *Journal of Internet Law*, 21(8), 1–27.

Brauneis, A., Mestel, R. (2018). Price Discovery of Cryptocurrencies: Bitcoin and Beyond. *Economics Letters*, 165, 58–61.

Ciaian, P., Rajcaniova, M., Kancs, D. (2016). The Digital Agenda of Virtual Currencies: Can BitCoin Become a Global Currency? *Information Systems and eBusiness Management,* 14(4), 883–919.

Coin Bundle Team (2018). Ethereum: Evolution. Retrieved from: https://medium.com/@coinbundle. Accessed February 29, 2020.

Coin Checkup Organization (2018). Purpose of Monero. Retrieved from Coin Checkup: The Crypto Research Platform: https://coincheckup.com/coins/monero/purpose.

CoinLore (n.d.). Retrieved from: Cryptocurrency Prices By Market Capitalization: https://www.coinlore.com/?gclid=Cj0KCQjw08XeBRC0ARIsAP_gaQAWg1QGoB3JIPvoIsgjH2PoqgmqSFk0_5Ruhr7ZiOJaPV-Wii7D4d4aAol9EALw_wcB.

Demchenko, O. (2017). Bitcoin: Legal Definition and Its Place in Legal Framework. *Journal of International Trade, Logistics and Law,* 3(1), 23–42.

Dika, A. (2017). Ethereum Smart Contracts: Security Vulnerabilities and Security Tools. *NTNU*, 8–20.

Etherscan. (n.d.). Retrieved from Total Ether Supply and Market Capitalization: https://etherscan.io/stat/supply.

Etheruem (2020). What is Etheruem? Retrieved from: https://ethereum.org/ what-is-ethereum/. Accessed February 29, 2020.

Gurgaon (2017). Doxis4 Adds a Whole New Level of Security to Content and Collaboration. *Doxis,* 4, 1.

Hanna, H. (2014). Competition in the Cryptocurrency Market. *SSRN Electronic Journal*, 5.

Hu, W., Maese, V. A., Wink, S. P., Valdez, Y. D., Yatter, D. K. (2017). What Do the SEC's Recent Bitcoin Disapproval Orders Really Mean for Investors? Retrieved from: https://corpgov.law.harvard.edu/2017/04/27/what-do-the-secs-recent-bitcoin-disapproval-orders-really-mean-for-investors/. Accessed February 29, 2020.

Kaushal, P. K., Bagga, A., Sobti, R. (2017). Evolution of Bitcoin and Security Risk in Bitcoin Wallets. In *2017 International Conference on Computer, Communications and Electronics (Comptelix).*

Kumar, A., Fischer, C., Tople, S., Saxena, P. (2018). A Traceability Analysis of Monero's Blockchain. *National University of Singapore*, 11.

Kurtz, J. A. (2017). *Hacking Wireless Access Points Cracking, Tracking and Signal Jacking.* Cambridge: Elsevier Inc.

Liu, Y., Li, R., Liu, X., Wang, J., Tang, C., Kang, H. (2018). Enhancing Anonymity of Bitcoin Based on Ring Signature Algorithm. In *2017 13th International Conference on Computational Intelligence and Security (CIS).*

Michalik, V. (2015). Dark Markets: Anonymity in Bitcoin; *M2 Presswire.*

NandarAugun, Y. (2017). Review of Ethereum: Smart Home Case Study. *INCIT*, 8–9.

The Evolution and Development of E-Commerce Market and E-Cash. In *2nd International Conference on Measurement and Control Engineering (ICMCE 2011)*, ASME Press.

Orcutt, M. (2018). No Ripple Isn't the Next Bitcoin. Retrieved from: https://www.technologyreview.com/s/609958/no-ripple-isnt-the-next-bitcoin/. Accessed February 29, 2020.

Romano, D., Schmid, G. (2017). Beyond Bitcoin: A Critical Look at Blockchain-based Systems. *Cryptography*, 1(2), 15.

Saberhagen, N. V. (2013). CryptoNote v 2.0. *CryptoNote Whitepaper*, 3.

Savare, M. (2017). *CoinDesk.* Retrieved from: https://www.coindesk.com/coders-beware-licensing-issues-abound-ethereum-apps/.

Severeijns, L. (2017). What is Blockchain? How is it going to. *Vrije Universiteit Amsterdam*, 15.

Statista Global (2018). Global Statista. Retrieved from Ecommerce Market: https://www.statista.com/outlook/243/100/ecommerce/worldwide.

Toyoda, K., Mathiopoulos, P. T., Sasase, I., Ohtsuki, T. (2017). A Novel Blockchain-Based Product Ownership Management System (POMS) for Anti-Counterfeits in the Post Supply Chain. *IEEE Access*, 5, 17465–17477.

Yazdanifard, A. (2011). The Evolution and Development of E-Commerce Market and E-Cash. In *International Conference on Measurement and Control Engineering*, Kolkata, India.

Chapter 10

Cryptocurrencies — An Assessment of Global Adoption Trends

Sam Goundar*, Niumaia Tabunakawai†, Jobe Tamata‡, Arpana Deb§ and Salsabil Nusair¶

The University of the South Pacific, Suva, Fiji

**sam.goundar@gmail.com*

†S11003552@student.usp.ac.fj

‡S02008742@student.usp.ac.fj

§arpana.deb@usp.ac.fj

¶nusair_s@usp.ac.fj

Abstract

Government and state approaches to any venture first begin with regulations being kept in place to safeguard its interests as well as those of its citizens. Cryptocurrency adoption on a global scale has been led by major players such as the U.S. and China, while some smaller countries have achieved comparable success. In this chapter, we analyze and assess a country's level of cryptocurrency adoption on the basis of its regulatory framework. We then classify this approach according to the business function that regulates the use of these cryptocurrencies. We also derive a gradual approach to cryptocurrency adoption and regulation, which can be used by fledgling countries new to cryptocurrency.

Introduction

Cryptocurrency (CC) is mainly known as digital cash or virtual currency that works as a medium of exchange using cryptography to process financial transactions, create new units and verify transactions (Supriya, 2018). CCs have been in existence for a while, but it was the introduction of Bitcoin by Nakamoto that sealed its future as the first truly decentralized system. Decentralization is achieved using an underlying framework known as the Blockchain, which enables peers to collectively maintain an encrypted digital ledger of all transactions. CCs like Bitcoin have gained popularity in recent times and are quickly becoming a viable alternative market for consumers, retailers and banks alike. In March 2017, (Chiu & Koeppl, 2017) Bitcoin's market value was approximately US$20 billion.

This chapter first looks at the history of CCs, including the emergence of Bitcoin and other popular altcoins. Included is a review of existing literature on the topic of government approaches to CC adoption. The next section presents the findings of a desktop review of papers, media and online databases on country/state regulations regarding the use of CCs. These approaches are then classified according to a bespoke categorization that reflects the area of business in which CC is being regulated. Using this information, potential challenges to CC adoption are then discussed as well as possible ways they can be addressed and mitigated effectively. Finally, we propose a framework for CC adoption that avoids the pitfalls experienced in other regions so as to have the best chances of succeeding.

The findings and analyses are provided as a starting reference point for future studies in the Pacific on the subject of CC adoption. Given its immense potential and popularity on the back of Bitcoin, many countries in the region will and have taken note. Preparations to utilize CCs, whether partially or in full will soon begin.

Cryptocurrency Background

In 2008, a person or a group of people under the pseudonym Satoshi Nakamoto created a peer-to-peer decentralized financial system called

"Bitcoin" (Nakamoto, 2008). Bitcoin was the first CC that was implemented, and it required no monitoring by a central authority due to its peer-to-peer characteristics. However, the system is not fully decentralized since wallet software, service providers, and bitcoin exchange are centralized (Kaushal *et al.*, 2017).

Bitcoin has a limit in its creation and circulation. The maximum amount of Bitcoins that can be created is about 21 million, and the 17th million coin was mined on April 26, 2018 (Cheng, 2018). The critics of Bitcoin argue that with a set limit, Bitcoin is subject to deflation. Supporters argue that because Bitcoin is divisible to eight decimal places, it would not be susceptible to deflation (Bohr & Bashir, 2014).

Countries that experienced financial crises have turned to CCs like Bitcoin to help their citizens. The Greek government debt crisis is a good example. With the imminent closure of banks in Greece around 2015, people turned to Bitcoin to allow them to buy goods online (Pagliery, 2015). These resulted in an increase in people using Bitcoin to purchase goods and services. Venezuela is another country whose citizens have been using Bitcoin to purchase medicines, food and other supplies (Chandler, 2018). The country has been ravaged by hyperinflation since 2014. Cross-border transaction using CCs is also cheap in a sense that there are cheaper fees charged for this transaction compared to fees charged on fiat currency.

Anonymity is another trait present in CC that has its advantages and disadvantages. This has its benefits in a sense that there is less information that people have to provide in regard to doing a purchase. However, in 2014, a site called silk road was shut down by the Federal Bureau of Investigation (FBI) (Martin, 2014). The site was accused of selling illicit drugs online, and there was no way to find out the sellers or buyers due to this feature present in CC.

CC has also been able to resolve the issue of "double-dipping", which is an issue when there is no central body that verifies buying and selling online. The use of blockchain technology to record a completed transaction in an immutable ledger that is verified, secure, transparent and permanent prevents the "dipping" scenario from happening (Holotescu, 2018). The immutability of the technology makes it hard to reverse transaction if there is a need to correct a mistake.

Problem Statement

CC has attracted substantial attention from consumers and businesses due to its media popularity. It has also become an interesting area of research for academics and financial analysts. What has been missing is an assured plan of adoption by Governments and regulators. Efforts by State Authorities to understand and engage with CC have been minimal or non-existent. A cause for this hesitance may be a lack of technical knowledge as well as apprehensions due to the dark history surrounding CCs and their use in suspect activities.

Aims & objectives

This chapter aims to assess and classify the levels of CC adoption by country from a regulatory perspective and identify factors that could influence adoption outcomes. Using the data and analyses from these classifications, we can then form a provisional approach to adopting CCs, which can be proactively followed by countries wanting to implement CCs.
The research objectives are as follows:

- Assess and determine level of CC adoption by country.
- Describe a classification of countries by the extent of its CC adoption.
- Propose a "best-practice" approach to be followed when adopting CC.

Review of Existing Literature

There currently exists vast literature regarding various CCs, their advantages and disadvantages, and speculation on what the future holds for each of them. There has also been coverage of government approaches via media and scholarly articles that offer varying degrees of detail. Bohr & Bashir (2014) explored biological, social and political factors that influenced a user's choice of and accumulation of Bitcoin wealth. Lansky (2018) has compiled a classification of state approaches to cryptocurrency via a bespoke grading model. A 2016 web article (Hansen, 2018) lists countries of the world that have begun interactions with CCs on a state level. Burnie *et al.* (2018) developed a framework for classifying CC tokens based on their functional attributes. This classification also helped to identify important issues that one must consider when deciding to engage in a CC network.

Methodology

Lansky defined a classification model of up to six levels based on regulatory measures. Our approach aims to achieve a more generic classification system that sorts government regulations according to the type of business case that it most greatly affects. Using this taxonomy, a desktop review was conducted on available regulatory information from various countries present in the library of Congress Report (Staff, 2018) and Hansen's list (Hansen, 2018). The country was then classified to reflect the level of adoption at consumer level as well as the status of state regulations on CCs. Information was sourced from research papers, government websites, news media and legal journals.

Findings

Data for this research was sourced from online country databases kept and updated by various legal and media organizations. Combining the sources allowed the team to extract a sampling of 92 countries categorized into 5 regions: Africa & Middle East, America & Caribbean, Asia, Europe (EU & Non EU) and the Pacific. For each country, the following classification was used to categorize the level of adoption and business activity under regulation. Appendix 1 contains the full country dataset showing their regulatory approach towards different CC usage scenarios.

Grouping of regulatory approach

Group 1 Undefined: The country has not acknowledged/recognized CCs or has warned against the use of CCs and its derivatives. This also covers countries where regulation is minimal or ambiguous on the subject.

Group 2 Acknowledgment: The Government/Central Bank/Tax Authority or other Regulatory body has released statements or advisory acknowledging the existence/use of CCs in the country. Further work or plans towards developing CCs and the financial sector may or may not be in place.

Group 3 Consumer Friendly: Provision has been made to allow use of CCs for the purchase of goods and services. The creation and provision of CC-related services are regulated. CC exchanges are supported and regulated to certain extent. Taxes may or may not be charged on CCs as a form of income or as an asset.

Group 4 Investor Friendly: State authorities have approved regulations recognizing CCs as an asset class that can be traded and used to build investment. Taxation is applied to such investments as well as any income/losses that are generated. This group is further subclassified into:

Group 4A Retail and Institutional Trading: These are normal citizens and companies that purchase CC's for the intention of using it as an asset to resell coins when prices are high enough to gain profit.

Group 4B Initial Coin Offering (ICO) Regulation: These are companies that sell coins to enthusiasts to support a project and in return enthusiasts are able to gain a return of investment once the project is successfully deployed.

Group 5 Illegal: The country has banned the use of CCs in trade or investments of all forms. This includes absolute and implicit bans via warnings and other regulations.

Table 1 shows the countries classified according to their approach to CC regulation and adoption. This assessment was conducted on the latest information gathered on each country outlining CC regulations and policies. Some states satisfied conditions for more than one group and were thus listed more than once.

Assessment of findings

Looking at the findings table, we have come up with a basic taxonomy tree (Figure 1) that basically highlights the steps that a country could take if it wants to adopt CC.

Table 1: Table of Countries Grouped According to Cryptocurrency Regulatory Approach

Regulatory Group	Countries Implementing CC Regulation
Group 1 **Undefined**	Jordan, Lebanon, Saudi Arabia, Tunisia, Belize, Bermuda, Brazil, Chile, Cuba, Kyrgyzstan, Portugal
Group 2 **Acknowledgment**	Colombia, Costa Rica, Ecuador, Guatemala, Honduras, FSM, Marshall Is, PNG, Samoa, Vanuatu, Indonesia, Republic of China, Philippines, Kazakhstan, Austria, Belarus, Belgium, Bulgaria, Finland, France, Greece, Greenland, Estonia, Hungary, Isle of Man, Israel, Italy, Latvia, Lithuania, Netherlands, Poland, Russia, Serbia, Slovenia, Spain, Sweden, Switzerland, United Kingdom
Group 3 **Consumer Friendly**	Israel, Senegal, Canada, United States, Singapore, Belgium, Bulgaria, Hungary, Isle of Man, Italy, Luxembourg, United Kingdom
Group 4 **Investor Friendly**	Abu Dhabi, South Africa, Argentina, Canada, Mexico, United States, Japan, South Korea, Malaysia, Singapore, Austria, Belarus, Belgium, Bulgaria, Cyprus, Czech Republic, Denmark, Finland, France, Germany, Iceland, Ireland, Isle of Man, Israel, Latvia, Lithuania, Malta, Netherlands, Poland, Russia, Spain, Sweden, Switzerland, United Kingdom, Turkey
Group 5 **Illegal**	Algeria, Egypt, Iran, Kuwait, Morocco, United Arab Emirates, Zimbabwe, Bolivia, Bangladesh, Colombia, China, Hong Kong SAR of PRC, India, Nepal, Republic of China, Thailand, Vietnam, Indonesia, Kazakhstan

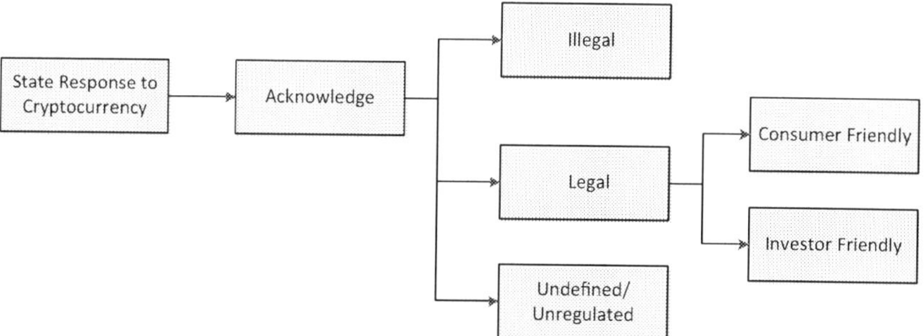

Figure 1: Taxonomy of Regulatory Approaches to Cryptocurrency

Challenges to Cryptocurrency Adoption

In the following, we discuss some of the challenges to CC regulation that countries have faced. These challenges have the potential to obstruct efforts to integrate CCs into an economy, whether by allowing people to avoid laws or weaken protection of consumers and businesses leading to exploitation of innocent users.

Market volatility

As experienced by Bitcoin (Comben, 2018), market share prices can have wild fluctuations over a short period of time. As a store of value, a currency needs to provide a level of assurance that its value will remain unchanged (or change very minutely) over a period of time. With CCs, the purchases that you make today may not be possible tomorrow due to the fact that your money has lost value compared to the product (or may even equate to zero).

Since the release of Bitcoin, work has already progressed to the next generation of CCs. A new category of CC, known as Stablecoin, (Munro, 2018) is designed to minimize price volatility. These coins are primarily used as stores of value and are backed by and valued against a fiat currency. Different programming designs allow the coins to remain stable, mostly pegging their value at US$1.

Transaction immutability & anonymity

An Immutable object is one whose state cannot be modified once it is created. This feature is displayed by most CCs, including Bitcoin. Another feature that opposes regulation efforts is the anonymity of users on a cryptonetwork. Bitcoin user identities are kept private via the cryptographic public key infrastructure. This allows users to create multiple public key identities, since the only way to decrypt these public signatures is with the user's private key. Privacy and irreversibility both pose related obstacles to regulation. It can be reasonably expected that in any economic setting, scenarios such as mistakes in payments, reneging on a transaction and refunds due to inadequate service/product do occur. The ability to reverse or annul a payment is an action that can be taken by banks, businesses or consumers to mitigate the effects of these scenarios. CCs that do not offer transaction reversal cannot expect to be adopted by mainstream consumers.

Fortunately, there are new developments in CC and Blockchain technology that allow reversible transactions (Menezes, 2014). Having a centralized body perform minimal functions to manage identities can overcome the problem of privacy. A more serious concern to regulators is not that of privacy but of transparent transactions. The inclusion of Know Your Customer (KYC) and Anti–Money Laundering (AML) mechanisms will make it difficult to keep one's identity private.

Learning curve & ease of use

The launching of Bitcoin not only brought focus onto the field of cryptography and public key encryption, it also introduced us to Blockchain technology and its associated decentralized ledger. The leap in technical requisites from Cash and Online payments to CCs has been huge. Add to this the immense number of different CCs, and the picture starts to get a little overwhelming. Older generations may prefer using physical over digital forms of business. As with all new technology, mass adoption is not feasible, rather a settling period will follow, and with time more and more will accept and adopt CCs.

Security & cyber-threats

Recently, Japan released news of one of its biggest CC exchanges being hacked (Partz, 2018). CC worth US$59 million were stolen by hackers. The virtual nature of CC wallets and CC exchanges opens them up to malicious attackers. But the same can also be said of current e-Payment systems and credit cards. Improved security procedures and improved monitoring can alert authorities to attacks on exchanges or user wallets as they occur. User vigilance and practising security measures such as two-factor authentication can also decrease the chances of CC theft. Payment intermediaries acting on behalf of both parties in a transaction ensure that the identities of buyer and seller are protected from unauthorized parties.

Conclusions

The research team found a lack of or ambiguous regulation on CCs in most countries, meaning that it has not been regulated or prohibited yet. Improved awareness of its potential benefits will lead to combined efforts among businesses, financial stakeholders and regulators towards adopting CCs, while at the same time preserving the founding principles. Such guidance and advice are needed, whether by governments or by small businesses, to navigate the numerous pitfalls encountered in these new and mostly unchartered waters of CC.

Discussion

At present, CCs may not be a good candidate as a replacement for fiat currencies as predicted by researchers (Ciaian & Rajcaniova, 2016). Rather we feel that it should complement and be viewed as an alternative option for consumers who prefer the advantages that it brings. We may even see currencies as an open market where users are free to choose and transact with the currency and mode of their choice. Despite the headway being made, there are still a lot of "gray areas" when it comes to CC adoption and regulation.

Fijian context & future research

We propose that adoption of CCs be managed in a phased approach, which can be gradually increased as the adoption model matures and regulation gets refined. Based on the findings, many countries were found to benefit from CCs in the form of taxation revenue on earnings and investments. The use of CC as legal tender in transactions for goods and services did not gain much traction and was found to suffer from wild variations in market price, affecting buying power.

The new wave of next-generation CCs are now incorporating centralized blockchains, (Milutinović, 2018) and this can be further looked at to garner more interest from governments that want to protect citizens from being targeted by unscrupulously dealers.

A centralized blockchain could be maintained by the central bank, and updates to this master copy can be propagated to the rest of the network once they have been verified.

References

Bohr, J., Bashir, M. (2014). *Who Uses Bitcoin? An Exploration of the Bitcoin Community*. Paper presented at the Conference on Privacy, Security and Trust (PST).

Burnie, A., Burnie, J., Henderson, A. (2018). Developing a Cryptocurrency Assessment Framework: Function over Form. *Ledger Journal*, 3, 24–47.

Chandler, S. (2018). How Venezuela came to be one of the Biggest Markets for Crypto in the World. *Cointelegraph*. Retrieved from: https://cointelegraph.com/news/how-venezuela-came-to-be-one-of-the-biggest-markets-for-crypto-in-the-world.

Cheng, E. (2018). There are now 17 million Bitcoins in Existance-only 4 million Left to "Mine". Retrieved from: https://www.cnbc.com/2018/04/26/there-are-now-17-million-bitcoins-in-existence--only-4-million-left-to-mine.html.

Chiu, J., Koeppl, T. V. (2017). The Economics of Cryptocurrencies–Bitcoin and Beyond. Available at SSRN 3048124.

Ciaian, P., Rajcaniova, M. (2016). The Digital Agenda of Virtual Currencies: Can BitCoin Become a Global Currency? *Information Systems and e-Business Management*, 14(4), 883–919.

Comben, C. (2018). 9 Major Barriers to Widespread Cryptocurrency Adoption. Retrieved from: https://coincentral.com/9-barriers-cryptocurrency-adoption/.

Hansen, J. D. (2018). Digital Currencies: International Actions and Regulations. Retrieved from: https://www.perkinscoie.com/en/news-insights/digital-currencies-international-actions-and-regulations.html.

Holotescu, C. (2018). *Understanding Blockchain Opportunities and Challenges*. Paper Presented at the International Scientific Conference eLearning and Software for Education, Bucharest.

Kaushal, P. K., Bagga, A., Sobti, R. (2017). *Evolution of Bitcoin and Security Risk in Bitcoin Wallets. Paper Presented at the International Conference on Computer, Communications and Electronics*, Manipal University Japan, Malaviya National Institute of Technology Jaipur, & IRISWORLD.

Lansky, J. (2018). Possible State Approaches to Cryptocurrencies. *Journal of Systems Integration*, 9(1), 19–31.

Martin, J. (2014). Lost on the Silk Road: Online Drug Distribution and the Cryptomarket. *Canadian Journal of Criminology and Criminal Justice,* 14, 351–367.

Menezes, N. (2014). ReverseCoin — World First Cryptocurrency with Reversible Transactions. Retrieved from: https://bitcoinist.com/reversecoin-worlds-first-cryptocurrency-reversible-transactions/.

Milutinović, M. (2018). Cryptocurrency. *Ekonomika*, 64(1), 105–122.

Munro, A. (2018). The Six Challenges and Solutions for Cryptocurrency Adoption. Retrieved from: https://www.finder.com.au/the-six-challenges-and-solutions-for-cryptocurrency-adoption.

Nakamoto, S. (2008). Bitcoin: A Peer-to-Peer Electronic Cash System [online]. Retrieved from: https://bitcoin.org/bitcoin.pdf.

Pagliery, J. (2015). Greeks are Rushing to Bitcoin. Retrieved from: https://money.cnn.com/2015/06/29/technology/greece-bitcoin/index.html.

Partz, H. (2018). Japanese Cryptocurrency Exchange Hacked, $59 million in Losses Reported. *Cointelegraph*. Retrieved from: https://cointelegraph.com/news/japanese-cryptocurrency-exchange-hacked-59-million-in-losses-reported.

Staff, G. I. R. D. (2018). Regulation of Cryptocurrency Around the World. Retrieved from: http://www.loc.gov/law/help/cryptocurrency/cryptocurrency-world-survey.pdf.

Supriya, R. (2018). Cryptocurrencies and its Relevance in this Day and Age Understanding Cryptocurrency and How it Works (News). (0970034X). Retrieved from Athena Information Solutions Pvt. Ltd.

Appendix 1

	Country	Government/ Regulatory Advisory	Legalized/Regulated (Y = Yes, N = No, U = Undefined)					Local CC
			Payments/ Transactions	Retail Investor Trading	Institutional Investor Trading	ICO Regulation	DCE Regulation	
	Africas & Middle East							
1	Abu Dhabi	Y	U	Y	Y	Y	Y	
2	Algeria	Y	N	N	N	N	N	
3	Egypt	Y	N	N	N	N	N	
4	Iran	Y	N	N	N	N	U	TBD
5	Israel	Y	Y	Y	Y	Y	U	
6	Jordan	Y	Not legal tender	N	N	N	N	
7	Kuwait	Y	N	N	N	U	U	TBD
8	Lebanon	Y	N	N	N	N	U	
9	Morocco	Y	N	N	N	N	U	
10	Saudi Arabia	Y	U	U	U	U	U	Riyal
11	Senegal	Y	Y	Y	Y	U	Y	eCFA
12	South Africa	Y	Not legal tender	Y	Y	Y	U	
13	Tunisia	N	U	U	U	U	U	eDinar
14	United Arab Emirates	Y	N	N	N	N	N	
15	Zimbabwe	Y	Not legal tender	N	N	N	U	

(*Continued*)

(*Continued*)

	Country	Government/ Regulatory Advisory	Legalized/Regulated (Y = Yes, N = No, U = Undefined)					Local CC
			Payments/ Transactions	Retail Investor Trading	Institutional Investor Trading	ICO Regulation	DCE Regulation	
	Africas & Middle East							
1	Argentina	Y	Not legal tender	U	U	U	U	
2	Belize	N	U	U	U	U	U	
3	Bermuda	Y	U	U	U	Y	Y	
4	Bolivia	Y	N	N	N	N	N	
5	Brazil	Y	U	U	U	U	U	NiobiumCoin
6	Canada	Y	Y	Y	Y	Y	Y	
7	Chile	Y	U	U	U	U	U	
8	Colombia	Y	Not legal tender	N	N	N	N	
9	Costa Rica	Y	N	N	N	N	N	
10	Cuba	N	U	U	U	U	U	
11	Ecuador	Y	N	N	N	N	N	TBD
12	El Salvador	Y	Not legal tender	N	N	N	N	
13	Guatemala	Y	Not legal tender	N	N	N	N	
14	Honduras	Y	N	N	N	U	U	
15	Mexico	Y	U	Y	Y	Y	U	
16	United States	Y	Y	Y	Y	Y	Y	

				Asia			
1	Bangladesh	Y	N	N	N	N	N
2	China	Y	N	N	N	N	N
3	Hong Kong SAR of PRC	Y	N	N	N	N	N
4	India	Y	Not legal tender	N	N	N	N
5	Indonesia	Y	N	N	N	N	N
6	Japan	Y	Y	Y	Y	U	Y
7	Kazakhstan	Y	N	N	N	N	N
8	Kyrgyzstan	Y	U	U	U	U	U
9	Malaysia	Y	Y	Y	Y	U	U
10	Nepal	Y	N	N	N	N	N
11	Philippines	Y	Not legal tender	N	N	U	N
12	Singapore	Y	Y	Y	Y	Y	U
13	South Korea	Y	Y	Y	Y	Y	Y
14	Republic of China	Y	Y	Y	Y	Y	Y
15	Thailand	Y	Y	Y	Y	Y	Y
16	Vietnam	Y	Not legal tender	N	N	N	N
				Europe (EU & Non-EU)			
1	Austria	Y	U	Y	Y	U	U
2	Belarus	Y	N	N	N	Y	Y
3	Belgium	Y	Not legal tender	U	U	U	U

(*Continued*)

(*Continued*)

	Country	Government/ Regulatory Advisory	Legalized/Regulated (Y = Yes, N = No, U = Undefined)					Local CC
			Payments/ Transactions	Retail Investor Trading	Institutional Investor Trading	ICO Regulation	DCE Regulation	
4	Bulgaria	Y	U	U	U	U	U	
5	Croatia	Y	U	U	U	U	U	
6	Cyprus	Y	Not legal tender	U	U	U	U	
7	Czech Republic	Y	U	U	U	U	U	
8	Denmark	Y	U	U	U	U	U	
9	Estonia	Y	Y	Y	Y	U	Y	
10	European Union	Y	Y	Y	Y	U	Y	
11	Finland	Y	U	U	U	U	U	
12	France	Y	Y	Y	Y	U	U	
13	Germany	Y	Y	Y	Y	Y	Y	
14	Greece	Y	U	U	U	U	U	
15	Hungary	Y	U	U	U	U	U	
16	Iceland	Y	N	U	N	N	N	Auroracoin
17	Ireland	Y	U	U	U	Y	U	IrishCoin
18	Isle of Man	Y	Y	U	U	U	U	
19	Italy	Y	Y	Y	U	U	Y	
20	Latvia	Y	Y	Y	Y	U	Y	

21	Lithuania	Y	N	N	U	Y	U	
22	Luxembourg	Y	U	U	U	U	U	
23	Malta	Y	Y	Y	Y	Y	Y	
24	Netherlands	Y	Y	Y	Y	U	Y	DNBCoin
25	Norway	Y	U	Y	Y	U	U	
26	Poland	Y	Not legal tender	N	N	U	U	
27	Portugal	Y	U	U	U	U	U	
28	Russia	Y	Y	Y	Y	Y	N	
29	Slovenia	Y	U	U	U	U	U	
30	Spain	Y	U	U	U	Y	U	
31	Sweden	Y	U	U	U	U	U	TBD
32	Switzerland	Y	Y	Y	Y	Y	U	
33	Turkey	Y	Y	Y	Y	U	U	Turkcoin
34	United Kingdom	Y	Y	Y	Y	U	U	
				Pacific				
1	Australia	Y	Y	Y	Y	Y	Y	
2	Cook Islands	N	N	Y	Y	N	N	
3	FSM	Y	Y	U	U	U	U	
4	Marshall Islands	Y	Y	N	N	U	U	Sovereign
5	New Zealand	Y	Y	Y	U	Y	Y	
6	Niue	N	U	U	U	Y	N	

(Continued)

(Continued)

	Country	Government/ Regulatory Advisory	Legalized/Regulated (Y = Yes, N = No, U = Undefined)					Local CC
			Payments/ Transactions	Retail Investor Trading	Institutional Investor Trading	ICO Regulation	DCE Regulation	
7	PNG	Y	N	U	U	Y	Y	Torokina
8	Samoa	Y	U	U	U	Y	N	
9	Tonga	N	N	N	N	N	N	
10	Tuvalu	N	N	N	N	N	N	
11	Vanuatu	Y	U	Y	Y	U	Y	

Chapter 11

An Overview of Cryptocurrencies for Online Payments of Enterprise Systems

Sam Goundar*, Anil Singh[†], Semiti Saini[‡], Fariha Tafsil[§], Shafina Shabnam[¶] and Krishneel Prakash[||]

The University of the South Pacific, Suva, Fiji

**sam.goundar@gmail.com*

[†]S11044939@student.usp.ac.fj

[‡]S02001094@student.usp.ac.fj

[§]S11109207@student.usp.ac.fj

[¶]S11031243@student.usp.ac.fj

[||]S11086868@student.usp.ac.fj

Abstract

Cryptocurrencies have evolved erratically and at unprecedented speed over the course of their short lifespans. Since the inception of Bitcoin in 2009, more than 1600 cryptocurrencies have been developed, with majority of them witnessing success in the market. With the advent of cryptocurrencies, the possibility of online trading has reached new heights. Thus, this chapter focuses on enterprise cryptocurrencies and provides a thorough analysis of the various opportunities that lie with the use of cryptocurrencies for online payments. This chapter is presented as there is a need to draw a fine line between using fiat currencies and using cryptocurrencies for online transactions. It is also important as there is not much research done on using cryptocurrencies in enterprise systems, and so this will give a fair idea to researchers and organizations and help them in making decisions while making corporate payments. We are basing our research using grounded theory, and our research will focus on the certainty of using cryptocurrencies.

Introduction

Computing, automatization and, ultimately, the Internet have contributed vastly to the growth and wealth of economies and cultures (Manyika & Roxburgh, 2011). Similarly, cryptocurrencies are rapidly becoming relevant to organizations when the topic of online trading is brought up as they provide competitive advantages to companies. The concept of electronic currency dates back to the late 1980s; however, the first successful decentralized cryptocurrency — Bitcoin — was launched in 2009 by an unidentifiable group of people known as Satoshi Nakomoto.

Cryptocurrencies function much like a standard currency as they are virtual coinage systems that allow for digital payments for goods and services without the presence of a central authority. The amount of alternate payment types is growing, and therefore the customary means of online payment (such as debit cards, credit cards) are being downgraded as they are fighting with competition from cryptocurrencies, which offer lower costs and more security. Thus, nowadays, there are lots of virtual currencies being used with more or less success on the Internet.

This chapter is outlined as follows: first, the research objectives will be stated, then a review of literature will be done on the existing usage of cryptocurrencies by organizations and the reasons why they are being used, though there is not much usage of cryptocurrencies in the Pacific Context; we have, however, based our research on journal articles. Then research findings on the cryptocurrency market — on usage of cryptocurrencies — will be discussed; these markets include those countries already accepting payments in digital currencies. Then our research questions will be answered and a discussion on the overall topic will be provided. All the works referred to during our research will be cited, and a reference list is provided at the end of this chapter.

Research Objectives

This research aims to meet the following objectives:

1. To investigate the different forms of payments available and compare them.
2. To investigate the usage of cryptocurrencies in online payments that make it viable for utilization in Enterprise Systems.
3. To identify the advantages and disadvantages of utilizing cryptocurrencies.

Literature Review

Cryptocurrencies are not hyped in Fiji, and there is not enough research conducted on usage of cryptocurrencies in Enterprise Systems, but our group has reviewed the applicable 15 journal articles related to our area of research.

Over the last two decades, Information Technology (IT) is emerging in the world and has made a noteworthy contribution to our quality of life and affects our social, public and personal life. Due to the advances in computer technology and telecommunication, IT now handles data and information represented in graphics, image, text, digital, and video and audio formats, and prints, processes and stores it as desired by the specific users. With the emergence of the Web and the Internet, organizations' business processes have undergone a radical change.

Decisive inroads in all walks of life have been made by IT, in factories, offices, hotels, airports, communications, entertainment, academia, banking, hospitals, transportation and shopping. It is being used extensively for decision-making, easing of operations, improvement of communication, record-keeping and for obtaining higher productivity from the system in which it is put to use. Paperless transactions, cash and checks are converted to electronic cash.

IT has initiated the era of managing business from anywhere without being in the office and enabled new functions in business such as secured payment processes and web-based business processes. All these changes have affected the working style of the organization staff. The management processes now need speed, precision and snapshot business status through relevant information technology support (O'Brien & Marakas, 2007).

Today, according to Morganwalp and Sage (2004), many organizations are concerned with how to successfully transition to organizations that utilize IT to its fullest strategic extent. "Most of the organizations are financing significant amounts of resources into developing their enterprise architecture as they are widely aware that an organization's enterprise architecture plays a key role in the shift.

Practically speaking, an enterprise architecture describes how all the information technology fundamentals — organizations, systems, processes, and people — in an organization work together as a whole. For an organization to continue to justify expending resources on enterprise architecture, it must be able to show positive effects of enterprise architecture efforts. However, demonstrating the positive effects of enterprise architecture is difficult because it is always changing and its effects cannot be directly or easily measured" (Morganwalp & Sage, 2004).

Organizations have abandoned legacy systems in favor of a new class of comprehensive packaged application software designed to integrate the core corporate activities of an organization known as Enterprise Systems. Enterprise Systems are commercial software packages that enable the integration of transaction-oriented data and business process throughout an organization. The shift from legacy systems to Enterprise Systems is in itself an expensive approach which, after successful implementation, reaps benefits for any organization (Farell, 2015).

However, to overcome the high costs associated with this implementation, organizations can make use of virtual currencies such as cryptocurrencies for payments to Enterprise Systems. Virtual currencies such as cryptocurrencies are becoming increasingly common in recent years. Cryptocurrencies first came to be known in the year 2009 when they were released by a group of individuals named Satoshi Nakomoto. Till date, there are no virtual currencies that are fiat currencies, and no government has accepted any cryptocurrency as its legal tender. Cryptocurrencies such as Bitcoins differ from other earlier currencies in that they are exchangeable with government-issued fiat currencies in the real economy (Baron *et al.*, 2015).

Since cryptocurrencies are not controlled by any entity, over the years it is possible for the organizations to create their own currencies with the availability of software and programs online. Virtual currencies are increasing exponentially, and according to the Cyber-Terrorism Activities Report Number 4, by mid-2013 there were three times as many types of virtual currencies extant as there were in the beginning of the year 2013 (Cyber-Terrorism Activities Report No. 4, 2013). Virtual currencies are easily transportable and do not need to transit through international borders as currency, which in turn increases their usage and reduces cross-border transaction costs.

Some of the inherent properties of cryptocurrencies make the underlying technology an appealing candidate for amending or eventually displacing incumbent payment and transaction infrastructure (Glaser & Bezzenberger, 2015). Among these are security (Grinberg, 2011), transaction speed (Karame *et al.*, 2012), scalability, entry barriers and, most importantly, lower costs (Barber *et al.*, 2012).

According to William Luther (2016), the amount of electronic transactions will increase mainly due to the fact that it is convenient to make digital payments and also as there is increase in online shopping (Luther, 2016). As payments to enterprise systems are a crucial topic, much attention needs to be paid when dealing with either developing it for an organization or modifying it. All levels of managers need to have their say in the decision-making process. The IT need to be consulted when such topics are discussed as they will be the department in charge of maintaining it. Therefore, the alternative option for payment using cryptocurrencies of enterprise systems needs to be assessed.

Research questions

- Why is there need for Cryptocurrencies in online payments?
- What are the perceived advantages of cryptocurrencies compared to other forms of electronic payments?
- What are some of the challenges of using cryptocurrencies for Enterprise systems?
- How do users and experts evaluate the future potential of cryptocurrencies as a serious alternative currency?

Findings and analysis

Nations are driving the charge with regard to business development and infrastructural support in the digital currency space. With the world moving towards digital era, fiat money is being replaced by digital currency for multiple reasons. Some common Digital currencies employed by enterprises are Bitcoin (BTC), Ethereum (Ether), Ripple (XRP), Bitcoin Cash (BCH), EOS, Cardano (ADA), Litecoin (LTC), Stellar (XLM), IOTA and NEO.

According to a website run by Ryan X. Charles, which rated the top one hundred Cryptocurrencies by Market Capitalization, BITCOIN was ranked as the most common in the digital currency market. Bitcoin, the world's most common and well-known cryptocurrency, has been increasing in popularity. It has the same fundamental structure as it did when introduced in 2008, but the changes in the world market have created a new demand for cryptocurrencies much greater than its initial showing.

Cryptocurrency allows its users to exchange currency online without any third-party insight (Figure 1). This in a way provides assurance to the client that the transaction that is taking place is rather very secure and safe.

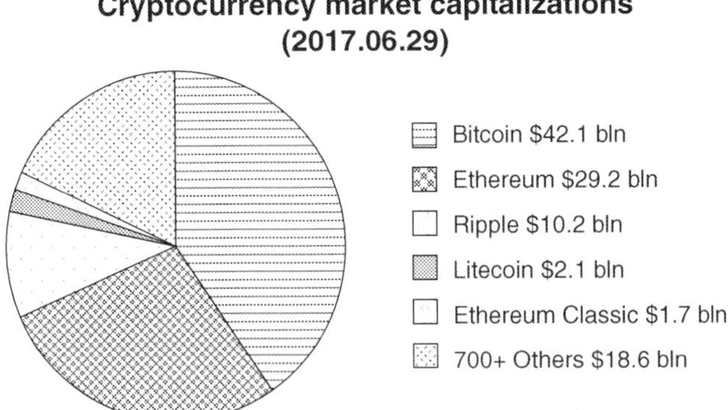

Figure 1: Capitalization of Tokens

Source: https://coinmarketcap.com/all/views/all/.

How does cryptocurrency function?

Cryptocurrency has a theory of solving encrypted algorithms, which are used to create unique hashes that are finite in number. This, when collaborated with a network of computers verifying transactions, allows users to exchange hashes as if exchanging physical currency. Taking Bitcoins as an example, there will always be a limited number of bitcoins that will ever be created, avoiding excess and guaranteeing its rarity. However, when compared with something vital for survival, like water, it is mostly classified as being free or of little cost because it is so abundant. If water in this case was rare, it would be of more value than gold. The reason for the value of bitcoins to always appreciate is due to its users having trust that if they accept it as payments, they could use it elsewhere to purchase something they want or need (Kelly, 2014). As long as the users maintain this faith, the valued object can be simply anything.

Bitcoin's value exists in its bionetwork very much in the same way as wampum — a seashell — was the currency of the land for Native Americans (Kelly, 2014). Cryptocurrencies do not have intrinsic value like gold in that they cannot be used to make physical objects like jewelry that have value. Nevertheless, value continues to exist due to trust and acceptance.

What is Bitcoin and how do digital forms of money (Bitcoin) work?

As indicated by Sarah Meiklejon *et al.* (2016), Bitcoin is completely online virtual cash, unbacked by either physical wares or self-governing commitment; rather, it depends on a mix of cryptographic security and a distributed convention for seeing repayments. Subsequently, Bitcoin has the unintuitive property that while the ownership of money is implicitly anonymous, its flow is globally visible. Bitcoin at first was presented by (the pseudonymous) Satoshi Nakamoto in 2008. From that time, it has encountered a gigantic growth and produced a huge number of benefits to those occupied with this business.

The future of digital currencies

According to Ivaschenko (2016), in general there are different and challenging opinions regarding the future of cryptocurrencies. While those with democratic views of life are optimistic and embrace the cryptocurrency system, other authors, economists and scholars from this field are not passionate about the use of cryptocurrency in the system of payments and financial transactions. "The optimistic view of cryptocurrencies use is backed by the fact that they make it easier to transfer funds between two parties in a transaction; these transactions are facilitated over the use of private and public keys for security reasons.

The entire fund transfer is mostly done with minimal processing fees, permitting users to avoid the abrupt fees charged by most of the banks. In addition, many countries have started to accept Crypto currencies as valid currencies. Particularly, countries that wish to get rid of cash have a very welcoming approach to cryptocurrencies. The promoters of bitcoin use an argument for Market Capitalization of bitcoin, ethereum and other cryptocurrencies, claiming that cryptocurrency market has become very enormous and powerful, so banning it would be too costly for any country" (Ivaschenko, 2016).

On the other hand, the cryptocurrencies are claimed to be very volatile by their opponents, can be used for financing illegal activities or money laundering. Therefore, Tymoigne (2015) is uninterested in using cryptocurrencies; hence, he provides reasons to support his idea of cryptocurrencies such as bitcoin not being viable digital currency. He observes that bitcoins are illiquid and have shown high price volatility, and that the discounted cash value of a bitcoin is zero. He further observes that such a currency lacks a central controller, and that there is no financial or economic basis for its creation. Therefore, the following section discusses the advantages and disadvantages of bitcoin as noted by Ivaschenko (2016).

Advantages of using cryptocurrency

Cryptocurrency has various advantages that makes it different from fiat currency. Some of these include peer-to-peer cryptocurrency network. There are no master servers that control all operations. Exchange of information (in this case money) is mostly between 2–3 or more software clients. All cryptocurrency software installed by a user's program-wallets are part of a bitcoin network. Each client stores a record of all committed transactions and the number of bitcoins in each wallet. Transactions are made by hundreds of distributed servers. Neither banks or taxes nor governments can control the exchange of money in between.

Speed of transaction is the next advantage (Figure 2). This is characterized by the ability to send money anywhere and to anyone in a matter of minutes after the digital currency network processes the payment. Lack of inflation is yet another advantage. There is a limit assigned to each cryptocurrency, which cannot be altered. As there are neither political forces nor corporations able to change this order, there is no possibility for development of inflation in the system. No chances to use some personal data for fraud — This is an important point.

Today, majority of purchases are made with credit cards. Credit cards are not reliable to some point. While filling forms on websites, customers are required to enter the following data: card number, expiration date and code. It is hard to come up with a less secure way to make payments. Therefore, credit cards are very often stolen. Digital Currency transactions do not require disclosure of any personal data. Instead, they use two keys: public and private. The public one is available to all (i.e. the address of Digital Currency wallet), but the private key is known only to the owner. The transaction needs to be signed by interacting private keys and by applying a mathematical function. This creates evidence that the transaction is performed by the owner.

Decentralization is yet another advantage. There is no central control authority in the network; the network is distributed to all participants, each computer mining digital currency is a member of this system. This means that the central authority has no power to dictate rules for owners of a particular cryptocurrency. And even if some part of the network goes offline, the payment system will continue to operate stably. Unlimited possibilities of transactions — each of the wallet holders can pay to anyone, anywhere and any amount.

The transaction cannot be controlled or prevented, so you can make transfers anywhere in the world wherever another user with a digital wallet is located. It belongs only to the wallet owner. There is a unique electronic payment system where the account belongs to the owner only. For example, on PayPal if for any reason the company decides that the owner somehow uses the account in a wrong way, the system has the right to freeze all funds on the account without even warning the owner about it. Verification of the proper usage of an account is the total responsibility of the owner. With cryptocurrency, the owner has a private key and a corresponding public key, which is the address to the digital currency wallet. No one but the owner can withdraw the digital currency.

One more advantage is anonymity. Transactions that take place are very anonymous, and at the same time fully transparent. Any company can create an infinite number of digital currency addresses without reference to name, address or any other information.

Open source code is used for mining crypto currency.

Cryptocurrencies employ the same algorithms that are used in online banking. The only difference between the two is that Internet banking discloses the information about the users, whereas cryptocurrency allows all information of the transaction about the network to be shared (how, when), but it stores no data about the recipient or the sender of the cryptocurrency (there is no access to the personal information of the owner's wallet, thus

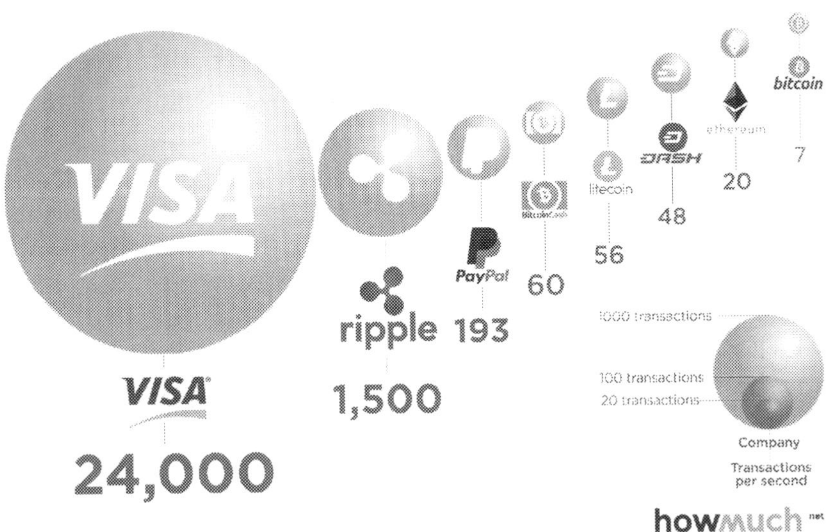

Figure 2: Cryptocurrencies Transaction Speeds

Source: https://howmuch.net/articles/crypto-transaction-speeds-compared.

making it very secure). Cryptocurrencies have no boundaries. Payments made in this system are impossible to cancel. The coins cannot be faked, copied or spent twice. These capabilities guarantee the integrity of the entire system.

Disadvantages of using cryptocurrency

Ivaschenko (2016) believes that there do exist some disadvantages of using cryptocurrencies, such as the large risks of investing in cryptocurrencies, that should be considered for the medium and long term. Strong volatility is one such area. Almost all of the ups and downs of the digital currency value depend directly on the declared statements of the governments of different countries. This volatility creates the problem in the short term.

According to Ivaschenko (2016), the opinion is that the list of cryptocurrency disadvantages is very extensive, and most of these are associated with the risk of terrorism, money laundering, lack of a central issuer and other illegal activity financings, implying that in the event of any bankruptcy there is no guaranty in any legal formal entity. Nevertheless, many professionals and scholars of this topic claim that the future of cryptocurrencies is optimistic since it would decrease the cost of transactions, it will remove trade barriers and intermediaries, and it will thus boost the economy and trade industries, although it is very difficult to predict. However, we should concentrate on the pessimistic voices in the academic world as well, and this lack of institutional backup makes the future of cryptocurrencies not very optimistic, especially when coupled with the hacking risks and the high risk of volatility.

Figure 3 illustrates the biggest problems cryptography traders face in the currently available exchanges, such as security, high trading fees, lack of liquidity, customer support, lack of cryptopairs, inconvenient user interface, high withdrawal fees, etc, and these are listed as some of the contributing factors and recent issues that are preventing the cryptorevolution from progressing to its next stage.

Figure 4 illustrates the countries that employ cryptocurrencies. As can be seen from the figure, United States is the largest contributor to cryptocurrencies, accounting for 28% of the global cryptocurrency markets. It is followed by Russia, contributing to 9%, United Kingdom 8%, Japan 6%,

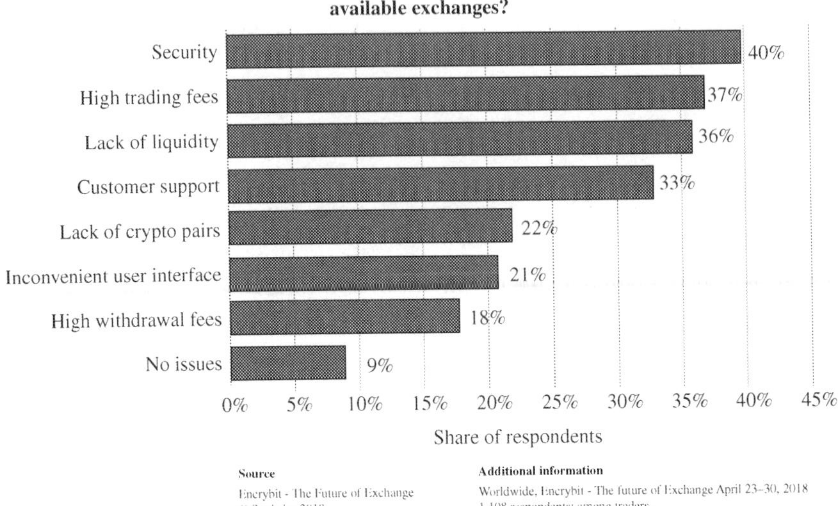

Figure 3: Problems with Cryptocurrency Traders

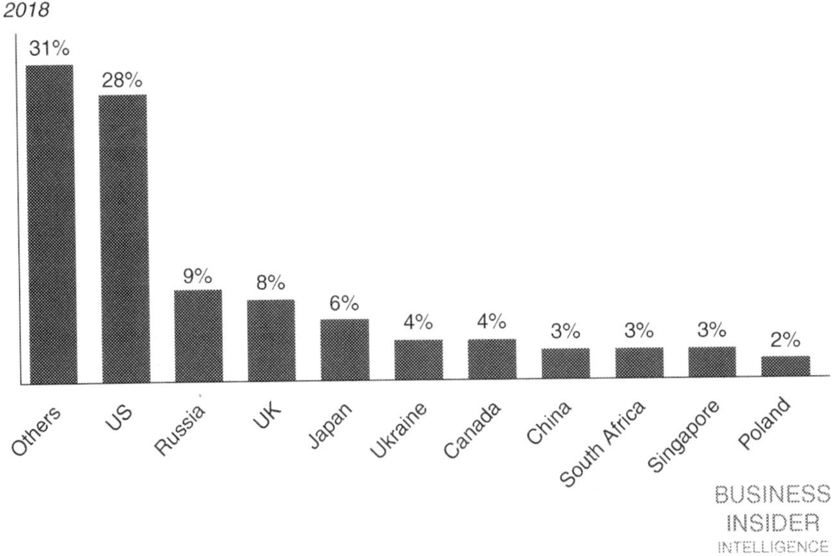

Figure 4: Sources of Traffic on Global Cryptocurrency Markets

Note: Percentage may not add to 100% due to rounding.

Source: SEMrush.

Ukraine 4%, Canada 4%, China, South Africa, Singapore 3%, and Poland 2%. Apart from this, the figure also shows a bar for "Others"; these are the countries that use cryptocurrency but do not put it as a priority or major means of exchange.

All in all, after scaling both the positive and the negative sides of cryptocurrency, it could be stated that cryptocurrency plays a vital role in this digital era. Looking at the positive aspects, which outscale the negative ones, it can be clearly seen that cryptocurrency is definitely a much more secure and convenient way to deal with currency than what is currently employed by organizations.

According to Eli Dourado and Jerry Brito (2014), "Cryptocurrency is an impressive technical achievement, but it remains a monetary experiment. Even if cryptocurrencies survive, they may not fully displace fiat currencies. As we have tried to show in this chapter, they provide an interesting new perspective from which to view economic questions surrounding currency governance, the characteristics of money, the political economy of financial intermediaries, and the nature of currency competition".

Contribution/Addition to the field of knowledge

Cryptocurrency is indeed unique and has a brighter future. With it being a major means of payment, an organization would indeed have a boost on the current legacy system in terms of security and many other features, as discussed in the chapter.

Methodology

A qualitative research method was used in this research as it allows for greater understanding of patterns and assists in gauging information needed to identify the current trends in cryptocurrency, and in this case the results may be more descriptive in nature. It is mainly used in areas where there is little or limited understanding of what can be found; therefore, discoveries may be novel. Qualitative research consists of gathering relevant information through techniques such as analyzing documents and observations. Qualitative studies have been used to understand current market trends in regard to payment through cryptocurrency, answer research questions and collect various findings.

Grounded theory is a methodology that involves construction of a theory based on empirical observations or data. This study uses grounded theory with an exploratory approach. For the purpose of this study, secondary data were derived from reports and previously published papers and articles, all of which are mentioned in the references to provide various insights into this research.

Discussion

"Cryptocurrency" is based on the primary concept of decentralized technology using blockchain and inherent encryption; there are various terms given to describe this. Some terms used to reference to it are: digital currency (Argentina, Thailand and Australia), virtual commodity (Canada, China, Republic of China), crypto-tokens (Germany), payment tokens (Switzerland), cyber-currency (Italy and Lebanon), electronic currency (Colombia and Lebanon) and virtual-asset (Honduras and Mexico).

Countries such as United States, Canada, Japan and Australia allow trade and investment in cryptocurrency, while it is totally banned in countries such as Iceland, Vietnam, Kyrgyzstan and Bolivia (Crypto Currency: A bright future? 2018).

One of the limitations cryptocurrencies currently face is the fact that digital fortune can be erased by a computer crash, or a virtual vault can be ransacked by a hacker, which has to be overcome through technological advancements. The number of organizations accepting cryptocurrency has increased, but they are still in the minority. Consumers need to accept cryptocurrency for it to be widely used; however, its complexity over conventional currencies dissuades most people apart from the technologically adroit. For cryptocurrency to become part of the mainstream financial system, a wide range of acceptance criteria need to be fulfilled: it has to be easy for consumers to understand but has to avoid fraud, decentralized but with necessary consumer protection, and preserve user anonymity without being a channel for money laundering.

Cryptocurrencies such as Bitcoins have come on the market today and have become so popular that it has become difficult to reason out where the market trends are moving. According to Charles and Darné (2019), bitcoins are managed by the an open-source software algorithm that uses the global internet; however, the issue of how it is measured and protected in the market is something that needs to be discussed in further research.

The main *limitation* of this research was that cryptocurrency is not used as a standard method of payment in Fiji, so the research was solely based on journal articles, research papers and online research on the current market. Australia is the only country in the South Pacific to accept cryptocurrency as a method of payment.

Conclusions

In accordance with the research findings, cryptocurrency is the future of the world; as a result, more e-commerce business owners are shifting towards virtual currency. Various advantages of a move towards cryptocurrency are secure transactions, as a result of Blockchain technology and "wallet"; privacy protection, since anonymity is maintained during transactions; decentralization feature, as the virtual counterpart is not acquiescent to any type of government or any organization; and faster and cheaper transactions, as payments are processed immediately upon request and the security feature of cryptocurrency eliminating any need for a third party, thus reducing transaction fees.

However, cryptocurrencies, mainly Bitcoin, still suffer from significant impediments that need to be overcome before they can completely replace the current currency systems. The opposition from financial institutions, which exert great power, can stifle the popularity of cryptocurrencies. Organizations, even though they are fast-paced, do not currently consider cryptocurrencies as stable enough to keep as assets for a long period. The whole idea of converting the entire world financial system to the Bitcoin, for example, can lead to massive increase in blockchain size, and thus the distributed ledger model would be impractical. Also, due to significant energy costs and diminished rewards over time in relation to the "mining" process, the users may bear unreasonable transaction costs.

Recommendation and Future Research

The literature review has identified numerous loopholes that would benefit from further research. One in particular is market trend in the Pacific Island Countries. It is recommended for future researchers to investigate how bitcoin will transit in Pacific countries. In line with same trend, research can also be done on how bitcoin can impact non-economic transactions if cryptocurrencies become effective. Thus, the implications in this area of research will bring forward a lot of interesting phenomena in the area of cryptocurrencies such as bitcoin.

Appendix

1. *Why is there need for cryptocurrencies in online payments?*

With the growing number of fiat-based payment processors, a variety of practical tools and methods of payment have been employed over the years. Adding cryptocurrency payments into the mix provides consumers and traders with benefits beyond compare. Some of these benefits include simplicity, lower overall cost, security, privacy and a greater level of control over one's funds.

2. *What are the perceived advantages of cryptocurrencies compared to other forms of electronic payments?*

Some arguments and encounters frame the use of cryptocurrency, but many organizations are accepting virtual currencies for transactions such as Bitcoin. And making use of the latest technologies in the marketplace is a great way to stand out from other businesses. Apart from that, cryptocurrency offers many other attractive proposals such as charging low or no fees, saving a lot of money compared to other payment methods, and transactions taking place instantly, which saves a lot of time.

3. *What are some of the challenges of using cryptocurrencies for enterprise systems?*

Some of the major challenges that the enterprises faced were security, high trading fees, lack of liquidity, lack of customer support, lack of cryptopairs, inconvenient user interface and high withdrawal fees.

4. *How do users and experts evaluate the future potential of cryptocurrencies as a serious alternative currency?*

As the world is moving towards the digital era, having a currency that is digital would take things to another level. Bearing these things in mind, before implementing or adapting to anything new, it is essential to do a thorough research on it to work the odds out or rather to have a more than 90% acuity for the idea to be a success.

References

Baig, A., Blau, B. M., Sabah, N. (2019). Price Clustering and Sentiment in Bitcoin. *Journal of Finance Research Letters*, 29, 111–116.

Barber, S., Boyen, X., Shi, E., Uzun, E. (2012). Bitter to Better — How to Make Bitcoin a Better Currency. In *International Conference on Financial Cryptography and Data Security*. Springer, Berlin: Heidelberg, pp. 399–414.

Baron, J., O'Mahony, A., Manheim, D., Dion-Schwarz, C. (2015). The Current State of Virtual Currencies. In *National Security Implications of Virtual Currency: Examining the Potential for Non-state Actor Deployment.* RAND Corporation. Retrieved from: http://www.jstor.org/stable/10.7249/j.ctt19rmd78.8.

Charles, A., Darné, O. (2019). Volatility Estimation for Bitcoin: Replication and Robustness. *Journal of International Economics*, 157, 23–32.

Charles, R. X. (2019). *Top 100 Cryptocurrencies by Market Capitalization.* Retrieved from: https://coinmarketcap.com/.

de la Horraa, L. P., de la Fuentea, G., Perote J. (2019). The Drivers of Bitcoin Demand: A Short and Long-Run Analysis. *Journal of International Review of Financial Analysis*, 62, 21–24.

Glaser, F., Bezzenberger, L. (2015). Beyond Cryptocurrencies — a Taxonomy of Decentralized Consensus Systems. In *23rd European Conference on Information Systems* (ECIS), Münster: Germany.

Grinberg, R. (2011). Bitcoin: An Innovative Alternative Digital Currency. *Hastings Science and Technology Law Journal*, 160. Retrieved from: https://papers.ssrn.com/sol3/papers.cfm?abstract_id=1817857.

Ivaschenko, A. I. (2016). Using Cryptocurrency in the Activities of Ukrainian Small and Medium Enterprises in Order to Improve their Investment Attractiveness. *Problems of Economics*, (3), 267–273.

Karame, G. O., Androulaki, E., Capkun, S. (2012). Double-pending Fast Payments in Bitcoin. In *Proceedings of the 2012 ACM Conference on Computer and Communications Security*, pp. 906–917.

Kelly, B. (2014). *The Bitcoin Big Bang: How Alternative Currencies are About to Change the World*. John Wiley & Sons.

Luther, W. J. (2016). Bitcoin and the Future of Digital Payments. *Independent Review,* 20(3), 397–404. Retrieved from: http://www.jstor.org/stable/24562161.

MBA Universe (2018). Crypto Currency: A Bright Future? Retrieved from https://www.mbauniverse.com/group-discussion/topic/business-economy/crypto-currency.

Morganwalp, J. M., Sage, A. P. (2004). Enterprise Architecture Measures of Effectiveness. *International Journal of Technology, Policy and Management,* 4(1). Retrieved from: https://doi.org/10.1504/IJTPM.2004.004569

O'Brien, J. A., Marakas, G. M. (2011). *Management Information Systems*. McGraw-Hill/Irwin, Vol. 9.

Stosic, D., Stosic, D., Ludermir, T. B., Stosic, T. (2019). Exploring Disorder and Complexity in the Cryptocurrency Space. *Journal of Physics A*, 19, 548–556.

Wing Hong Chan, Minh Le, Yan Wendy Wu. (2019). Holding Bitcoin Longer: The Dynamic Hedging Abilities of Bitcoin. *Journal of Quarterly Review of Economic Finance,* 71, 107–113.

Index

C

Printed in the United States
by Baker & Taylor Publisher Services